SYSTEMATIC THEOLOGY

SYSTEMATIC THEOLOGY

VOLUME I

Reason and Revelation
Being and God

PAUL TILLICH

THE UNIVERSITY OF CHICAGO PRESS

THE UNIVERSITY OF CHICAGO PRESS, CHICAGO 60637
James Nisbet & Co., Limited, London W. 1, England
Copyright 1951 by The University of Chicago. All rights reserved
Published 1951. Printed in the United States of America

00 99 98 97 96 95 94   20 21 22 23 24 25

ISBN: 0-226-80337-6 (paperbound)
Library of Congress Catalog Card Number: 51-2235

TO MY FORMER STUDENTS
HERE AND ABROAD

PREFACE

FOR a quarter of a century I have wanted to write a systematic theology. It always has been impossible for me to think theologically in any other than a systematic way. The smallest problem, if taken seriously and radically, drove me to all other problems and to the anticipation of a whole in which they could find their solution. But world history, personal destiny, and special problems kept me from fulfilling this self-chosen task. Somehow the mimeographed propositions which I have used for my lectures became a substitute for the system for my pupils and friends. The present volume deals with the problems contained in the Introduction and the first two parts of the propositions. The content of the propositions has been preserved and expanded, while the propositional form has been dissolved and replaced by a continuous text. The scope of a theological system can be almost unlimited, as the Scholastic and Protestant Orthodox "Summae" show. Personal, practical limitations, as well as the problem of space, have kept me from moving even in the direction of a "Summa." It has been impossible to deal with all the traditional problems of a theological system. Those which are not decisive for the structure of the system have had to be omitted, while others are only mentioned because they have been discussed by me in other writings. Furthermore, it has been impossible to make extensive references to the Bible or the classical theologians. The elaboration of the line of thought has consumed all effort and all space. The biblical and ecclesiastical character of the solutions to theological problems presented in this volume will not be difficult to recognize, although it is more implicit than explicit. Finally, it has been impossible to enter into an open discussion with the different representatives of contemporary theology and philosophy, although an "underground" discussion with them is going on on almost every page.

My purpose, and I believe it is a justified purpose, has been to present the method and the structure of a theological system written from an apologetic point of view and carried through in a continuous correlation with philosophy. The subject of all sections of this system is the method of correlation and its systematic consequences illustrated in a discussion of the main theological problems. If I have succeeded in proving the

vii

apologetic adequacy and the systematic fertility of this method, I shall not regret the limitations of the system.

This volume could not have been written without the help of some of my younger friends who really proved that they were friends by the selfless way in which they read and criticized the first and second drafts, from the theological as well as the stylistic point of view. First, I want to mention Professor A. T. Mollegen, professor of Christian ethics at The Seminary, Alexandria, Virginia, who offered important material and formal criticisms concerning large sections of the first draft. The main burden, however, was carried by my former assistant, John Dillenberger, of the Department of Religion, Columbia University, and by my present assistant, Cornelius Loew, who in regular conferences formulated the final text and took care of the entire technical side of the preparation of the manuscript. I also wish to mention my former secretary, the late Mrs. Hilde Frankel, who with great toil transferred my handwritten pages to typewritten copy, making it available to all those who helped me. I am grateful to the publishers, the University of Chicago Press, who waited patiently for several years for the completion of the manuscript.

I dedicate this book to my students, here and in Germany, who from year to year have urged me to publish the theological system with which they became acquainted in my lectures. Their desire to have in print what they heard in the classroom was the strongest psychological force in overcoming my hesitations, my perfectionism, and my awareness of my limitations. My ardent desire is that they shall find in these pages something of what they expect—a help in answering the questions they are asked by people inside and outside their churches.

A help in answering questions: this is exactly the purpose of this theological system.

NEW YORK CITY

TABLE OF CONTENTS

INTRODUCTION

ix

PART II. BEING AND GOD

INDEX

INTRODUCTION

INTRODUCTION

A. THE POINT OF VIEW

1. MESSAGE AND SITUATION

THEOLOGY, as a function of the Christian church, must serve the needs of the church. A theological system is supposed to satisfy two basic needs: the statement of the truth of the Christian message and the interpretation of this truth for every new generation. Theology moves back and forth between two poles, the eternal truth of its foundation and the temporal situation in which the eternal truth must be received. Not many theological systems have been able to balance these two demands perfectly. Most of them either sacrifice elements of the truth or are not able to speak to the situation. Some of them combine both shortcomings. Afraid of missing the eternal truth, they identify it with some previous theological work, with traditional concepts and solutions, and try to impose these on a new, different situation. They confuse eternal truth with a temporal expression of this truth. This is evident in European theological orthodoxy, which in America is known as fundamentalism. When fundamentalism is combined with an antitheological bias, as it is, for instance, in its biblicistic-evangelical form, the theological truth of yesterday is defended as an unchangeable message against the theological truth of today and tomorrow. Fundamentalism fails to make contact with the present situation, not because it speaks from beyond every situation, but because it speaks from a situation of the past. It elevates something finite and transitory to infinite and eternal validity. In this respect fundamentalism has demonic traits. It destroys the humble honesty of the search for truth, it splits the conscience of its thoughtful adherents, and it makes them fanatical because they are forced to suppress elements of truth of which they are dimly aware.

Fundamentalists in America and orthodox theologians in Europe can point to the fact that their theology is eagerly received and held by many people just because of the historical or biographical situation in which men find themselves today. The fact is obvious, but the interpretation is wrong. "Situation," as one pole of all theological work, does not refer to the psychological or sociological state in which individuals or groups live. It refers to the scientific and artistic, the economic, political, and ethical

3

forms in which they express their interpretation of existence. The "situation" to which theology must speak relevantly is not the situation of the individual as individual and not the situation of the group as group. Theology is neither preaching nor counseling; therefore, the success of a theology when it is applied to preaching or to the care of souls is not necessarily a criterion of its truth. The fact that fundamentalist ideas are eagerly grasped in a period of personal or communal distintegration does not prove their theological validity, just as the success of a liberal theology in periods of personal or communal integration is no certification of its truth. The "situation" theology must consider is the creative interpretation of existence, an interpretation which is carried on in every period of history under all kinds of psychological and sociological conditions. The "situation" certainly is not independent of these factors. However, theology deals with the cultural expression they have found in practice as well as in theory and not with these conditioning factors as such. Thus theology is not concerned with the political split between East and West, but it *is* concerned with the political interpretation of this split. Theology is not concerned with the spread of mental diseases or with our increasing awareness of them, but it *is* concerned with the psychiatric interpretation of these trends. The "situation" to which theology must respond is the totality of man's creative self-interpretation in a special period. Fundamentalism and orthodoxy reject this task, and, in doing so, they miss the meaning of theology.

"Kerygmatic" theology is related to fundamentalism and orthodoxy in so far as it emphasizes the unchangeable truth of the message (kerygma) over against the changing demands of the situation. It tries to avoid the shortcomings of fundamentalism by subjecting every theology, including orthodoxy, to the criterion of the Christian message. This message is contained in the Bible, but it is not identical with the Bible. It is expressed in the classical tradition of Christian theology, but it is not identical with any special form of that tradition. Reformation theology and, in our own day, the neo-Reformation theology of Barth and his school are outstanding examples of kerygmatic theology. In his day Luther was attacked by orthodox thinkers, and now Barth and his followers are under heavy attack by fundamentalists. This means that it is not entirely fair to call Luther "orthodox" or Barth "neo-orthodox." Luther was in danger of becoming orthodox, and Barth is in danger of becoming so; but this was not their intention. Both made a serious attempt to rediscover the eternal message *within* the Bible and tradition, over against a distorted tradition and a mechanically misused Bible. Luther's criticism of the Roman system of mediations and degrees in the name of the decisive biblical categories of judgment and grace, his rediscovery of the Pauline message, and, at the same time, his courageous evaluation of the spiritual value of the biblical books were a genuine kerygmatic theology. Barth's criticism of the neo-Protestant–bourgeois synthesis achieved by liberal theology, his rediscovery of the Christian paradox, and, at the same time, the freedom of his spiritual exegesis of the Epistle to the Romans and his acceptance of radical historical criticism were a genuine kerygmatic theology. In both cases there was an emphasis on the eternal truth over against the human situation and its demands. In both cases this emphasis had prophetic, shaking, and transforming power. Without such kerygmatic reactions theology would lose itself in the relativities of the "situation"; it would become a "situation" itself—for instance, the religious nationalism of the so-called German Christians and the religious progressivism of the so-called humanists in America.

Yet the "situation" cannot be excluded from theological work. Luther was unprejudiced enough to use his own nominalist learning and Melanchthon's humanist education for the formulation of theological doctrines. But he was not conscious enough of the problem of the "situation" to avoid sliding into orthodox attitudes, thus preparing the way for the period of Protestant orthodoxy. Barth's greatness is that he corrects himself again and again in the light of the "situation" and that he strenuously tries not to become his own follower. Yet he does not realize that in doing so he ceases to be a merely kerygmatic theologian. In attempting to derive every statement directly from the ultimate truth—for instance, deriving the duty of making war against Hitler from the resurrection of the Christ[1]—he falls into using a method which can be called "neo-orthodox," a method which has strengthened all trends toward a theology of repristination in Europe. The pole called "situation" cannot be neglected in theology without dangerous consequences. Only a courageous participation in the "situation," that is, in all the various cultural forms which express modern man's interpretation of his existence, can overcome the present oscillation of kerygmatic theology between the freedom implied in the genuine kerygma and its orthodox fixation. In

1. Karl Barth, "A Letter to Great Britain from Switzerland," in *This Christian Cause* (New York: Macmillan Co., 1941).

other words, kerygmatic theology needs apologetic theology for its completion.

2. Apologetic Theology and the Kerygma

Apologetic theology is "answering theology." It answers the questions implied in the "situation" in the power of the eternal message and with the means provided by the situation whose questions it answers.

The term "apologetic," which had such a high standing in the early church, has fallen into disrepute because of the methods employed in the abortive attempts to defend Christianity against attacks from modern humanism, naturalism, and historism. An especially weak and disgusting form of apologetics used the *argumentum ex ignorantia;* that is, it tried to discover gaps in our scientific and historical knowledge in order to find a place for God and his actions within an otherwise completely calculable and "immanent" world. Whenever our knowledge advanced, another defense position had to be given up; but eager apologetes were not dissuaded by this continuous retreat from finding in the most recent developments of physics and historiography new occasions to establish God's activity in new gaps of scientific knowledge. This undignified procedure has discredited everything which is called "apologetics."

There is, however, a more profound reason for the distrust of apologetic methods, especially on the part of the kerygmatic theologians. In order to answer a question, one must have something in common with the person who asks it. Apologetics presupposes common ground, however vague it may be. But kerygmatic theologians are inclined to deny any common ground with those outside the "theological circle." They are afraid that the common ground will destroy the uniqueness of the message. They point to the early Christian Apologists who saw a common ground in the acceptance of the Logos; they point to the Alexandrian school which found a common ground in Platonism; they point to Thomas Aquinas' use of Aristotle; above all, they point to the common ground which apologetic theology believed itself to have found with the philosophy of the Enlightenment, with Romanticism, with Hegelianism and Kantianism, with humanism and naturalism. They try to demonstrate that in each case what was assumed to be common ground actually was the ground of the "situation"; that theology lost its own ground when it entered the situation. Apologetic theology in all these forms—and that means practically all nonfundamentalist theology since the beginning of the eighteenth century—is, from the point of view

Going deep to deep

of recent kerygmatic theologians, a surrender of the kerygma, of the immovable truth. If this is an accurate reading of theological history, then the only real theology is kerygmatic theology. The "situation" cannot be entered; no answer to the questions implied in it can be given, at least not in terms which are felt to be an answer. The message must be thrown at those in the situation—thrown like a stone. This certainly can be an effective method of preaching under special psychological conditions, for instance, in revivals; it can even be effective if expressed in aggressive theological terms; but it does not fulfil the aim of the theological function of the church. And, beyond all this, it is impossible. Even kerygmatic theology must use the conceptual tools of its period. It cannot simply repeat biblical passages. Even when it does, it cannot escape the conceptual situation of the different biblical writers. Since language is the basic and all-pervasive expression of every situation, theology cannot escape the problem of the "situation." Kerygmatic theology must give up its exclusive transcendence and take seriously the attempt of apologetic theology to answer the questions put before it by the contemporary situation.

On the other hand, apologetic theology must heed the warning implied in the existence and the claim of kerygmatic theology. It loses itself if it is not based on the kerygma as the substance and criterion of each of its statements. More than two centuries of theological work have been determined by the apologetic problem. "The Christian message and the modern mind" has been the dominating theme since the end of classical orthodoxy. The perennial question has been: Can the Christian message be adapted to the modern mind without losing its essential and unique character? Most theologians have believed that it is possible; some have deemed it impossible either in the name of the Christian message or in the name of the modern mind. No doubt the voices of those who have emphasized the contrast, the *diastasis*, have been louder and more impressive—men usually are more powerful in their negations than in their affirmations. But the continuous toil of those who have tried to find a union, a "synthesis," has kept theology alive. Without them traditional Christianity would have become narrow and superstitious, and the general cultural movement would have proceeded without the "thorn in the flesh" which it needed, namely, an honest theology of cultural high standing. The wholesale condemnations of theology during the last two centuries of theology which are fashionable in traditional and neo-orthodox groups are profoundly wrong (as Barth himself has acknowledged in his *Die protestantische Theologie im neunzehnten Jahrhundert*). Yet certainly it is necessary to ask in every special case whether or not the apologetic bias has dissolved the Christian message. And it is further necessary to seek a theological method in which message and situation are related in such a way that neither of them is obliterated. If such a method is found, the two centuries' old question of "Christianity and the modern mind" can be attacked more successfully. The following system is an attempt to use the "method of correlation" as a way of uniting message and situation. It tries to correlate the questions implied in the situation with the answers implied in the message. It does not derive the answers from the questions as a self-defying apologetic theology does. Nor does it elaborate answers without relating them to the questions as a self-defying kerygmatic theology does. It correlates questions and answers, situation and message, human existence and divine manifestation.

Obviously, such a method is not a tool to be handled at will. It is neither a trick nor a mechanical device. It is itself a theological assertion, and, like all theological assertions, it is made with passion and risk; and ultimately it is not different from the system which is built upon it. System and method belong to each other and are to be judged with each other. It will be a positive judgment if the theologians of the coming generations acknowledge that it has helped them, and nontheological thinkers as well, to understand the Christian message as the answer to the questions implied in their own and in every human situation.

B. THE NATURE OF SYSTEMATIC THEOLOGY

3. THE THEOLOGICAL CIRCLE

Attempts to elaborate a theology as an empirical-inductive or a metaphysical deductive "science," or as a combination of both, have given ample evidence that no such an attempt can succeed. In every assumedly scientific theology there is a point where individual experience, traditional valuation, and personal commitment must decide the issue. This point, often hidden to the authors of such theologies, is obvious to those who look at them with other experiences and other commitments. If an inductive approach is employed, one must ask in what direction the writer looks for his material. And if the answer is that he looks in every direction and toward every experience, one must ask what characteristic of reality or experience is the empirical basis of his theology. Whatever the answer may be, an a priori of experience and valuation is implied.

The same is true of a deductive approach, as developed in classical idealism. The ultimate principles in idealist theology are rational expressions of an ultimate concern; like all metaphysical ultimates, they are religious ultimates at the same time. A theology derived from them is determined by the hidden theology implied in them.

In both the empirical and the metaphysical approaches, as well as in the much more numerous cases of their mixture, it can be observed that the a priori which directs the induction and the deduction is a type of mystical experience. Whether it is "being-itself" (Scholastics) or the "universal substance" (Spinoza), whether it is "beyond subjectivity and objectivity" (James) or the "identity of spirit and nature" (Schelling), whether it is "universe" (Schleiermacher) or "cosmic whole" (Hocking), whether it is "value creating process" (Whitehead) or "progressive integration" (Wieman), whether it is "absolute spirit" (Hegel) or "cosmic person" (Brightman)—each of these concepts is based on an immediate experience of something ultimate in value and being of which one can become intuitively aware. Idealism and naturalism differ very little in their starting point when they develop theological concepts. Both are dependent on a point of identity between the experiencing subject and the ultimate which appears in religious experience or in the experience of the world as "religious." The theological concepts of both idealists and naturalists are rooted in a "mystical a priori," an awareness of something that transcends the cleavage between subject and object. And if in the course of a "scientific" procedure this a priori is discovered, its discovery is possible only because it was present from the very beginning. This is the circle which no religious philosopher can escape. And it is by no means a vicious one. Every understanding of spiritual things (*Geisteswissenschaft*) is circular.

But the circle within which the theologian works is narrower than that of the philosopher of religion. He adds to the "mystical a priori" the criterion of the Christian message. While the philosopher of religion tries to remain general and abstract in his concepts, as the concept "religion" itself indicates, the theologian is consciously and by intention specific and concrete. The difference, of course, is not absolute. Since the experiential basis of every philosophy of religion is partly determined by the cultural tradition to which it belongs—even mysticism is culturally conditioned—it inescapably includes concrete and special elements. The philosopher as philosopher, however, tries to abstract from these elements and to create generally valid concepts concerning religion. The theologian, on the other hand, claims the universal validity of the Christian message in spite of its concrete and special character. He does not justify this claim by abstracting from the concreteness of the message but by stressing its unrepeatable uniqueness. He enters the theological circle with a concrete commitment. He enters it as a member of the Christian church to perform one of the essential functions of the church —its theological self-interpretation.

The "scientific" theologian wants to be more than a philosopher of religion. He wants to interpret the Christian message generally with the help of his method. This puts him before two alternatives. He may subsume the Christian message under his concept of religion. Then Christianity is considered to be one example of religious life beside other examples, certainly the highest religion, but not the final one and not unique. Such a theology does not enter the theological circle. It keeps itself within the religious-philosophical circle and its indefinite horizons —horizons which beckon toward a future which is open for new and perhaps higher examples of religion. The scientific theologian, in spite of his desire to be a theologian, remains a philosopher of religion. Or he becomes really a theologian, an interpreter of his church and its claim to uniqueness and universal validity. Then he enters the theological circle and should admit that he has done so and stop speaking of himself as a scientific theologian in the ordinary sense of "scientific."

But even the man who has entered the theological circle consciously and openly faces another serious problem. Being inside the circle, he must have made an existential decision; he must be in the situation of faith. But no one can say of himself that he is in the situation of faith. No one can call himself a theologian, even if he is called to be a teacher of theology. Every theologian is committed *and* alienated; he is always in faith *and* in doubt; he is inside *and* outside the theological circle. Sometimes the one side prevails, sometimes the other; and he is never certain which side really prevails. Therefore, one criterion alone can be applied: a person can be a theologian as long as he acknowledges the content of the theological circle as his ultimate concern. Whether this is true does not depend on his intellectual or moral or emotional state; it does not depend on the intensity and certitude of faith; it does not depend on the power of regeneration or the grade of sanctification. Rather it depends on his being ultimately concerned with the Christian message even if he is sometimes inclined to attack and to reject it.

This understanding of "theological existence" resolves the conflict be-

tween the orthodox and the pietist theologians over the *theologia irre-*
genitorum ("theology of the irregenerate"). The pietists realized that
one cannot be a theologian without faith, decision, commitment, without being in the theological circle. But they identified theological existence with an experience of regeneration. The orthodox protested against
this, arguing that no one can be certain of his regeneration and, beyond
this, that theology deals with objective materials which can be handled
by any thinker inside or outside the theological circle who meets the
intellectual preconditions. Today orthodox and pietist theologians are
allied against the assumedly unbelieving critical theologians, while the
heritage of orthodox objectivism has been taken over by the program
(not the achievement) of empirical theology. In view of this age-old
struggle it must be restated that the theologian belongs inside the theological circle but that the criterion whether or not he is in it is the acceptance of the Christian message as his ultimate concern.

The doctrine of the theological circle has a methodological consequence: neither the introduction nor any other part of the theological
system is the logical basis for the other parts. Every part is dependent
on every other part. The introduction presupposes the Christology and
the doctrine of the church and vice versa. The arrangement is only a
matter of expediency.

4. Two Formal Criteria of Every Theology

The last remark applies significantly to this Introduction, which is an
attempt to give criteria for every theological enterprise. The criteria are
formal, since they are abstracted from the concrete materials of the theological system. They are, however, derived from the whole of the Christian message. Form and content can be distinguished but not separated
(this is the reason why even formalized logic cannot escape the philosophical circle). Form and content do not function as the basis of a deductive system; but they are methodological guardians at the boundary
line of theology.

We have used the term "ultimate concern" without explanation. Ultimate concern is the abstract translation of the great commandment:
"The Lord, our God, the Lord is one; and you shall love the Lord your
God with all your heart, and with all your soul and with all your mind,
and with all your strength."[2] The religious concern is ultimate; it excludes all other concerns from ultimate significance; it makes them pre-

2. Mark 12:29 (Revised Standard Version).

liminary. The ultimate concern is unconditional, independent of any conditions of character, desire, or circumstance. The unconditional concern is total: no part of ourselves or of our world is excluded from it; there is no "place" to flee from it.[3] The total concern is infinite: no moment of relaxation and rest is possible in the face of a religious concern which is ultimate, unconditional, total, and infinite.

The word "concern" points to the "existential" character of religious experience. We cannot speak adequately of the "object of religion" without simultaneously removing its character as an object. That which is ultimate gives itself only to the attitude of ultimate concern. It is the correlate of an unconditional concern but not a "highest thing" called "the absolute" or "the unconditioned," about which we could argue in detached objectivity. It is the object of total surrender, demanding also the surrender of our subjectivity while we look at it. It is a matter of infinite passion and interest (Kierkegaard), making us its object whenever we try to make it our object. For this reason we have avoided terms like *"the* ultimate," *"the* unconditioned," *"the* universal," *"the* infinite," and have spoken of ultimate, unconditional, total, infinite concern. Of course, in every concern there is *something* about which one is concerned; but this something should not appear as a separated object which could be known and handled without concern. This, then, is the first formal criterion of theology: *The object of theology is what concerns us ultimately. Only those propositions are theological which deal with their object in so far as it can become a matter of ultimate concern for us.*

The negative meaning of this proposition is obvious. Theology should never leave the situation of ultimate concern and try to play a role within the arena of preliminary concerns. Theology cannot and should not give judgments about the aesthetic value of an artistic creation, about the scientific value of a physical theory or a historical conjecture, about the best methods of medical healing or social reconstruction, about the solution of political or international conflicts. The theologian *as* theologian is no expert in any matters of preliminary concern. And, conversely, those who are experts in these matters should not *as such* claim to be experts in theology. The first formal principle of theology, guarding the boundary line between ultimate concern and preliminary concerns, protects theology as well as the cultural realms on the other side of the line.

But this is not its entire meaning. Although it does not indicate the

3. Psalm 139.

[margin note: 1st criterion: object of theology.]

content of the ultimate concern and its relation to the preliminary concerns, it has implications in both respects. There are three possible relations of the preliminary concerns to that which concerns us ultimately. The first is mutual indifference, the second is a relation in which a preliminary concern is elevated to ultimacy, and the third is one in which a preliminary concern becomes the vehicle of the ultimate concern without claiming ultimacy for itself. The first relation is predominant in ordinary life with its oscillation between conditional, partial, finite situations and experiences and moments when the question of the ultimate meaning of existence takes hold of us. Such a division, however, contradicts the unconditional, total, and infinite character of the religious concern. It places our ultimate concern beside other concerns and deprives it of its ultimacy. This attitude sidesteps the ultimacy of the biblical commandments and that of the first theological criterion. The second relation is idolatrous in its very nature. Idolatry is the elevation of a preliminary concern to ultimacy. Something essentially conditioned is taken as unconditional, something essentially partial is boosted into universality, and something essentially finite is given infinite significance (the best example is the contemporary idolatry of religious nationalism). The conflict between the finite basis of such a concern and its infinite claim leads to a conflict of ultimates; it radically contradicts the biblical commandments and the first theological criterion. The third relation between the ultimate concern and the preliminary concerns makes the latter bearers and vehicles of the former. That which is a finite concern is not elevated to infinite significance, nor is it put beside the infinite, but in and through it the infinite becomes real. Nothing is excluded from this function. In and through every preliminary concern the ultimate concern can actualize itself. Whenever this happens, the preliminary concern becomes a possible object of theology. But theology deals with it only in so far as it is a medium, a vehicle, pointing beyond itself.

Pictures, poems, and music can become objects of theology, not from the point of view of their aesthetic form, but from the point of view of their power of expressing some aspects of that which concerns us ultimately, in and through their aesthetic form. Physical or historical or psychological insights can become objects of theology, not from the point of view of their cognitive form, but from the point of view of their power of revealing some aspects of that which concerns us ultimately in and through their cognitive form. Social ideas and actions, legal projects and procedures, political programs and decisions, can become

the third relation: vehicle, not the message itself

objects of theology, not from the point of view of their social, legal, and political form, but from the point of view of their power of actualizing some aspects of that which concerns us ultimately in and through their social, legal, and political forms. Personality problems and developments, educational aims and methods, bodily and mental healing, can become objects of theology, not from the point of view of their ethical and technical form, but from the point of view of their power of mediating some aspects of that which concerns us ultimately in and through their ethical and technical form.

The question now arises: What is the content of our ultimate concern? What *does* concern us unconditionally? The answer, obviously, cannot be a special object, not even God, for the first criterion of theology must remain formal and general. If more is to be said about the nature of our ultimate concern, it must be derived from an analysis of the concept "ultimate concern." *Our ultimate concern is that which determines our being or not-being. Only those statements are theological which deal with their object in so far as it can become a matter of being or not-being for us.* This is the second formal criterion of theology.

Nothing can be of ultimate concern for us which does not have the power of threatening and saving our being. The term "being" in this context does not designate existence in time and space. Existence is continuously threatened and saved by things and events which have no ultimate concern for us. But the term "being" means the whole of human reality, the structure, the meaning, and the aim of existence. All this is threatened; it can be lost or saved. Man is ultimately concerned about his being and meaning. "To be or not to be" in *this* sense is a matter of ultimate, unconditional, total, and infinite concern. Man is infinitely concerned about the infinity to which he belongs, from which he is separated, and for which he is longing. Man is totally concerned about the totality which is his true being and which is disrupted in time and space. Man is unconditionally concerned about that which conditions his being beyond all the conditions in him and around him. Man is ultimately concerned about that which determines his ultimate destiny beyond all preliminary necessities and accidents.

The second formal criterion of theology does not point to any special content, symbol, or doctrine. It remains formal and, consequently, open for contents which are able to express "that which determines our being or nonbeing." At the same time it excludes contents which do not have this power from entering the theological realm. Whether it is a god who

Theology is the methodical interpretation of the contents of the Christian faith.

is a being beside others (even a highest being) or an angel who inhabits a celestial realm (called the realm of "spirits") or a man who possesses supranatural powers (even if he is called a god-man)—none of these is an object of theology if it fails to withstand the criticism of the second formal criterion of theology, that is, if it is not a matter of being or nonbeing for us.

5. Theology and Christianity

Theology is the methodical interpretation of the contents of the Christian faith. This is implicit in the preceding statements about the theological circle and about theology as a function of the Christian church. The question now arises whether there is a theology outside Christianity and, if so, whether or not the idea of theology is fulfilled in Christian theology in a perfect and final way. Indeed, this is what Christian theology claims; but is it more than a claim, a natural expression of the fact that the theologian works within the theological circle? Has it any validity beyond the periphery of the circle? It is the task of apologetic theology to prove that the Christian claim also has validity from the point of view of those outside the theological circle. Apologetic theology must show that trends which are immanent in all religions and cultures move toward the Christian answer. This refers both to doctrines and to the theological interpretation of theology.

If taken in the broadest sense of the word, theology, the *logos* or the reasoning about *theos* (God and divine things), is as old as religion. Thinking pervades all the spiritual activities of man. Man would not be spiritual without words, thoughts, concepts. This is especially true in religion, the all-embracing function of man's spiritual life.[4] It was a misunderstanding of Schleiermacher's definition of religion ("the feeling of absolute dependence") and a symptom of religious weakness when successors of Schleiermacher located religion in the realm of feeling as one psychological function among others. The banishment of religion into the nonrational corner of subjective emotions in order to have the realms of thought and action free from religious interference was an easy way of escaping the conflicts between religious tradition and modern thought. But this was a death sentence against religion, and religion did not and could not accept it.

---

4. The term "spiritual" (with a lower-case *s*) must be sharply distinguished from "Spiritual" (with a capital *S*). The latter refers to activities of the divine Spirit in man; the former, to the dynamic-creative nature of man's personal and communal life.

Every myth contains a theological thought which can be, and often has been, made explicit. Priestly harmonizations of different myths sometimes disclose profound theological insights. Mystical speculations, as in Vedanta Hinduism, unite meditative elevation with theological penetration. Metaphysical speculations, as in classical Greek philosophy, unite rational analysis with theological vision. Ethical, legal, and ritual interpretations of the divine law create another form of theology on the soil of prophetic monotheism. All this is "theo-logy," *logos* of *theos*, a rational interpretation of the religious substance of rites, symbols, and myths.

Christian theology is no exception. It does the same thing, but it does it in a way which implies the claim that it is *the* theology. The basis of this claim is the Christian doctrine that the Logos became flesh, that the principle of the divine self-revelation has become manifest in the event "Jesus as the Christ." If this message is true, Christian theology has received a foundation which transcends the foundation of any other theology and which itself cannot be transcended. Christian theology has received something which is absolutely concrete and absolutely universal at the same time. No myth, no mystical vision, no metaphysical principle, no sacred law, has the concreteness of a personal life. In comparison with a personal life everything else is relatively abstract. And none of these relatively abstract foundations of theology has the universality of the Logos, which itself is the principle of universality. In comparison with the Logos everything else is relatively particular. Christian theology is *the* theology in so far as it is based on the tension between the absolutely concrete and the absolutely universal. Priestly and prophetic theologies can be very concrete, but they lack universality. Mystical and metaphysical theologies can be very universal, but they lack concreteness.

It seems paradoxical if one says that only that which is absolutely concrete can also be absolutely universal and vice versa, but it describes the situation adequately. Something that is merely abstract has a limited universality because it is restricted to the realities from which it is abstracted. Something that is merely particular has a limited concreteness because it must exclude other particular realities in order to maintain itself as concrete. Only that which has the power of representing everything particular is absolutely concrete. And only that which has the power of representing everything abstract is absolutely universal. This leads to a point where the absolutely concrete and the absolutely universal are identical. And this is the point at which Christian theology emerges, the point which is described as the "Logos who has become flesh."[5] The Logos doctrine as the doctrine of the identity of the absolutely concrete with the absolutely universal is not one theological doctrine among others; it is the only possible foundation of a Christian theology which claims to be *the* theology. It is not necessary to call the absolutely universal the *logos;* other words, derived from other traditions, could replace it. The same is true of the term "flesh" with its Hellenistic connotations. But it is necessary to accept the vision of early Christianity that if Jesus is called the Christ he must represent everything particular and must be the point of identity between the absolutely concrete and the absolutely universal. In so far as he is absolutely concrete, the relation to him can be a completely existential concern. In so far as he is absolutely universal, the relation to him includes potentially all possible relations and can, therefore, be unconditional and infinite. The biblical reference to the one side is found in the letters of Paul when he speaks of "being in Christ."[6] We cannot be *in* anything particular because of the self-seclusion of the particular against the particular. We can be only *in* that which is absolutely concrete and absolutely universal at the same time. The biblical reference to the other side also is given in Paul's writings when he speaks of the subjection of the cosmic powers to the Christ.[7] Only that which is absolutely universal and, at the same time, absolutely concrete can conquer cosmic pluralism.

It was not a cosmological interest (Harnack) but a matter of life and death for the early church which led to the use of the Stoic-Philonic *logos* doctrine in order to express the universal meaning of the event "Jesus the Christ." In so doing, the church announced its faith in the victory of the Christ over the demonic-natural powers which constitute polytheism and prevent salvation. For this reason the church fought desperately against the attempt of Arianism to make the Christ into one of the cosmic powers, although the highest, depriving him of both his absolute universality (he is less than God) and his absolute concreteness (he is more than man). The half-God Jesus of Arian theology is neither uni-

---

5. The Logos doctrine is misunderstood if the tension between universal and concrete is interpreted as a tension between abstract and particular. Abstraction negates parts of that from which it abstracts. Universality includes every part because it includes concreteness. Particularity excludes every particular from every other one. Concreteness represents every other concrete because it includes universality. Christian theology moves between the poles of the universal and the concrete and not between those of the abstract and the particular.

6. II Cor. 5:17.

7. Romans, chap. 8.

versal enough nor concrete enough to be the basis of Christian theology.

It is obvious that these arguments do not prove the assertion of faith that in Jesus Christ the Logos has become flesh. But they show that, if this assertion is accepted, Christian theology has a foundation which infinitely transcends the foundations of everything in the history of religion which could be called "theology."

theology

6. THEOLOGY AND PHILOSOPHY: A QUESTION

Theology claims that it constitutes a special realm of knowledge, that it deals with a special object and employs a special method. This claim places the theologian under the obligation of giving an account of the way in which he relates theology to other forms of knowledge. He must answer two questions: What is the relationship of theology to the special sciences (*Wissenschaften*) and what is its relationship to philosophy? The first question has been answered implicitly by the preceding statement of the formal criteria of theology. If nothing is an object of theology which does not concern us ultimately, theology is unconcerned about scientific procedures and results and vice versa. Theology has no right and no obligation to prejudice a physical or historical, sociological or psychological, inquiry. And no result of such an inquiry can be directly productive or disastrous for theology. The point of contact between scientific research and theology lies in the philosophical element of both, the sciences and theology. Therefore, the question of the relation of theology to the special sciences merges into the question of the relation between theology and philosophy.

The difficulty of this question lies partly in the fact that there is no generally accepted definition of philosophy. Every philosophy proposes a definition which agrees with the interest, purpose, and method of the philosopher. Under these circumstances the theologian can only suggest a definition of philosophy which is broad enough to cover most of the important philosophies which have appeared in what usually is called the history of philosophy. The suggestion made here is to call philosophy *that cognitive approach to reality in which reality as such is the object*. Reality as such, or reality as a whole, is not the whole of reality; it is the structure which makes reality a whole and therefore a potential object of knowledge. Inquiring into the nature of reality as such means inquiring into those structures, categories, and concepts which are presupposed in the cognitive encounter with every realm of reality. From this point of view philosophy is by definition critical. It separates the multifarious materials of experience from those structures which make experience possible. There is no difference in this respect between constructive idealism and empirical realism. The question regarding the character of the general structures that make experience possible is always the same. It is *the* philosophical question.

The critical definition of philosophy is more modest than those philosophical enterprises which try to present a complete system of reality, including the results of all the special sciences as well as the general structures of prescientific experience. Such an attempt can be made from "above" or from "below." Hegel worked from "above" when he filled the categorical forms, developed in his *Logic*, with the available material of the scientific knowledge of his time and adjusted the material to the categories. Wundt worked from "below" when he abstracted general and metaphysical principles from the available scientific material of his time, with the help of which the entire sum of empirical knowledge could be organized. Aristotle worked from both "above" and "below" when he carried through metaphysical and scientific studies in interdependence. This also was the ideal of Leibniz when he sketched a universal calculus capable of subjecting all of reality to mathematical analysis and synthesis. But in all these cases the limits of the human mind, the finitude which prevents it from grasping the whole, became visible. No sooner was the system finished than scientific research trespassed its boundaries and disrupted it in all directions. Only the general principles were left, always discussed, questioned, changed, but never destroyed, shining through the centuries, reinterpreted by every generation, inexhaustible, never antiquated or obsolete. These principles are the material of philosophy.

This understanding of philosophy is, on the other hand, less modest than the attempt to reduce philosophy to epistemology and ethics, which was the goal of the Neo-Kantian and related schools in the nineteenth century, and less modest also than the attempt to reduce it to logical calculus, which has been the goal of logical positivism and related schools in the twentieth century. Both attempts to avoid the ontological question have been unsuccessful. The later adherents of the Neo-Kantian philosophy recognized that every epistemology contains an implicit ontology. It cannot be otherwise. Since knowing is an act which participates in being or, more precisely, in an "ontic relation," every analysis of the act of knowing must refer to an interpretation of being (cf. Nicolai Hartmann). At the same time the problem of values pointed toward an ontological foundation of the validity of value-judgments. If values have no *fundamentum in re* (cf. Plato's identification of the good with the essential structures, the ideas of being), they float in the air of a transcendent validity, or else they are subjected to pragmatic tests which are arbitrary and accidental unless they introduce an ontology of essences surreptitiously. It is not necessary to discuss the pragmatic-naturalistic line of philosophical thought, for, in spite of the antimetaphysical statements of some of its adherents, it has expressed itself in definite ontological terms such as life, growth, process, experience, being (understood in an all-embracing sense), etc. But it is necessary to compare the ontological definition of philosophy, suggested above, with the radical attempts to reduce philosophy to scientific logic. The question is whether the elimination of almost all traditional philosophical problems by logical positivism is a successful escape from ontology. One's first reaction is the feeling that such an attitude pays too high a price, namely, the price of making philosophy irrelevant. But, beyond this impression, the following argument can be put forward. If the restriction of philosophy to the logic of the sciences is a matter of taste, it need not be taken seriously. If it is based on an analysis of the limits of human knowledge, it is based, like every epistemology, on ontological assumptions. There is always at least one problem about which logical positivism, like all semantic philosophies, must make a decision. What is the relation of signs, symbols, or logical operations to reality? Every answer to this question says something about the structure of being. It is ontological. And a philosophy which is so radically critical of all other philosophies should be sufficiently self-critical to see and to reveal its own ontological assumptions.

Philosophy asks the question of reality as a whole; it asks the question of the structure of being. And it answers in terms of categories, structural laws, and universal concepts. It must answer in ontological terms. Ontology is not a speculative-fantastic attempt to establish a world behind the world; it is an analysis of those structures of being which we encounter in every meeting with reality. This was also the original meaning of metaphysics; but the preposition *meta* now has the irremediable connotation of pointing to a duplication of this world by a transcendent realm of beings. Therefore, it is perhaps less misleading to speak of ontology instead of metaphysics.

Philosophy necessarily asks the question of reality as a whole, the question of the structure of being. Theology necessarily asks the same question, for that which concerns us ultimately must belong to reality as a whole; it must belong to being. Otherwise we could not encounter it, and it could not concern us. Of course, it cannot be one being among others; then it would not concern us infinitely. It must be the ground of our being, that which determines our being or not-being, the ultimate and unconditional power of being. But the power of being, its infinite ground or "being-itself," expresses itself in and through the structure of being. Therefore, we can encounter it, be grasped by it, know it, and act toward it. Theology, when dealing with our ultimate concern, presupposes in every sentence the structure of being, its categories, laws, and concepts. Theology, therefore, cannot escape the question of being any more easily than can philosophy. The attempt of biblicism to avoid nonbiblical, ontological terms is doomed to failure as surely as are the corresponding philosophical attempts. The Bible itself always uses the categories and concepts which describe the structure of experience. On every page of every religious or theological text these concepts appear: time, space, cause, thing, subject, nature, movement, freedom, necessity, life, value, knowledge, experience, being and not-being. Biblicism may try to preserve their popular meaning, but then it ceases to be theology. It must neglect the fact that a philosophical understanding of these categories has influenced ordinary language for many centuries. It is surprising how casually theological biblicists use a term like "history" when speaking of Christianity as a historical religion or of God as the "Lord of history." They forget that the meaning they connect with the word "history" has been formed by thousands of years of historiography and philosophy of history. They forget that historical being is one kind of being in addition to others and that, in order to distinguish it from the word "nature," for instance, a general vision of the structure of being is presupposed. They forget that the problem of history is tied up with the problems of time, freedom, accident, purpose, etc., and that each of these concepts has had a development similar to the concept of history. The theologian must take seriously the meaning of the terms he uses. They must be known to him in the whole depth and breadth of their meaning. Therefore, the systematic theologian must be a philosopher in critical understanding even if not in creative power.

The structure of being and the categories and concepts describing this structure are an implicit or explicit concern of every philosopher and of every theologian. Neither of them can avoid the ontological question. Attempts from both sides to avoid it have proved abortive. If this is the situation, the question becomes the more urgent: What is the relation between the ontological question asked by the philosopher and the onto-logical question asked by the theologian?

7. THEOLOGY AND PHILOSOPHY: AN ANSWER

Philosophy and theology ask the question of being. But they ask it from different perspectives. Philosophy deals with the structure of being in itself; theology deals with the meaning of being for us. From this difference convergent and divergent trends emerge in the relation of theology and philosophy.

The first point of divergence is a difference in the cognitive attitude of the philosopher and the theologian. Although driven by the philo-sophical *erōs*, the philosopher tries to maintain a detached objectivity toward being and its structures. He tries to exclude the personal, social, and historical conditions which might distort an objective vision of re-ality. His passion is the passion for a truth which is open to general approach, subject to general criticism, changeable in accordance with every new insight, open and communicable. In all these respects he feels no different from the scientist, historian, psychologist, etc. He collabo-rates with them. The material for his critical analysis is largely supplied by empirical research. Just as all sciences have their origin in philosophy, so they contribute in turn to philosophy by giving to the philosopher new and exactly defined material far beyond anything he could get from a prescientific approach to reality. Of course, the philosopher, as a phi-losopher, neither criticizes nor augments the knowledge provided by the sciences. This knowledge forms the basis of his description of the cate-gories, structural laws, and concepts which constitute the structure of being. In this respect the philosopher is as dependent on the scientist as he is dependent on his own prescientific observation of reality—often more dependent. This relation to the sciences (in the broad sense of *Wissenschaften*) strengthens the detached, objective attitude of the phi-losopher. Even in the intuitive-synthetic side of his procedure he tries to exclude influences which are not purely determined by his object.[8]

The theologian, quite differently, is not detached from his object but is involved in it. He looks at his object (which transcends the character of being an object) with passion, fear, and love. This is not the *erōs* of

8. The concept of a "philosophical faith" appears questionable from this point of view (see Karl Jaspers, *The Perennial Scope of Philosophy* [New York: Philosophical Library, 1949]).

the philosopher or his passion for objective truth; it is the love which accepts saving, and therefore personal, truth. The basic attitude of the theologian is commitment to the content he expounds. Detachment would be a denial of the very nature of this content. The attitude of the theologian is "existential." He is involved—with the whole of his existence, with his finitude and his anxiety, with his self-contradictions and his despair, with the healing forces in him and in his social situation. Every theological statement derives its seriousness from these elements of existence. The theologian, in short, is determined by his faith. Every theology presupposes that the theologian is in the theological circle. This contradicts the open, infinite, and changeable character of philosophical truth. It also differs from the way in which the philosopher is dependent on scientific research. The theologian has no direct relation to the scientist (including the historian, sociologist, psychologist). He deals with him only in so far as philosophical implications are at stake. If he abandons the existential attitude, as some of the "empirical" theologians have done, he is driven to statements the reality of which will not be acknowledged by anybody who does not share the existential presuppositions of the assumedly empirical theologian. Theology is necessarily existential, and no theology can escape the theological circle.

The second point of divergence between the theologian and the philosopher is the difference in their sources. The philosopher looks at the whole of reality to discover within it the structure of reality as a whole. He tries to penetrate into the structures of being by means of the power of his cognitive function and its structures. He assumes—and science continuously confirms this assumption—that there is an identity, or at least an analogy, between objective and subjective reason, between the *logos* of reality as a whole and the *logos* working in him. Therefore, this *logos* is common; every reasonable being participates in it, uses it in asking questions and criticizing the answers received. There is no particular place to discover the structure of being; there is no particular place to stand to discover the categories of experience. The place to look is all places; the place to stand is no place at all; it is pure reason.

The theologian, on the other hand, must look where that which concerns him ultimately is manifest, and he must stand where its manifestation reaches and grasps him. The source of his knowledge is not the universal *logos* but the Logos "who became flesh," that is, the *logos* manifesting itself in a particular historical event. And the medium through which he receives the manifestation of the *logos* is not common rationality but the church, its traditions and its present reality. He speaks in the church about the foundation of the church. And he speaks because he is grasped by the power of this foundation and by the community built upon it. The concrete *logos* which he sees is received through believing commitment and not, like the universal *logos* at which the philosopher looks, through rational detachment.

The third point of divergence between philosophy and theology is the difference in their content. Even when they speak about the same object, they speak about something different. The philosopher deals with the categories of being in relation to the material which is structured by them. He deals with causality as it appears in physics or psychology; he analyzes biological or historical time; he discusses astronomical as well as microcosmic space. He describes the epistemological subject and the relation of person and community. He presents the characteristics of life and spirit in their dependence on, and independence of, each other. He defines nature and history in their mutual limits and tries to penetrate into ontology and logic of being and nonbeing. Innumerable other examples could be given. They all reflect the cosmological structure of the philosophical assertions. The theologian, on the other hand, relates the same categories and concepts to the quest for a "new being." His assertions have a soteriological character. He discusses causality in relation to a *prima causa*, the ground of the whole series of causes and effects; he deals with time in relation to eternity, with space in relation to man's existential homelessness. He speaks of the self-estrangement of the subject, about the spiritual center of personal life, and about community as a possible embodiment of the "New Being." He relates the structures of life to the creative ground of life and the structures of spirit to the divine Spirit. He speaks of the participation of nature in the "history of salvation," about the victory of being over nonbeing. Here also the examples could be increased indefinitely; they show the sharp divergence of theology from philosophy with respect to their content.

The divergence between philosophy and theology is counterbalanced by an equally obvious convergence. From both sides converging trends are at work. The philosopher, like the theologian, "exists," and he cannot jump over the concreteness of his existence and his implicit theology. He is conditioned by his psychological, sociological, and historical situation. And, like every human being, he exists in the power of an ultimate concern, whether or not he is fully conscious of it, whether or not he admits it to himself and to others. There is no reason why even the most scientific philosopher should not admit it, for without an ultimate concern his philosophy would be lacking in passion, seriousness, and creativity. Wherever we look in the history of philosophy, we find ideas and systems which claim to be ultimately relevant for human existence. Occasionally the philosophy of religion openly expresses the ultimate concern behind a system. More often it is the character of the ontological principles, or a special section of a system, such as epistemology, philosophy of nature, politics and ethics, philosophy of history, etc., which is most revealing for the discovery of the ultimate concern and the hidden theology within it. Every creative philosopher is a hidden theologian (sometimes even a declared theologian). He is a theologian in the degree to which his existential situation and his ultimate concern shape his philosophical vision. He is a theologian in the degree to which his intuition of the universal *logos* of the structure of reality as a whole is formed by a particular *logos* which appears to him on his particular place and reveals to him the meaning of the whole. And he is a theologian in the degree to which the particular *logos* is a matter of active commitment within a special community. There is hardly a historically significant philosopher who does not show these marks of a theologian. But the philosopher does not intend to be a theologian. He wants to serve the universal *logos*. He tries to turn away from his existential situation, including his ultimate concern, toward a place above all particular places, toward pure reality. The conflict between the intention of becoming universal and the destiny of remaining particular characterizes every philosophical existence. It is its burden and its greatness.

The theologian carries an analogous burden. Instead of turning away from his existential situation, including his ultimate concern, he turns toward it. He turns toward it, not in order to make a confession of it, but in order to make clear the universal validity, the *logos* structure, of what concerns him ultimately. And he can do this only in an attitude of detachment from his existential situation and in obedience to the universal *logos*. This obligates him to be critical of every special expression of his ultimate concern. He cannot affirm any tradition and any authority except through a "No" and a "Yes." And it is always possible that he may not be able to go all the way from the "No" to the "Yes." He cannot join the chorus of those who live in unbroken assertions. He must take the risk of being driven beyond the boundary line of the theological circle. Therefore, the pious and powerful in the church are suspicious of him, although they live in dependence upon the work of the former theologians who were in the same situation. Theology, since it serves not only the concrete but also the universal *logos*, can become a stumbling block for the church and a demonic temptation for the theologian. The detachment required in honest theological work can destroy the necessary involvement of faith. This tension is the burden and the greatness of every theological work.

The duality of divergence and convergence in the relation between theology and philosophy leads to the double question: Is there a necessary conflict between the two and is there a possible synthesis between them? Both questions must be answered negatively. Neither is a conflict between theology and philosophy necessary, nor is a synthesis between them possible.

A conflict presupposes a common basis on which to fight. But there is no common basis between theology and philosophy. If the theologian and the philosopher fight, they do so either on a philosophical or on a theological basis. The philosophical basis is the ontological analysis of the structure of being. If the theologian needs this analysis, either he must take it from a philosopher or he must himself become a philosopher. Usually he does both. If he enters the philosophical arena, conflicts as well as alliances with other philosophers are unavoidable. But all this happens on the philosophical level. The theologian has no right whatsoever to argue for a philosophical opinion in the name of his ultimate concern or on the basis of the theological circle. He is obliged to argue for a philosophical decision in the name of the universal *logos* and from the place which is no place: pure reason. It is a disgrace for the theologian and intolerable for the philosopher if in a philosophical discussion the theologian suddenly claims an authority other than pure reason. Conflicts on the philosophical level are conflicts between two philosophers, one of whom happens to be a theologian, but they are not conflicts between theology and philosophy.

Often, however, the conflict is fought on the theological level. The hidden theologian in the philosopher fights with the professed theologian. This situation is more frequent than most philosophers realize. Since they have developed their concepts with the honest intention of obeying the universal *logos*, they are reluctant to recognize the existentially conditioned elements in their systems. They feel that such elements, while they give color and direction to their creative work, diminish its truth value. In such a situation the theologian must break the resistance of the philosopher against a theological analysis of his ideas.

He can do this by pointing to the history of philosophy, which discloses that in every significant philosopher existential passion (ultimate concern) and rational power (obedience to the universal *logos*) are united and that the truth value of a philosophy is dependent on the amalgamation of these two elements in every concept. The insight into this situation is, at the same time, an insight into the fact that two philosophers, one of whom happens to be a theologian, can fight with each other and that two theologians, one of whom happens to be a philosopher, can fight with each other; but there is no possible conflict between theology and philosophy because there is no common basis for such a conflict. The philosopher may or may not convince the philosopher-theologian. And the theologian may or may not convert the theologian-philosopher. In no case does the theologian as such stand against the philosopher as such and vice versa.

Thus there is no conflict between theology and philosophy, and there is no synthesis either—for exactly the same reason which insures that there will be no conflict. A common basis is lacking. The idea of a synthesis between theology and philosophy has led to the dream of a "Christian philosophy." The term is ambiguous. It can mean a philosophy whose existential basis is historical Christianity. In this sense all modern philosophy is Christian, even if it is humanistic, atheistic, and intentionally anti-Christian. No philosopher living within Western Christian culture can deny his dependence on it, as no Greek philosopher could have hidden his dependence on an Apollonian-Dionysian culture, even if he was a radical critic of the gods of Homer. The modern vision of reality and its philosophical analysis is different from that of pre-Christian times, whether one is or is not existentially determined by the God of Mount Zion and the Christ of Mount Golgotha. Reality is encountered differently; experience has different dimensions and directions than in the cultural climate of Greece. No one is able to jump out of this "magic" circle. Nietzsche, who tried to do so, announced the coming of the Anti-Christ. But the Anti-Christ is dependent on the Christ against whom he arises. The early Greeks, for whose culture Nietzsche was longing, did not have to fight the Christ; indeed, they unconsciously prepared his coming by elaborating the questions to which he gave the answer and the categories in which the answer could be expressed. Modern philosophy is not pagan. Atheism and anti-Christianity are not pagan. They are anti-Christian in Christian terms. The scars of the Christian tradition cannot be erased; they are a *character indelebilis*. Even the paganism of naziism was not really a relapse to paganism (just as bestiality is not a relapse to the beast).

But the term "Christian philosophy" is often meant in a different sense. It is used to denote a philosophy which does not look at the universal *logos* but at the assumed or actual demands of a Christian theology. This can be done in two ways: either the church authorities or its theological interpreters nominate one of the past philosophers to be their "philosophical saint" or they demand that contemporary philosophers should develop a philosophy under special conditions and with a special aim. In both cases the philosophical *erōs* is killed. If Thomas Aquinas is officially named *the* philosopher of the Roman Catholic church, he has ceased to be for Catholic philosophers a genuine partner in the philosophical dialogue which goes on through the centuries. And if present-day Protestant philosophers are asked to accept the idea of personality as their highest ontological principle because it is the principle most congenial to the spirit of the Reformation, the work of these philosophers is mutilated. There is nothing in heaven and earth, or beyond them, to which the philosopher must subject himself except the universal *logos* of being as it gives itself to him in experience. Therefore, the idea of a "Christian philosophy" in the narrower sense of a philosophy which is intentionally Christian must be rejected. The fact that every modern philosophy has grown on Christian soil and shows traces of the Christian culture in which it lives has nothing to do with the self-contradicting ideal of a "Christian philosophy."

Christianity does not need a "Christian philosophy" in the narrower sense of the word. The Christian claim that the *logos* who has become concrete in Jesus as the Christ is at the same time the universal *logos* includes the claim that wherever the *logos* is at work it agrees with the Christian message. No philosophy which is obedient to the universal *logos* can contradict the concrete *logos,* the Logos "who became flesh."

C. THE ORGANIZATION OF THEOLOGY

Theology is the methodical explanation of the contents of the Christian faith. This definition is valid for all theological disciplines. Therefore, it is unfortunate if the name "theology" is reserved for systematic theology. Exegesis and homiletics are as theological as systematics. And systematics can fail to be theological as readily as can the others. The criterion of every theological discipline is whether or not it deals with the Christian message as a matter of ultimate concern.

The tension between the universal and the concrete poles in the Christian faith leads to the division of theological work into historical and constructive groups of disciplines. This is foreshadowed in the division of the New Testament into gospels (including the acts of the apostles) and epistles. It is significant, however, that in the Fourth Gospel there is a complete amalgamation of the historical and the constructive elements. This points to the fact that in the Christian message history is theological and theology is historical. Nevertheless, reasons of expediency make a division into historical and constructive disciplines unavoidable, since each of them has a different nontheological side. Historical theology includes historical research; systematic theology includes philosophical discussion. The historian and the philosopher, both of them members of the theological faculty, must unite in the theological task of interpreting the Christian message, each with his special cognitive tools. But more is involved in their co-operation. In every moment of his work the historical theologian presupposes a systematic point of view; otherwise he would be a historian of religion, not a historical theologian. This mutual immanence of the historical and the constructive elements is a decisive mark of Christian theology.

Historical theology can be subdivided into the biblical disciplines, church history, and the history of religion and culture. Biblicistic theologians are inclined to admit only the former group to full theological standing and to exclude the third group completely. Even Barth considers church history only as *Hilfswissenschaft* (a supporting science). This, of course, is a systematic-theological assertion, and, seen in the light of the critical principles, a misguided one, for all three groups combine a nontheological with a theological element. There is much nontheological research in the biblical disciplines; there can be a radically theological interpretation of the history of religion and culture from the point of view of our ultimate concern; and both assertions are true of church history. In spite of the basic significance of the biblical disciplines, it is not justifiable to exclude the two other groups from a full theological standing. This is confirmed by the fact that the three groups are largely interdependent. In some respects, the biblical literature is a section not only of church history but also of the history of religion and culture. The influence of nonbiblical religions and cultures on Bible and church history is too obvious to be denied (cf., for instance, the intertestamental period). The criterion whether or not a discipline is theological is not its assumedly supranatural origin but its significance for the interpretation of our ultimate concern.

Systematic theology is more difficult to organize than historical theology. Questions of truth and questions of expediency must be answered before adequate organization is possible. The first problem is created by the fact that the section on "natural theology" in the classical tradition has been replaced (definitely, since Schleiermacher) by a general and autonomous philosophy of religion. But while "natural theology" was, so to speak, a preamble to the theology of revelation, developed in view of the latter and under its control, philosophy of religion is an independent philosophical discipline. Or, more exactly, philosophy of religion is a dependent part of a philosophical whole and in no sense a theological discipline. Schleiermacher was aware of this situation, and he spoke of propositions borrowed by theology from "ethics"[9]—ethics meaning to him philosophy of culture. But Schleiermacher did not answer the question of the relation of this "borrowed" philosophical truth to theological truth. If philosophical truth lies outside the theological circle, how can it determine the theological method? And if it lies within the theological circle, it is not autonomous and theology need not borrow it. This problem has worried all those modern theologians who have neither adhered to the traditional precritical natural theology (as Catholics and orthodox Protestants have done) nor dismissed natural theology as well as philosophy of religion by exclusively maintaining a theology of revelation (as the neo-orthodox theologians have done).

The solution which underlies the present system, and which is fully explained only by means of the whole system, accepts the philosophical and theological criticism of natural theology in its traditional sense. It also accepts the neo-orthodox criticism of a general philosophy of religion as the basis of systematic theology. At the same time, it tries to do justice to the theological motives behind natural theology and philosophy of religion. It takes the philosophical element into the structure of the system itself, using it as the material out of which questions are developed. The questions are answered by the theological concepts. The problem, "Natural theology or philosophy of religion?" is answered by a third way—the "method of correlation" (see below, p. 59). For the organization of systematic theology this means that no special discipline called "philosophy of religion" belongs to the realm of systematic the-

9. Friedrich Schleiermacher, *The Christian Faith*, trans. H. R. Mackintosh (Edinburgh: T. & T. Clark, 1928), pp. 5 ff.

ology. This decision does not mean, however, that the problems currently included in what is called "philosophy of religion" must be refused consideration in the theological curriculum.

A second problem of the organization of systematic theology is the position of apologetics. Modern theologians usually have identified it with philosophy of religion, while in traditional theology the section on natural theology contained much apologetic material. The exclusion of these two methods makes another solution necessary. One contribution to a solution has been given in the second section of this system, "Apologetic Theology and the Kerygma." It points to the fact that systematic theology is "anwering theology." It must answer the questions implied in the general human and the special historical situation. Apologetics, therefore, is an omnipresent element and not a special section of systematic theology. The "method of correlation" applied in the present system gives pointed expression to the decisive character of the apologetic element in systematic theology.

This solution is also valid for the ethical element in systematic theology. It was not until the later orthodox period that, under the influence of modern philosophy, ethics was separated from dogmatics. The positive result was a much richer development of theological ethics; the negative result was an unsolved conflict with philosophical ethics. Today, in spite of the fact that some theological faculties have well-developed departments of Christian ethics, a trend toward taking theological ethics back into the unity of the system can be seen. This trend has been supported by the neo-orthodox movement's rejection of an independent theological ethic. A theology which, like the present system, emphasizes the existential character of theology must follow this trend all the way to its very end. The ethical element is a necessary—and often predominant—element in every theological statement. Even such formal statements as the critical principles point to the decision of the ethical individual about his "being or nonbeing." The doctrines of finitude and existence, or of anxiety and guilt, are equally ontological and ethical in character, and in the sections on "The Church" and "The Christian" the ethical element (social and personal) is predominant. These are only examples which show that an "existential" theology implies ethics in such a way that no special section for ethical theology is needed. Reasons of expediency may, nevertheless, justify the preservation of departments of Christian ethics.

The third and most significant element in systematic theology is the dogmatic element. For a long period it supplied the name for the whole of systematic theology. Dogmatics is the statement of the doctrinal tradition for our present situation. The word "dogmatics" emphasizes the importance of the formulated and officially acknowledged dogma for the work of the systematic theologian. And in this sense the terminology is justified, for the theologian exercises a function of the church within the church and for the church. And the church is based on a foundation whose protective formulation is given in the creeds. The word "dogma" itself originally expressed this function. In the later Greek philosophical communities it designated the special doctrines accepted as the tradition of a special school. *Dogmata* were distinctive philosophical doctrines. In this sense the Christian community had its *dogmata* too. But the word received another meaning in the history of Christian thought. The function of the creeds as a protection against destructive heresies made their acceptance a matter of life and death for Christianity. The heretic was considered a demonic enemy of the message of Christ. With the complete union of church and state after Constantine, the doctrinal laws of the church also became civil laws of the state, and the heretic was considered a criminal. The destructive consequences of this situation, the demonic activities of states and churches, Catholic as well as Protestant, against theological honesty and scientific autonomy have discredited the words "dogma" and "dogmatics" to such a degree that it is hardly possible to re-establish their genuine meaning. This does not reduce the significance of the formulated *dogmata* for systematic theology, but it makes use of the term "dogmatics" impossible. "Systematic theology," embracing apologetics, dogmatics, and ethics, seems to be the most adequate term.

The organization of theological work is not complete without the inclusion of what is usually called "practical theology." Although Schleiermacher praised it as the crown of theology, it is not a third part in addition to the historical and the systematic parts. It is the technical theory through which these two parts are applied to the life of the church. A technical theory describes the adequate means for a given end. The given end of practical theology is the life of the church. While the doctrine of the church about its nature and its functions is a matter of systematic theology, practical theology deals with the institutions through which the nature of the church is actualized and its functions are performed. It does not deal with them from the historical point of view, telling what has been and is still going on in the church, but it looks at them from the technical point of view, asking how to act most effectively. If the practical theologian makes a study of the history of the Protestant hymn, he works in the realm of historical theology. And if he writes an essay on the aesthetic function of the church, he works in the realm of systematic theology. But if he uses the material and the principles gained through his historical or systematic studies in order to make suggestions for the use of hymns or for the design of church buildings, he works in the realm of practical theology. It is the technical point of view that distinguishes practical from theoretical theology. As occurs in every cognitive approach to reality, a bifurcation between pure and applied knowledge takes place in theology. And since for modern feeling in contrast to ancient feeling, pure sciences have no higher dignity than technical sciences, practical theology has no less theological standing than theoretical theology. And finally just as there is a continuous exchange of knowledge between the pure and the technical approaches in all scientific realms, so practical and theoretical theology are interdependent. This also follows from the existential character of theology, for in the state of ultimate concern the difference between theory and practice vanishes.

The organization of practical theology is implicit in the doctrine of the functions of the church. Each function is a necessary consequence of the nature of the church and therefore an end for which institutional means exist, however poorly developed they may be. Each function needs a practical discipline to interpret, to criticize, and to transform the existing institutions and to suggest new ones if necessary. Theology itself is such a function, and its institutional realization within the life of the church is one of the many concerns of practical theology.

Like historical and systematic theology, practical theology has a non-theological side. In order to discuss the institutional expressions of the life of the church, the practical theologian must use (1) our present knowledge of the general psychological and sociological structures of man and society; (2) a practical and theoretical understanding of the psychological and sociological situation of special groups; and (3) a knowledge of the cultural achievements and problems within the realms of his special interest: education, arts, music, medicine, politics, economics, social work, public communication, etc. In this way practical theology can become a bridge between the Christian message and the human situation, generally and specially. It can put new questions before the systematic theologian, questions arising out of the cultural life of the period, and it can induce the historical theologian to make new researches from points of view which come out of the actual needs of his contemporaries. It can preserve the church from traditionalism and dogmatism, and it can induce society to take the church seriously. But it can do all this only if, in unity with historical and systematic theology, it is driven by the ultimate concern which is concrete and universal at the same time.

D. THE METHOD AND STRUCTURE OF SYSTEMATIC THEOLOGY

8. The Sources of Systematic Theology

Every methodological reflection is abstracted from the cognitive work in which one actually engages. Methodological awareness always follows the application of a method; it never precedes it. This fact has often been forgotten in recent discussions on the use of the empirical method in theology. The adherents of this method made it a kind of fetish, hoping that it would "work" in every cognitive approach to every subject. Actually they had found the basic structure of their theology before they reflected on the method to be used. And the method they described could be called "empirical" only with great difficulty and artificiality. The following methodological considerations describe the method actually used in the present system. Since the method is derived from a preceding understanding of the subject of theology, the Christian message, it anticipates the decisive assertions of the system. This is an unavoidable circle. Whether the "method of correlation" (the name I suggest without special emphasis) is empirical, constructive, or something else is unimportant as long as it proves adequate to its subject.

If the task of systematic theology is to explain the contents of the Christian faith, three questions immediately arise: What are the sources of systematic theology? What is the medium of their reception? What is the norm determining the use of the sources? The first answer to these questions might be the Bible. The Bible is the original document about the events on which Christianity is based. Although this cannot be denied, the answer is insufficient. In dealing with the question of the sources of systematic theology, we must reject the assertion of neo-orthodox biblicism that the Bible is the *only* source. The biblical message cannot be understood and could not have been received had there been no preparation for it in human religion and culture. And the biblical message would not have become a message for anyone, including the theologian himself, without the experiencing participation of the church and of every Christian. If the "Word of God" or the "act of revelation" is called the source of systematic theology, it must be emphasized that the "Word of God" is not limited to the words of a book and that the act of revelation is not the "inspiring" of a "book of revelations," even if the book is the document of the final "Word of God," the fulfilment and criterion of all revelations. The biblical message embraces more (and less) than the biblical books. Systematic theology, therefore, has additional sources beyond the Bible.

The Bible, however, is the basic source of systematic theology because it is the original document about the events on which the Christian church is founded. If we use the word "document" for the Bible, we must exclude legal connotations. The Bible is not a legally conceived, formulated, and sealed record about a divine "deed" on the basis of which claims can be decided. The documentary character of the Bible is identical with the fact that it contains the original witness of those who participated in the revealing events. Their participation was their response to the happenings which became revealing events through this response. The inspiration of the biblical writers is their receptive and creative response to potentially revelatory facts. The inspiration of the writers of the New Testament is their acceptance of Jesus as the Christ, and with him, of the New Being, of which they became witnesses. Since there is no revelation unless there is someone who receives it as revelation, the act of reception is a part of the event itself. The Bible is both original event and original document; it witnesses to that of which it is a part.

The biblical material as a source of systematic theology is presented in a methodological way by the historical theologian. Biblical theology, in co-operation with the other disciplines of historical theology, opens the Bible as the basic source of systematic theology. But how it does this is by no means obvious. The biblical theologian, to the degree to which he is a theologian (which includes a systematic point of view), does not present pure facts to us; he gives us theologically interpreted facts. His exegesis is pneumatic (Spiritual) or, as we would call it today, "existential." He speaks of the results of his philosophical and detached interpretation as matters of ultimate concern to him. He unites philology and devotion in dealing with the biblical texts. It is not easy to do this with fairness to both points of view. A comparison of any recent scientific commentary on Romans (e.g., C. H. Dodd or Sanday and Headlam) with Barth's pneumatic-existential interpretation of it lays bare the un-bridged gap between both methods. All theologians, and especially the students of systematic theology, suffer because of this situation. System-atic theology needs a biblical theology which is historical-critical without any restrictions and, at the same time, devotional-interpretative, taking account of the fact that it deals with matters of ultimate concern. It is possible to fulfil this demand, for that which concerns us ultimately is not linked with any special conclusion of historical and philological research. A theology which is dependent on predetermined results of the historical approach is bound to something conditional which claims to be unconditional, that is, with something demonic. And the demonic character of any demand imposed on the historian for definite results becomes visible in the fact that it destroys his honesty. Being ultimately concerned about what is really ultimate liberates the theologian from all "sacred dishonesty." It makes conservative as well as revolutionary his-torical criticism open to him. Only such free historical work, united with the attitude of ultimate concern, can open the Bible to the systematic theologian as his basic source.

The genesis of the Bible is an event in church history—an event in a comparatively late stage of early church history. The systematic theo-logian, therefore, in using the Bible as a source, implicitly uses church history as a source. He must do this explicitly. Systematic theology has a direct and definite relation to church history. On this point there is a real difference between the Catholic and the Protestant attitude, and no systematic theologian can escape a decision about it. The decision is easy for those who are bound by the authority of the Roman church. It is also easy for those who believe that Protestantism means a radical biblicism and who assume that radical biblicism is a possible theological position. But most theologians in the non-Roman churches are not willing to accept this alternative. It is obvious to them that the radical biblicistic attitude is a self-deception. No one is able to leap over two thousand years of church history and become contemporaneous with the writers of the New Testament, except in the Spiritual sense of accepting Jesus as the Christ. Every person who encounters a biblical text is guided in his religious understanding of it by the understanding of all previous gener-ations. Even the Reformers were dependent on the Roman tradition against which they protested. They directed special elements of the eccle-siastical tradition against others in order to fight the distortion which had affected the whole tradition, but they did not and could not jump out of the tradition into the situation of Matthew and Paul. The Reformers were aware of this situation, and their orthodox systematizers were still aware of it. Evangelical biblicism, both past and present, is unaware of it and produces a "biblical" theology which actually is dependent on definite dogmatic developments of the post-Reformation period. Through historical scholarship the difference between the dogmatic teaching of most American evangelistic churches and the original meaning of the biblical texts can easily be shown. Church history cannot be evaded; therefore, it is a religious as well as a scholarly necessity that the relationship of systematic theology to the ecclesiastical tradition be stated frankly and pointedly.

Another approach which is not acceptable to most non-Roman theologians is the subjection of systematic theology to the decisions of councils and popes. Roman Catholic dogmatics uses those doctrinal traditions which have gained legal standing (*de fide*) as the real source of systematic theology. It presupposes dogmatically, with or without a posteriori proofs, that those doctrines whose validity is guaranteed by canon law agree essentially with the biblical message. The work of the systematic theologian is an exact and, at the same time, polemic interpretation of the statements *de fide*. This is the reason for the dogmatic sterility of Roman Catholic theology, in contrast to its liturgical and ethical creativity and the great scholarship it develops in areas of church history which are free from dogmatic prohibitions. It is important for the ecumenical character of systematic theology that Greek Orthodox theologians, although they accept the authority of tradition, deny the legalization of tradition by papal authority. This gives the Greek Orthodox theologian creative possibilities from which Roman theologians are excluded. Protestant theology protests in the name of the Protestant principle (see Part V, Sec. II) against the identification of our ultimate concern with any creation of the church, including the biblical writings in so far as their witness to what is really ultimate concern is also a conditioned expression of their own spirituality. Therefore, it is able to use all the materials provided by church history. It can make use of Greek and Roman and German and modern concepts in interpreting the biblical message; it can make use of the decisions of sectarian protests against official theology; but it is not bound to any of these concepts and decisions.

A special problem arises from the fact that no one is actually able to handle all these materials, because the denominational structures operate as an unconscious and conscious principle of selection. This cannot be avoided, and it has a creative side. The ecclesiastical and theological climate in which the theologian grows up or for which he has later made a personal decision produces understanding through familiarity. Without such familiarity no existential use of the church-historical material is possible. The systematic theologian encounters in the concrete life of his denomination, in its liturgy and hymns, its sermons and sacraments, that which concerns him ultimately—the New Being in Jesus as the Christ. Therefore, the denominational tradition is a decisive source for the systematic theologian, however ecumenically he may use it.

The biblical source is made available to the systematic theologian through a critical and ultimately concerned biblical theology. In the same way church history is made available to the systematic theologian through a historically critical and ultimately concerned history of Christian thought, formerly called "history of dogma." The traditional term "dogmatics" implies a concern which the more recent term does not express. The "history of Christian thought" can mean a detached description of the ideas of theological thinkers through the centuries. Some of the critical histories of Christian thought are not far removed from such an attitude. The historical theologian must show that in all periods Christian thought has dealt with matters of ultimate concern and that therefore it is itself a matter of ultimate concern. Systematic theology needs a history of Christian thought written from a point of view which is radically critical and, at the same time, existentially concerned.

A broader source of systematic theology than all those mentioned so far is the material presented by the history of religion and culture. Its impact on the systematic theologian begins with the language he uses and the cultural education he has received. His spiritual life is shaped by his social and individual encounter with reality. This is expressed in the language, poetry, philosophy, religion, etc., of the cultural tradition in which he has grown up and from which he takes some content in every moment of his life, in his theological work and also outside it. Beyond this immediate and unavoidable contact with his culture and religion, the systematic theologian deals with them directly in many ways. He uses culture and religion intentionally as his means of expression, he points to them for confirmation of his statements, he fights against them as contradictions of the Christian message, and, above all, he formulates the existential questions implied in them, to which his theology intends to be the answer.

This continuous and never ending use of cultural and religious contents as a source of systematic theology raises the question: How are these contents made available for use in a way parallel to the method by which the biblical theologian makes the biblical materials available and the historian of Christian thought makes the doctrinal materials available? There is no established answer to this question, since neither a theological history of religion nor a theological history of culture has been theoretically conceived and practically established.

A theological history of religion should interpret theologically the material produced by the investigation and analysis of the prereligious and religious life of mankind. It should elaborate the motives and types of religious expression, showing how they follow from the nature of the religious concern and therefore necessarily appear in all religions, including Christianity in so far as it is a religion. A theological history of religion also should point out demonic distortions and new tendencies in the religions of the world, pointing to the Christian solution and preparing the way for the acceptance of the Christian message by the adherents of non-Christian religions. One could say that a theological history of religion should be carried through in the light of the missionary principle that the New Being in Jesus as the Christ is the answer to the question asked implicitly and explicitly by the religions of mankind. Some materials taken from a theological history of religion appear in the present theological system.

A theological history of culture cannot be a continuous historical report (this is also true of the theological history of religion). It can only be what I like to call a "theology of culture,"[10] which is the attempt to analyze the theology behind all cultural expressions, to discover the ultimate concern in the ground of a philosophy, a political system, an artistic style, a set of ethical or social principles. This task is analytic rather than synthetic, historical rather than systematic. It is a preparation for the work of the systematic theologian. At the present time a theology of culture is continuously being constructed from the nontheological and, less vigorously, from the theological side. It has become an important part of the many critical analyses of the present world situation, of the cultural decline of the West, of developments in special realms. Theological analysis has been carried on in connection with the history of

10. Paul Tillich, "Ueber die Idee einer Theologie der Kultur," in *Kantstudien* (Berlin: Pan-Verlag, Rolf Heise, 1920); see also my *The Religious Situation* (New York: Henry Holt & Co., 1932).

modern thought, art, science, social movements (called in German *Geistesgeschichte,* "the history of spiritual life"). It should, however, be worked out in a more organized way by theologians. It should be taught as "the theology of culture" in all institutions of theological learning; for instance, as theological history of philosophy, the arts, etc. Concerning the method of such a theological analysis of culture the following might be said. The key to the theological understanding of a cultural creation is its style. Style is a term derived from the realm of the arts, but it can be applied to all realms of culture. There is a style of thought, of politics, of social life, etc. The style of a period expresses itself in its cultural forms, in its choice of objects, in the attitudes of its creative personalities, in its institutions and customs. It is an art as much as a science to "read styles," and it requires religious intuition, on the basis of an ultimate concern, to look into the depth of a style, to penetrate to the level where an ultimate concern exercises its driving power. This, however, is what is demanded of the theological historian of culture, and in performing this function he opens up a creative source for systematic theology.

This survey of the sources of systematic theology has shown their almost unlimited richness: Bible, church history, history of religion and culture. It has further shown that there are degrees of importance in this immense source material, corresponding with its more direct or more indirect relationship to the central event on which the Christian faith is based, the appearance of the New Being in Jesus as the Christ. But two decisive questions have neither been asked nor answered—the question of the medium through which this material is received by the systematic theologian and the question of the norm to be used by him in evaluating the sources.

9. EXPERIENCE AND SYSTEMATIC THEOLOGY

The sources of systematic theology can be sources only for one who participates in them, that is, through experience. Experience is the medium through which the sources "speak" to us, through which we can receive them. The question of experience, therefore, has been a central question whenever the nature and method of theology have been discussed. The theologians of the early Franciscan school were well aware of what today is called an "existential" relation to truth. For them theology was practical knowledge, based on a participation of the knowing subject in the spiritual realities, a touching and tasting (*haptus* and *gustus*) of that with which he deals. Alexander of Hales and Bonaven-

tura were strictly "experiential" theologians. They dedicated much labor
to an analysis of the nature of the especially religious experience as dis-
tinct from other forms of experience. Behind their endeavors stood the
mystical-Augustinian principle of the immediate awareness of "being-
itself," which is, at the same time, "truth-itself" (*esse ipsum—verum
ipsum*). While the predominant theology under the guidance of Thomas
Aquinas and Duns Scotus replaced the mystical immediacy of the early
Franciscans with analytical detachment, the Augustinian-Franciscan tradition never lost its power. The principle of experience was preserved by
sectarian movements (largely dependent on the enthusiasm of the Franciscan radicals) in the pre-Reformation and Reformation periods. An
evangelical enthusiast like Thomas Muenzer had almost all the characteristic traits of what is called today "existential experience," including
the elements of anxiety and despair, the "boundary situation," the experience of "meaninglessness"; and, on the other hand, he had the ecstatic experience of a Spiritual power driving and guiding him in the
practical decisions of his personal and social life. Although the victory
of ecclesiastical or biblical authority in all Continental churches and the
rise of classical orthodoxy suppressed the principle of experience, it never
eradicated it. The principle of experience reappeared in full strength
in Continental Pietism and Anglo-American Independentism, Method-
ism, and Evangelicalism. In these forms it survived the period of the
Enlightenment and found classical theological expression in Schleiermacher's theological method.

No present-day theology should avoid a discussion of Schleiermacher's
experiential method, whether in agreement or disagreement. One of the
causes for the disquieting effect of neo-orthodox theology was that it detached itself completely from Schleiermacher's method, consequently
denying the theological development of the last two hundred years (one
hundred before and one hundred after Schleiermacher). The crucial
question of theology today is whether or not, or to what degree, this denial is justified. Certainly it would not be justified if it were based only
on a mistaken interpretation of Schleiermacher. But more than this is
involved in the neo-orthodox judgment. A psychological interpretation
of Schleiermacher's famous definition of religion is mistaken and even
unfair, inasmuch as it can easily be avoided. When he defined religion as
the "feeling of absolute dependence," "feeling" meant the immediate
awareness of something unconditional in the sense of the Augustinian-
Franciscan tradition. This tradition was mediated to him religiously by

his Moravian education, philosophically by Spinoza and Schelling. "Feeling," in this tradition, referred not to a psychological function but to the awareness of that which transcends intellect and will, subject and object. "Dependence," in Schleiermacher's definition, was, on the Christian level, "teleological" dependence—a dependence which has moral character, which includes freedom and excludes a pantheistic and deterministic interpretation of the experience of the unconditional. Schleiermacher's "feeling of absolute dependence" was rather near to what is called in the present system "ultimate concern about the ground and meaning of our being." Understood in this way, it lies beyond much of the usual criticism directed against it.[11]

On the other hand, criticism must be directed against Schleiermacher's method in his *Glaubenslehre* (*The Christian Faith*). He tried to derive all contents of the Christian faith from what he called the "religious consciousness" of the Christian. In a similar way his followers, notably the Lutheran "School of Erlangen," which included the theologians Hofmann and Frank, tried to establish an entire system of theology by deriving the contents from the experience of the regenerated Christian. This was an illusion, as Frank's system clearly proves. The event on which Christianity is based (he called it "Jesus of Nazareth") is not derived from experience; it is *given* in history. Experience is not the source from which the contents of systematic theology are taken but the medium through which they are existentially received.

Another form of experiential theology not exposed to the same criticism has grown out of the evangelical tradition of American Christianity. It is distinguished from the Continental theology of experience by its alliance with philosophical empiricism and pragmatism. It tries to create an "empirical theology" on the basis of mere experience in line with the philosophical empiricists. For the method of systematic theology everything depends on the sense in which the term "experience" is used. A careful analysis of present philosophical and theological discussion shows that it is used in three ways: in an ontological, a scientific, and a mystical sense. The ontological sense of experience is a consequence of philosophical positivism. The positively given is, according to this theory, the only reality of which we can meaningfully speak. And positively given means given in experience. Reality is identical with experience. Pragmatism, as developed by William James and partly by John Dewey, reveals the philo-

11. It is fortunate that Barth has rejected Brunner's book on Schleiermacher, *Die Mystik und das Wort* (Tübingen: J. C. B. Mohr, 1924), for this very reason.

sophical motive behind this elevation of experience to the highest ontological rank. The motive is to deny the split between an ontological subject and ontological objects, for, once established, this split cannot be
overcome, the possibility of knowledge cannot be explained, and the
unity of life and its processes remains a mystery. The dynamic naturalism of recent philosophy involves the ontological concept of experience,
whether this naturalism is more realistic or more idealistic or more mystical in its emphasis.

If experience in this sense is used as the source of systematic theology,
nothing can appear in the theological system which transcends the whole
of experience. A divine being in the traditional sense is excluded from
such a theology. Since, on the other hand, the whole of experience cannot
be of ultimate concern, a special experience or a special quality of the
whole experience must be the source of systematic theology. For instance,
the value-producing processes (Whitehead) or the uniting processes
(Wieman) or the character of wholeness (Hocking) can be called the
especially religious experience. But if this is done, one must have a concept of what a religious experience is. Otherwise one would not recognize it within the whole of experience. This means that there must be
another kind of experience, an immediate participation in religious reality, preceding any theological analysis of reality as a whole. And this
is the actual situation. The empirical theologians who use the ontological
concept of experience do not derive their theology from this experience.
They derive it from their participation in a concrete religious reality,
from their religious experience in the mystical sense of experience. And
they try to discover the corresponding elements within the whole of experience. They seek a cosmological confirmation of their personal religious life.

In spite of its circular arguing, empirical theology of this type has made
a definite contribution to systematic theology. It has shown that the religious objects are not objects among others but that they are expressions
of a quality or dimension of our general experience. In this, American
empirical theology agrees with Continental phenomenological theology
(e.g., Rudolph Otto and Max Scheler). Whenever the question is asked,
"What does the 'holy' mean?" rather than the question, "Does God
exist?" we are in the line of thought in which pragmatism and phenomenology agree.[12]

12. Cf. also my own "Religionsphilosophie" in Max Dessoir's *Lehrbuch der Philosophie*
(Berlin: Ullstein, 1925).

The second sense in which experience is used is derived from the experimentally tested experience of science. Experience in this sense constitutes an articulated world. It does not designate the given as such but the given in its recognizable structure. It combines rational and perceptive elements and is the result of a never finished process of experimenting and testing. Some of the empirical theologians tried to apply the method of scientific experience to theology, but they never succeeded and could not succeed for two reasons. First, the object of theology (namely, our ultimate concern and its concrete expressions) is not an object within the whole of scientific experience. It cannot be discovered by detached observation or by conclusions derived from such observation. It can be found only in acts of surrender and participation. Second, it cannot be tested by scientific methods of verification. In these methods the testing subject keeps himself outside the test situation. And if this is partially impossible, as, for example, in microphysics, he includes the effects of this fact in his calculations. The object of theology can be verified only by a participation in which the testing theologian risks himself in the ultimate sense of "to be or not to be." This test is never finished, not even in a complete life of experience. An element of risk remains and makes an experimental verification in time and space impossible.

This is confirmed by the results of scientific-experiential theology. If an epistemological analysis of experience leads to embracing concepts like "cosmic person" (Brightman) or "cosmic mind" (Boodin) or "creative process" (Wieman), these concepts are neither scientific nor theological. They are not scientific but ontological. They do not describe a being beside other beings; they point to a quality of being-itself. This is not accomplished by scientific experience but by a vision in which scientific and nonscientific elements are united. On the other hand, these concepts are not theological. Certainly they can and must be used by systematic theology. But the "cosmic person" and the "creative process" are not in themselves matters of ultimate concern. They are philosophical possibilities with the tentative character of such. They are not religious necessities. They are theoretical, not existential. If, however, they claim religious significance—a genuine possibility of all ontological concepts—their scientific function is dropped, and they must be discussed in theological terms as symbolic expressions of our ultimate concern. In no case can scientific experience as such produce a foundation and source of systematic theology.

Mystical experience, or experience by participation, is the real problem of experiential theology. It is secretly presupposed by the ontological as well as by the scientific concept of experience. Without an experience of participation neither the whole of experience nor articulated experience would reveal anything about our ultimate concern. But the question is: What does experience by participation reveal? For the Reformers experience was not a source of revelation. The divine Spirit testifies in us to the biblical message. No new revelations are given by the Spirit. Nothing new is mediated by the experience of the Spiritual power in us. Evangelical enthusiasm, on the other hand, derived new revelations from the presence of the Spirit. The experience of the man who has the Spirit is the source of religious truth and therefore of systematic theology. The letter of the Bible and the doctrines of the church remain letter and law if the Spirit does not interpret them in the individual Christian. Experience as the inspiring presence of the Spirit is the ultimate source of theology.

The enthusiasts of the Reformation period did not envisage Spiritual experiences transcending the Christian message. Even if, following Joachim de Fiore, they hoped for a "third period" in the history of revelation, the period of the Spirit, they did not describe it as a post-Christian period. The Spirit is the Spirit of the Son who rules the second period and of the Father who rules the first period. The third period is a transformation of the second without a change in substance. This still was the attitude of Schleiermacher, but it has not been that of recent experiential theology. The encounter with great non-Christian religions, the evolutionary scheme of thought, the openness for the new which characterizes the pragmatic method, have had the consequence that experience has become not only the main source of systematic theology but an inexhaustible source out of which new truths can be taken continually. Being open for new experiences which might even pass beyond the confines of Christian experience is now the proper attitude of the theologian. He is not bound to a circle the center of which is the event of Jesus as the Christ. Of course, as a theologian, he also works in a circle but in a circle whose periphery is extendable and whose center is changeable. "Open experience" is the source of systematic theology.

Against this conception neo-orthodoxy turns back to the Reformers, and evangelical biblicism turns back to the Reformation sects. Both deny that a religious experience which goes beyond the Christian circle can be a source of systematic theology; and neo-orthodoxy denies that experience can become a source of systematic theology at all.

If experience is called the medium through which the objective sources are received, this excludes the reliance of the theologian on a possibly post-Christian experience. But it also denies the assertion that experience is a theological source. And, finally, it denies the belief in experiences which, although remaining in the Christian circle, add some new material to the other sources. Christian theology is based on the unique event Jesus the Christ, and in spite of the infinite meaning of this event it remains *this* event and, as such, the criterion of every religious experience. This event is given to experience and not derived from it. Therefore, experience receives and does not produce. Its productive power is restricted to the transformation of what is given to it. But this transformation is not intended. The act of reception intends to receive and only to receive. If transformation is intended, the reception becomes falsification. The systematic theologian is bound to the Christian message which he must derive from other sources than his experience under the criterion of the norm (see next section). This excludes any intentional subjectivity, yet it gives to the subjectivity of the theologian that influence which a medium has on what is mediated through it. The medium colors the presentation and determines the interpretation of what it receives. Two extremes must be avoided in this procedure: the influence of the medium, the experience of the theologian, should not be so small that the result is a repetition instead of a transformation, and it should not be so large that the result is a new production instead of a transformation. While the first failure was predominant in several former periods of the history of Christian thought, the second failure has become more conspicuous in the modern period. The ultimate reason for this change is a change in the theological doctrine of man. Man's religious experience could become an independent source of systematic theology only if man were united with the source of all religious experience, the Spiritual power in him. Only if his spirit and the divine Spirit in him were one could his experience have revealing character. This unity is implied in the modern doctrine of man. But, as the Reformers realistically stressed against the Enthusiasts, this unity is not a fact. Even the saint must listen to what the Spirit says to his spirit, because the saint is also a sinner. There may be revelation through him, as there was through prophets and apostles. But this revelation comes against him and to him and not from him. Insight into the human situation destroys every theology which makes experience an independent source instead of a dependent medium of systematic theology.

10. The Norm of Systematic Theology

The discussion of the sources and of the medium of systematic theology has left a decisive question unanswered—the question of the criterion to which the sources as well as the mediating experience must be subjected. The necessity of such a criterion is obvious in view of the breadth and variety of the material and in view of the indefiniteness of the mediating function of experience. Sources and medium can produce a theological system only if their use is guided by a norm.

The question of the norm of Christian doctrine arose very early in the history of the church. It received a material and a formal answer. On the material side the church created a creed which, with the baptismal confession to Jesus as the Christ at its center, was supposed to contain the doctrinal norm. On the formal side the church established a hierarchy of authorities—bishops, councils, the pope—who were supposed to safeguard the norm against heretical distortions. In the Catholic churches (Roman, Greek, Anglican) the second answer became so predominant that the need for a material norm disappeared. Here Christian doctrine is what the church declares it to be through its official authorities. This is the reason for the lack of an organizing principle even in the otherwise radically organized scholastic systems. It is the reason for the final identification of the tradition with papal decisions (Council of Trent). And it is the reason why the Bible has had such little influence on the later dogmatic development of the Greek and Roman churches.

The question of the norm again became crucial in Protestantism as soon as the ecclesiastical authorities lost their standing. A formal norm and a material norm were established, not by intentional choice, but, as in the beginnings of Christianity, by the demands of the situation. Luther broke through the Roman system in the power of the material norm which, following Paul, he called "justification through faith" and with the authority of the biblical (especially the Pauline) message. Justification and Bible in mutual interdependence were the norms of the Lutheran Reformation. In Calvinism justification was more and more replaced by predestination, and the mutuality of the material and the formal norms was weakened by a more literalistic understanding of biblical authority. But the problem and the line of solution were the same.

If we look at the whole of church history in the light of the explicit statement of the material norm by the Reformers, we find analogous norms implicit in all periods. While the norm for the early Greek church was the liberation of finite man from death and error by the incarnation of immortal life and eternal truth, for the Roman church it was salvation from guilt and disruption by the actual and sacramental sacrifice of the God-man. For modern Protestantism it was the picture of the "synoptic" Jesus, representing the personal and social ideal of human existence; and for recent Protestantism it has been the prophetic message of the Kingdom of God in the Old and New Testaments. These symbols were the unconscious or conscious criteria for the way in which systematic theology dealt with its sources and judged the mediating experience of the theologian.

The growth of these norms is a historical process which, in spite of many conscious decisions, is on the whole unconscious. It happens in and through the encounter of the church with the Christian message. This encounter is different in each generation, and its difference becomes visible in the successive periods of church history. The norm grows; it is not produced intentionally; its appearance is not the work of theological reflection but of the Spiritual life of the church, for the church is the "home" of systematic theology. Here alone do the sources and the norms of theology have actual existence. At this place alone can experience occur as the medium of systematic theology. The lonely reader of the Bible is by no means outside the church. He has received the Bible, collected and preserved by the church through the centuries; he has received the book through the activity of the church or some of its members; he has received it as interpreted by the church even if this interpretation comes to him simply by way of the accepted translation into his own language. The experience of the systematic theologian is shaped by the sources which are mediated through it. And the most concrete and nearest of these formative sources is the church in which he lives and its collective experience. This is his "place of work" as a systematic theologian. It is, of course, his place even if he lives and works in protest against it. Protest is a form of communion.

The norm used as criterion in the present system can be stated only with reservations. In order to be a genuine norm, it must not be a private opinion of the theologian but the expression of an encounter of the church with the Christian message. Whether this is the case cannot be known at the present time.

The norm of systematic theology is not identical with the "critical principle for all theology." The latter is negative and protective; the norm must be positive and constructive. The critical principle is abstract; the norm must be concrete. The critical principle has been formulated under the pressure of the apologetic situation, in order to prevent mutual interference between theology and other forms of knowledge. The norm must be formulated under the pressure of the dogmatic situation in modern Protestantism, which is characterized by the lack of a formal authority and the quest for a material principle.

The norms of systematic theology which have been effective in church history did not exclude each other in content; they excluded each other in emphasis. The norm to be stated below is different in emphasis from that of the Reformers and from that of modern liberal theology, but it claims to preserve the same substance and to bring it out in a form more adequate to the present situation and to the biblical source.

It is not an exaggeration to say that today man experiences his present situation in terms of disruption, conflict, self-destruction, meaninglessness, and despair in all realms of life. This experience is expressed in the arts and in literature, conceptualized in existential philosophy, actualized in political cleavages of all kinds, and analyzed in the psychology of the unconscious. It has given theology a new understanding of the demonic-tragic structures of individual and social life. The question arising out of this experience is not, as in the Reformation, the question of a merciful God and the forgiveness of sins; nor is it, as in the early Greek church, the question of finitude, of death and error; nor is it the question of the personal religious life or of the Christianization of culture and society. It is the question of a reality in which the self-estrangement of our existence is overcome, a reality of reconciliation and reunion, of creativity, meaning, and hope. We shall call such a reality the "New Being," a term whose presuppositions and implications can be explained only through the whole system. It is based on what Paul calls the "new creation" and refers to its power of overcoming the demonic cleavages of the "old reality" in soul, society, and universe. If the Christian message is understood as the message of the "New Being," an answer is given to the question implied in our present situation and in every human situation.

But this answer is not sufficient. It leads immediately to the further question, "Where is this New Being manifest?" Systematic theology answers this question by saying: "In Jesus the Christ." This answer also has presuppositions and implications which it is the main purpose of the whole system to develop. Only this must be said here—that this formula accepts the ancient Christian baptismal confession of Jesus as the Christ. He who is the Christ is he who brings the new eon, the new reality. And it is the man Jesus who in a paradoxical assertion is called the Christ. Without this paradox the New Being would be an ideal, not a reality, and consequently not an answer to the question implied in our human situation.

The material norm of systematic theology, used in the present system and considered the most adequate to the present apologetic situation, is the "New Being in Jesus as the Christ." If this is combined with the critical principle of all theology, one can say that the material norm of systematic theology today is the New Being in Jesus as the Christ as our ultimate concern. This norm is the criterion for the use of all the sources of systematic theology.

The most important question is how this norm is related to the basic source, the Bible. If the Bible *itself* is called the norm of systematic theology, nothing concrete is said, for the Bible is a collection of religious literature written, collected, and edited through the centuries. Luther was aware of this situation in a way which elevates him above most Protestant theologians. He gave a material norm according to which the biblical books should be interpreted and evaluated, namely, the message of Christ or of justification through faith. In the light of this norm he interpreted and judged all the biblical books. Their normative value is identical with the degree to which they express the norm, although, on the other hand, the norm is derived from them. The Bible can be called the norm of systematic theology only because the norm is derived from the Bible. But it is derived from it in an encounter of the church with the biblical message. The norm derived from the Bible is, at the same time, the criterion for the use of the Bible by systematic theology. Practically, this always has been the attitude of theology. The Old Testament was never directly normative. It was measured by the New Testament, and the New Testament was never equally influential in all its parts. Paul's influence almost disappeared in the post-apostolic period. John took his place. The more the gospel was understood as the "new law," the more the Catholic letters and the corresponding synoptic passages became decisive. Pauline reactions occurred again and again, in a conservative way in Augustine and in a revolutionary way in the Reformers. The predominance of the Synoptic Gospels over against Paul and John characterizes modern Protestantism; and in recent times the Old Testament in a prophetic interpretation has overshadowed even the New Testament.[13] The Bible as such never has been the norm of systematic the-

13. The biblical foundation of the present system is indicated by the wording of the material norm: the New Being in Jesus as the Christ. This refers above all to Paul's doctrine

ology. The norm has been a principle derived from the Bible in an encounter between Bible and church.

This gives a point of view for the question of the canonicity of the biblical books. The church closed the canon rather late, and there is no agreement among the Christian churches about the number of books belonging to the biblical canon. When the Roman church accepted and the Protestant churches rejected the Old Testament apocrypha as canonical books, the reason for both judgments was their respective norms of systematic theology. Luther even wanted to exclude more than the apocrypha. This situation shows that there is an element of indefiniteness in the composition of the biblical canon. This confirms very strongly the distinction between the theological norm and the Bible as the basic source from which the norm is derived. The norm decides the canonicity of books. It posits some of them on the boundary line (*antilegomena* in the early church). It is the Spirit which has created the canon, and, like all things Spiritual, the canon cannot be fixed legally in a definite way. The partial openness of the canon is a safeguard of the Spirituality of the Christian church.

This relation of the Bible as the basic source of systematic theology to the norm derived from it suggests a new approach to the question of the normative character of church history. A way must be found which lies between the Roman Catholic practice of making ecclesiastical decisions not only a source but also the actual norm of systematic theology and the radical Protestant practice of depriving church history not only of its normative character but also of its function as a source. The latter already has been discussed. The normative character of church history is implied in the fact that the norm, although derived from the Bible, is produced in an encounter between the church and the biblical message. Every period of church history, this is the implication, unconsciously or consciously contributes through its special situation to the establishment of a theological norm. Beyond this, however, church decisions have no directly normative character. The systematic theologian cannot claim validity for the norm he uses by pointing to Church Fathers, councils, creeds, etc. The possibility that all these have fallen into error must be maintained by Protestant theology as radically as Rome maintains the opposite in its doctrine of papal infallibility. The indirectly normative

---

of the Spirit. While Barth's Pauline protest against liberal theology agrees with that of the Reformers and is dependent on Paul's protective doctrine of justification through faith, the Paulinism of the present system is dependent on Paul's constructive doctrine of the New Creation in Christ which included the prophetic-eschatological message of the "new eon."

character of ecclesiastical decisions consists in their function as signposts, pointing to dangers for the Christian message which once have been overcome by such decisions. They offer a very serious warning and a constructive help to the theologian. But they do not determine authoritatively the direction of his work. He applies his norm to the church-historical material, irrespective of whether it has been affirmed by the most important or the least important authorities.

Even more indirect is the contribution of the history of religion and culture to the norm of systematic theology. An influence of religion and culture on the norm of systematic theology is noticeable only in so far as the encounter of the church with the biblical message is partly conditioned by the religious and cultural situation in which the church lives. There is no reason to deny or to reject such an influence. Systematic theology is not the message itself; and, while the message itself is beyond our grasp and never at our disposal (though it might grasp us and dispose of us), its theological interpretation is an act of the church and of individuals within the church. It is, therefore, religiously and culturally conditioned, and even its norm and criterion cannot claim independence of man's existential situation. The attempts of biblicism and orthodoxy to create an "unconditioned" theology contradict the correct and indispensable first principle of the neo-orthodox movement that "God is in heaven and man is on earth"—even if man is a systematic theologian. And "being on earth" not only means having personal shortcomings; it also means being historically conditioned. The attempt of neo-orthodox theologians to escape this mark of finitude is a symptom of that religious arrogance against which these very same theologians are fighting.

Since the norm of systematic theology is the result of an encounter of the church with the biblical message, it can be called a product of the collective experience of the church. But such an expression is dangerously ambiguous. It could be understood to mean that the collective experience produces the content of the norm. However, the content of the norm is the biblical message. Collective as well as individual experiences are the mediums through which the message is received, colored, and interpreted. The norm grows within the medium of experience. But it is, at the same time, the criterion of any experience. The norm judges the medium in which it grows; it judges the weak, interrupted, distorted character of all religious experience, although it is only through this feeble medium that a norm can come into existence at all.

11. The Rational Character of Systematic Theology

The questions of the source, the medium, and the norm of systematic theology are related to its concrete-historical foundation. But systematic theology is not a historical discipline (as Schleiermacher wrongly asserted);[14] it is a constructive task. It does not tell us what people have thought the Christian message to be in the past; rather it tries to give us an interpretation of the Christian message which is relevant to the present situation. This raises the question, "To what extent does systematic theology have a rational character?" Certainly reason must be used constructively in building a theological system. Nevertheless, there have been and still are many doubts and controversies concerning the role of reason in systematic theology.

The first problem is an adequate definition of "rational" in the present context. Providing such a definition would, however, involve an extensive discussion of reason in its various structures and functions (Part I, Sec. I). Since such a discussion is impossible in this Introduction, we must make the following anticipatory statements. There is a kind of cognition implied in faith which is qualitatively different from the cognition involved in the technical, scholarly work of the theologian. It has a completely existential, self-determining, and self-surrendering character and belongs to the faith of even the intellectually most primitive believer. Whoever participates in the New Being participates also in its truth. The theologian, in addition, is supposed not only to participate in the New Being but also to express its truth in a methodical way. We shall call the organ with which we receive the contents of faith "self-transcending," or ecstatic, reason, and we shall call the organ of the theological scholar "technical," or formal, reason. In both cases reason is not a source of theology. It does not produce its contents. Ecstatic reason is reason grasped by an ultimate concern. Reason is overpowered, invaded, shaken by the ultimate concern. Reason does not produce an object of ultimate concern by logical procedures, as a mistaken theology tried to do in its "arguments for the existence of God." The contents of faith grasp reason. Nor does the technical or formal reason of the theologian produce its content, as has been shown in the discussion of his sources and his medium.

But the situation is not so simple as it would be if the act of reception were merely a formal act without any influence on what is received. This

---

14. *Kurtze Darstellung des theologischen Studiums zum Gebrauche für Vorlesungen* (2d ed., 1830).

is not the case. Content and form, giving and receiving, have a more dialectical relationship than the words seem to connote. At this point a difficulty arises. The difficulty is obvious in the formulation of the theological norm. This formulation is a matter of personal and communal religious experience and, at the same time, a matter of the methodological judgment of the theologian. It is simultaneously received by ecstatic reason and conceived through technical reason. Traditional and neo-orthodox theologies do not differ at this point. The ambiguity cannot be avoided so long as there is theology, and it is one of the factors which make theology a "questionable" enterprise. The problem could be solved only if man's formal reason were in complete harmony with his ecstatic reason, if man were living in a complete theonomy, that is, in the fulness of the Kingdom of God. One of the basic Christian truths to which theology must witness is that theology itself, like every human activity, is subject to the contradictions of man's existential situation.

Although the problem of the rational character of systematic theology finally must remain unsolved, some directing principles can be stated.

The first principle determining the rational character of systematic theology is a semantic one. There are words which are used in philosophical, scientific, and popular language. If the theologian uses these words, he often can assume that the content indicates the realm of discourse within which the term stands. But this is not always the case. There are terms which for centuries have been adopted by theology, although, at the same time, they have retained religious, philosophical, and other meanings. In this situation the theologian must apply *semantic rationality*. The glory of scholasticism was that it had become a semantic clearing-house for theology as well as for philosophy. And it is almost always a shortcoming and sometimes the shame of modern theology that its concepts remain unclarified and ambiguous. It may be added, however, that the chaotic state of the philosophical and the scientific terminologies makes this situation more or less inevitable.

The principle of semantic rationality must not be confused with the attempt to construct a pan-mathematical formalism. In the realm of spiritual life words cannot be reduced to mathematical signs, nor can sentences be reduced to mathematical equations. The power of words denoting spiritual realities lies in their connotations. The removal of these connotations leaves dead bones which have no meaning in any realm. In such instances the logical positivists are right in rejecting them. When theology employs a term like "Spirit," connotations are present which point to philosophical and psychological concepts of spirit, to the magic world view in which breath and spirit are identical, to the mystic-ascetic experience of Spirit in opposition to matter or flesh, to the religious experience of the divine power grasping the human mind. The principle of semantic rationality does not demand that these connotations should be excluded but that the main emphasis should be elaborated by relating it to the connotations. Thus "Spirit," for example, must be related to "spirit" (with a lower-case *s*); the primitive magic sense must be excluded, the mystical connotations must be discussed in relation to the personalistic connotations, etc.

Another example is the term "New Being." Being carries connotations of a metaphysical and logical character; it has mystical implications when used in relation to God as being-itself. "New" in connection with "Being" has connotations of creativity, regeneration, eschatology. These elements of meaning always are present when a term like "New Being" appears. The principle of semantic rationality involves the demand that all connotations of a word should consciously be related to each other and centered around a controlling meaning. If the word "history" is used, the different levels of the scientific meaning of history are more in the foreground than in the two preceding examples. But the specific modern emphasis on history as progressive, the specific prophetic emphasis on God as acting through history, and the specific Christian emphasis on the historical character of revelation are united with the scientific meanings whenever history is discussed in a theological context. These examples illustrate the immense importance of the principle of semantic rationality for the systematic theologian. They also suggest how difficult it is to apply this principle—a difficulty which is rooted in the fact that every significant theological term cuts through several levels of meaning and that all of them contribute to the theological meaning.

The semantic situation makes it evident that the language of the theologian cannot be a sacred or revealed language. He cannot restrict himself to the biblical terminology or to the language of classical theology. He could not avoid philosophical concepts even if he used only biblical words; and even less could he avoid them if he used only the words of the Reformers. Therefore, he should use philosophical and scientific terms whenever he deems them helpful for his task of explaining the contents of the Christian faith. The two things he must watch in doing so are semantic clarity and existential purity. He must avoid conceptual ambiguity and a possible distortion of the Christian message by the intrusion of anti-Christian ideas in the cloak of a philosophical, scientific, or poetic terminology.

The second principle determining the rational character of theology is *logical rationality*. This principle refers first of all to the structures which determine any meaningful discourse and which are formulated in the discipline of logic. Theology is as dependent on formal logic as any other science. This must be maintained against both philosophical and theological protests.

The philosophical protest against the all-controlling position of formal logic has been made in the name of dialectical thinking. In dialectics yes and no, affirmation and negation, demand each other. But in formal logic they exclude each other. However, there is no real conflict between dialectics and formal logic. Dialectics follows the movement of thought or the movement of reality through yes and no, but it describes it in logically correct terms. The same concept always is used in the same sense; and, if the meaning of the concept changes, the dialectician describes in a logically correct way the intrinsic necessity which drives the old into the new. Formal logic is not contradicted when Hegel describes the identity of being and nonbeing by showing the absolute emptiness of pure being in reflective thought. Nor is formal logic contradicted when, in the dogma of the trinity, the divine life is described as a trinity within a unity. The doctrine of the Trinity does not affirm the logical nonsense that three is one and one is three; it describes in dialectical terms the inner movement of the divine life as an eternal separation from itself and return to itself. Theology is not expected to accept a senseless combination of words, that is, genuine logical contradictions. Dialectical thinking is not in conflict with the structure of thinking. It transforms the static ontology behind the logical system of Aristotle and his followers into a dynamic ontology, largely under the influence of voluntaristic and historical motives rooted in the Christian interpretation of existence. This change in ontology opens new vistas for the task of logic in describing and interpreting the structure of thought. It posits in a new way the question of the relation of the structure of thought to the structure of being.

Theological dialectics does not violate the principle of logical rationality. The same is true of the paradoxical statements in religion and theology. When Paul points to his situation as an apostle and to that of Christians generally in a series of *paradoxa* (II Corinthians), he does not intend to say something illogical; he intends to give the adequate, under-

standable, and therefore logical expression of the infinite tensions of
Christian existence. When he speaks about the paradox of the justification of the sinner (in Luther's formula, *simul peccator et iustus*), and
when John speaks about the Logos becoming flesh (later expressed in the
paradoxa of the creed of Chalcedon), neither of them wishes to indulge
in logical contradictions.[15] They want to express the conviction that
God's acting transcends all possible human expectations and all necessary human preparations. It transcends, but it does not destroy, finite
reason; for God acts through the Logos which is the transcendent and
transcending source of the *logos* structure of thought and being. God
does not annihilate the expressions of his own Logos. The term "paradox" should be defined carefully, and paradoxical language should
be used with discrimination. Paradoxical means "against the opinion,"
namely, the opinion of finite reason. Paradox points to the fact that in
God's acting finite reason is superseded but not annihilated; it expresses
this fact in terms which are not logically contradictory but which are
supposed to point beyond the realm in which finite reason is applicable.
This is indicated by the ecstatic state in which all biblical and classical
theological *paradoxa* appear. The confusion begins when these *paradoxa*
are brought down to the level of genuine logical contradictions and people are asked to sacrifice reason in order to accept senseless combinations
of words as divine wisdom. But Christianity does not demand such intellectual "good works" from anyone, just as it does not ask artificial
"works" of practical asceticism. There is, in the last analysis, only *one*
genuine paradox in the Christian message—the appearance of that which
conquers existence under the conditions of existence. Incarnation, re-
demption, justification, etc., are implied in this paradoxical event. It is
not a logical contradiction which makes it a paradox but the fact that it
transcends all human expectations and possibilities. It breaks into the
context of experience or reality, but it cannot be derived from it. The
acceptance of this paradox is not the acceptance of the absurd, but it is
the state of being grasped by the power of that which breaks into our
experience from above it. Paradox in religion and theology does not conflict with the principle of logical rationality. Paradox has its logical place.

The third principle determining the rational character of systematic
theology is the principle of *methodological rationality*. It implies that

15. It is the mistake of Brunner in *The Mediator* that he makes the offense of logical
rationality the criterion of Christian truth. This "offense" is neither that of Kierkegaard
nor that of the New Testament.

theology follows a method, that is, a definite way of deriving and stating its propositions. The character of this method is dependent on many non-rational factors (see chap. i), but, once it has been established, it must be carried through rationally and consistently. The final expression of consistency in applying methodological rationality is the theological system. If the title "Systematic Theology" has any justification, the systematic theologian should not be afraid of the system. It is the function of the systematic form to guarantee the consistency of cognitive assertions in all realms of methodological knowledge. In this sense some of the most passionate foes of the system are most systematic in the totality of their utterances. And it often happens that those who attack the systematic form are very impatient when they discover an inconsistency in someone else's thought. On the other hand, it is easy to discover gaps in the most balanced system, because life continuously breaks through the systematic shell. One could say that in each system an experienced fragment of life and vision is drawn out constructively even to cover areas where life and vision are missing. And, conversely, one could say that in each fragment a system is implied which is not yet explicated. Hegel's imposing system was built on his early fragmentary paragraphs on the dialectics of life, including the dialectics of religion and the state. The "blood" of his system, as well as its immense historical consequences, were rooted in this fragmentary vision of existence. The lines he later drew with the help of his logical tools soon became obsolete. Nietzsche's many fragments seem to be permanently contradictory. But in all of them a system is implicit, the demonic strength of which has become manifest in the twentieth century. A fragment is an implicit system; a system is an explicit fragment.

The systematic form frequently has been attacked from three points of view. The first attack is based on a confusion between "system" and "deductive system." The history of science, philosophy, and theology shows that a deductive system has very rarely even been attempted except in the field of mathematics. Spinoza made the attempt in his *Ethics*, which he elaborated *more geometrico;* it was envisaged, though not executed, by Leibniz when he suggested a *mathesis universalis* which would describe the cosmos in mathematical terms. Classical physicists, having reached their principles inductively, tried to be deductively systematic, but again in mathematical terms. With the exception of Raimundus Lullus, theology never has attempted to construct a deductive system of Christian truth. Because of the existential character of the Christian truth, such an attempt would have been a contradiction in terms. A system is a totality made up of consistent, but not of deduced, assertions.

The second criticism of the system is that it seems to close the doors to further research. Behind this feeling lies the violent reaction of science since the second half of the nineteenth century against the Romantic philosophy of nature. This reaction has now spent its power and should determine neither our attitude to the scientific achievements of the philosophy of nature (for instance, in the doctrine of man and the psychology of the unconscious) nor our attitude to the systematic form in all realms of cognition. It is a historical fact that the great systems have stimulated research at least as much as they have inhibited it. The system gives meaning to a whole of factual or rational statements, showing their implications and consequences. Out of such a total view, and out of the difficulties involved in carrying it through, new questions arise. The balance sheet of positive and negative consequences of "the system" for empirical research is at least equal.

The third reason for enmity against the system is largely emotional. It seems like a prison in which the creativity of spiritual life is stifled. Acceptance of a system seems to imply that "adventures in ideas" are prohibited. History shows that this is not the case. The great schools of Greek philosophy produced many creative pupils who remained in the school, accepted the system on which it was based, and, at the same time, transformed the ideas of the founder. The same was true of the theological schools of the nineteenth century. The history of human thought has been, and still is, identical with the history of the great systems.

The distinction between three terms may conclude the discussion of the systematic character of systematic theology and of its methodological rationality. System stands between *summa* and essay. The *summa* deals explicitly with *all actual* and many potential problems. The essay deals explicitly with *one actual* problem. The system deals with a group of *actual* problems which demand a solution in a special situation. In the Middle Ages the *summa* was predominant, though by no means exclusively so. At the beginning of the modern period the essay became predominant, although the systematic trend never ceased to exist. Today a need for systematic form has arisen in view of the chaos of our spiritual life and the impossibility of creating a *summa*.

12. The Method of Correlation

The principle of methodological rationality implies that, like all scientific approaches to reality, systematic theology follows a method. A method is a tool, literally a way around, which must be adequate to its subject matter. Whether or not a method is adequate cannot be decided a priori; it is continually being decided in the cognitive process itself. Method and system determine each other. Therefore, no method can claim to be adequate for every subject. Methodological imperialism is as dangerous as political imperialism; like the latter, it breaks down when the independent elements of reality revolt against it. A method is not an "indifferent net" in which reality is caught, but the method is an element of the reality itself. In at least one respect the description of a method is a description of a decisive aspect of the object to which it is applied. The cognitive relation itself, quite apart from any special act of cognition, reveals something about the object, as well as about the subject, in the relation. The cognitive relation in physics reveals the mathematical character of objects in space (and time). The cognitive relation in biology reveals the structure (Gestalt) and spontaneous character of objects in space and time. The cognitive relation in historiography reveals the individual and value-related character of objects in time (and space). The cognitive relation in theology reveals the existential and transcending character of the ground of objects in time and space. Therefore, no method can be developed without a prior knowledge of the object to which it is applied. For systematic theology this means that its method is derived from a prior knowledge of the system which is to be built by the method.

Systematic theology uses the method of correlation. It has always done so, sometimes more, sometimes less, consciously, and must do so consciously and outspokenly, especially if the apologetic point of view is to prevail. The method of correlation explains the contents of the Christian faith through existential questions and theological answers in mutual interdependence.

The term "correlation" may be used in three ways. It can designate the correspondence of different series of data, as in statistical charts; it can designate the logical interdependence of concepts, as in polar relations; and it can designate the real interdependence of things or events in structural wholes. If the term is used in theology, all three meanings have important applications. There is a correlation in the sense of correspondence between religious symbols and that which is symbolized by them. There is a correlation in the logical sense between concepts denoting the human and those denoting the divine. There is a correlation in the factual sense between man's ultimate concern and that about which he is ultimately concerned. The first meaning of correlation refers to the central problem of religious knowledge (Part I, Sec. I). The second meaning of correlation determines the statements about God and the world; for example, the correlation of the infinite and the finite (Part II, Sec. I). The third meaning of correlation qualifies the divine-human relationship within religious experience.[16] The third use of correlative thinking in theology has evoked the protest of theologians such as Karl Barth, who are afraid that any kind of divine-human correlation makes God partly dependent on man. But although God in his abysmal nature[17] is in no way dependent on man, God in his self-manifestation to man is dependent on the way man receives his manifestation. This is true even if the doctrine of predestination, namely, that this way is foreordained by God and entirely independent of human freedom, is maintained. The divine-human relation, and therefore God as well as man within this relation, changes with the stages of the history of revelation and with the stages of every personal development. There is a mutual interdependence between "God for us" and "we for God." God's wrath and God's grace are not contrasts in the "heart" of God (Luther), in the depth of his being; but they are contrasts in the divine-human relationship. The divine-human relation is a correlation. The "divine-human encounter" (Emil Brunner) means something real for both sides. It is an actual correlation, in the third sense of the term.

The divine-human relationship is a correlation also in its cognitive side. Symbolically speaking, God answers man's questions, and under the impact of God's answers man asks them. Theology formulates the questions implied in human existence, and theology formulates the answers implied in divine self-manifestation under the guidance of the questions implied in human existence. This is a circle which drives man to a point where question and answer are not separated. This point, however, is not a moment in time. It belongs to man's essential being, to the unity of his finitude with the infinity in which he was created (see Part II) and from which he is separated (see Part III). A symptom of both the essential unity and the existential separation of finite man from his infinity is his ability to ask about the infinite to which he belongs: the fact that he must ask about it indicates that he is separated from it.

The answers implied in the event of revelation are meaningful only in so far as they are in correlation with questions concerning the whole of our existence, with existential questions. Only those who have experi-

16. Luther: "As you believe him so you have him."
17. Calvin: "In his essence."

I need not have been and they will pass away...

enced the shock of transitoriness, the anxiety in which they are aware of their finitude, the threat of nonbeing, can understand what the notion of God means. Only those who have experienced the tragic ambiguities of our historical existence and have totally questioned the meaning of existence can understand what the symbol of the Kingdom of God means. Revelation answers questions which have been asked and always will be asked because they are "we ourselves." Man is the question he asks about himself, before any question has been formulated. It is, therefore, not surprising that the basic questions were formulated very early in the history of mankind. Every analysis of the mythological material shows this.[18] Nor is it surprising that the same questions appear in early childhood, as every observation of children shows. Being human means asking the questions of one's own being and living under the impact of the answers given to this question. And, conversely, being human means receiving answers to the question of one's own being and asking questions under the impact of the answers.

Hope in Tillich's theology

In using the method of correlation, systematic theology proceeds in the following way: it makes an analysis of the human situation out of which the existential questions arise, and it demonstrates that the symbols used in the Christian message are the answers to these questions. The analysis of the human situation is done in terms which today are called "existential." Such analyses are much older than existentialism; they are, indeed, as old as man's thinking about himself, and they have been expressed in various kinds of conceptualization since the beginning of philosophy. Whenever man has looked at his world, he has found himself in it as a part of it. But he also has realized that he is a stranger in the world of objects, unable to penetrate it beyond a certain level of scientific analysis. And then he has become aware of the fact that he himself is the door to the deeper levels of reality, that in his own existence he has the only possible approach to existence itself.[19] This does not mean that man is more approachable than other objects as material for scientific research. The opposite is the case! It does mean that the immediate experience of one's own existing reveals something of the nature of existence generally. Whoever has penetrated into the nature of his

18. Cf. H. Gunkel, *The Legends of Genesis* (Chicago: Open Court Publishing Co., 1901).
19. Cf. Augustine's doctrine of truth dwelling in the soul and transcending it at the same time; the mystical identification of the ground of being with the ground of self; the use of psychological categories for ontological purposes in Paracelsus, Böhme, Schelling, and in the "philosophy of life" from Schopenhauer to Bergson; Heidegger's notion of "Dasein" (being there) as the form of human existence and the entrance to ontology.

own finitude can find the traces of finitude in everything that exists. And he can ask the question implied in his finitude as the question implied in finitude universally. In doing so, he does not formulate a doctrine of man; he expresses a doctrine of existence as experienced in him as man. When Calvin in the opening sentences of the *Institutes* correlates our knowledge of God with our knowledge of man, he does not speak of the doctrine of man as such and of the doctrine of God as such. He speaks of man's misery, which gives the existential basis for his understanding of God's glory, and of God's glory, which gives the essential basis for man's understanding of his misery. Man as existing, representing existence generally and asking the question implied in his existence, is one side of the cognitive correlation to which Calvin points, the other side being the divine majesty. In the initial sentences of his theological system Calvin expresses the essence of the method of correlation.[20]

The analysis of the human situation employs materials made available by man's creative self-interpretation in all realms of culture. Philosophy contributes, but so do poetry, drama, the novel, therapeutic psychology, and sociology. The theologian organizes these materials in relation to the answer given by the Christian message. In the light of this message he may make an analysis of existence which is more penetrating than that of most philosophers. Nevertheless, it remains a philosophical analysis. The analysis of existence, including the development of the questions implicit in existence, is a philosophical task, even if it is performed by a theologian, and even if the theologian is a reformer like Calvin. The difference between the philosopher who is not a theologian and the theologian who works as a philosopher in analyzing human existence is only that the former tries to give an analysis which will be part of a broader philosophical work, while the latter tries to correlate the material of his analysis with the theological concepts he derives from the Christian faith. This does not make the philosophical work of the theologian heteronomous. As a theologian he does not tell himself what is philosophically true. As a philosopher he does not tell himself what is theologically true. But he cannot help seeing human existence and existence generally in such a way that the Christian symbols appear meaningful and understandable to him. His eyes are partially focused by his ulti-

20. "The knowledge of ourselves is not only an incitement to seek after God, but likewise a considerable assistance towards finding him. On the other hand, it is plain that no man can arrive at the true knowledge of himself, without having first contemplated the divine character, and then descended to the consideration of his own" (John Calvin, *Institutes*, I, 48).

mate concern, which is true of every philosopher. Nevertheless, his act of seeing is autonomous, for it is determined only by the object as it is given in his experience. If he sees something he did not expect to see in the light of his theological answer, he holds fast to what he has seen and reformulates the theological answer. He is certain that nothing he sees can change the substance of his answer, because this substance is the *logos* of being, manifest in Jesus as the Christ. If this were not his presupposition, he would have to sacrifice either his philosophical honesty or his theological concern.

The Christian message provides the answers to the questions implied in human existence. These answers are contained in the revelatory events on which Christianity is based and are taken by systematic theology *from* the sources, *through* the medium, *under* the norm. Their content cannot be derived from the questions, that is, from an analysis of human existence. They are "spoken" *to* human existence from beyond it. Otherwise they would not be answers, for the question is human existence itself. But the relation is more involved than this, since it is correlation. There is a mutual dependence between question and answer. In respect to content the Christian answers are dependent on the revelatory events in which they appear; in respect to form they are dependent on the structure of the questions which they answer. God is the answer to the question implied in human finitude. This answer cannot be derived from the analysis of existence. However, if the notion of God appears in systematic theology in correlation with the threat of nonbeing which is implied in existence, God must be called the infinite power of being which resists the threat of nonbeing. In classical theology this is being-itself. If anxiety is defined as the awareness of being finite, God must be called the infinite ground of courage. In classical theology this is universal providence. If the notion of the Kingdom of God appears in correlation with the riddle of our historical existence, it must be called the meaning, fulfilment, and unity of history. In this way an interpretation of the traditional symbols of Christianity is achieved which preserves the power of these symbols and which opens them to the questions elaborated by our present analysis of human existence.

The method of correlation replaces three inadequate methods of relating the contents of the Christian faith to man's spiritual existence. The first method can be called supranaturalistic, in that it takes the Christian message to be a sum of revealed truths which have fallen into the human situation like strange bodies from a strange world. No mediation to the human situation is possible. These truths themselves create a new situation before they can be received. Man must become something else than human in order to receive divinity. In terms of the classical heresies one could say that the supranaturalistic method has docetic-monophysitic traits, especially in its valuation of the Bible as a book of supranatural "oracles" in which human receptivity is completely overlooked. But man cannot receive answers to questions he never has asked. Furthermore, man has asked and is asking in his very existence and in every one of his spiritual creations questions which Christianity answers.

The second method to be rejected can be called "naturalistic" or "humanistic." It derives the Christian message from man's natural state. It develops its answer out of human existence, unaware that human existence itself *is* the question. Much of liberal theology in the last two centuries was "humanistic" in this sense. It identified man's existential with his essential state, overlooking the break between them which is reflected in the universal human condition of self-estrangement and self-contradiction. Theologically this meant that the contents of the Christian faith were explained as creations of man's religious self-realization in the progressive process of religious history. Questions and answers were put on the same level of human creativity. Everything was said by man, nothing to man. But revelation is "spoken" to man, not by man to himself.

The third method to be rejected can be called "dualistic," inasmuch as it builds a supranatural structure on a natural substructure. This method, more than others, is aware of the problem which the method of correlation tries to meet. It realizes that, in spite of the infinite gap between man's spirit and God's spirit, there must be a positive relation between them. It tries to express this relation by positing a body of theological truth which man can reach through his own efforts or, in terms of a self-contradictory expression, through "natural revelation." The so-called arguments for "the existence of God," which itself is another self-contradictory term, are the most important section of natural theology. These arguments are true (see Part II, Sec. I) in so far as they analyze human finitude and the question involved in it. They are false in so far as they derive an answer from the form of the question. This mixture of truth and falsehood in natural theology explains why there always have been great philosophers and theologians who have attacked natural theology, especially the arguments for the existence of God, and why others equally great have defended it. The method of correlation solves this historical and systematic riddle by resolving natural theology into the analysis of existence and by resolving supranatural theology into the answers given to the questions implied in existence.

13. THE THEOLOGICAL SYSTEM

The structure of the theological system follows from the method of correlation. The method of correlation requires that every part of the system should include one section in which the question is developed by an analysis of human existence and existence generally, and one section in which the theological answer is given on the basis of the sources, the medium, and the norm of systematic theology. This division must be maintained. It is the backbone of the structure of the present system.

One could think of a section which mediates between the two main sections by interpreting historical, sociological, and psychological materials in the light of both the existential questions and the theological answers.[21] Since these materials from the sources of systematic theology are used not as they appear in their historical, sociological, or psychological setting but in terms of their significance for the systematic solution, they belong to the theological answer and do not constitute a section of their own.

In each of the five parts of the system which are derived from the structure of existence in correlation with the structure of the Christian message, the two sections are correlated in the following ways. In so far as man's existence has the character of self-contradiction or estrangement, a double consideration is demanded, one side dealing with man as he essentially is (and ought to be) and the other dealing with what he is in his self-estranged existence (and should not be). These correspond to the Christian distinction between the realm of creation and the realm of salvation. Therefore, one part of the system must give an analysis of man's essential nature (in unity with the essential nature of everything that has being), and of the question implied in man's finitude and finitude generally; and it must give the answer which is God. This part, therefore, is called "Being and God." A second part of the system must give an analysis of man's existential self-estrangement (in unity with the self-destructive aspects of existence generally) and the question implied in this situation; and it must give the answer which is the Christ. This part, therefore, is called "Existence and Christ." A third part is based on

21. In former outlines, especially in the "Propositions" prepared for my lectures, such a section always was inserted.

Theological System

the fact that the essential as well as the existential characteristics are abstractions and that in reality they appear in the complex and dynamic unity which is called "life." The power of essential being is ambiguously present in all existential distortions. Life, that is, being in its actuality, displays such a character in all its processes. Therefore, this part of the system must give an analysis of man as living (in unity with life generally) and of the question implied in the ambiguities of life; and it must give the answer which is the Spirit. This part, therefore, is called "Life and the Spirit." These three parts represent the main body of systematic theology. They embrace the Christian answers to the questions of existence. But for practical reasons it is necessary to "split off" some of the material from each part and combine it to form an epistemological part. This part of the system must give an analysis of man's rationality, especially his cognitive rationality (in unity with the rational structure of reality as a whole), and of the questions implied in the finitude, the self-estrangement, and the ambiguities of reason; and it must give the answer which is Revelation. This part, therefore, is called "Reason and Revelation."

Finally, life has a dimension which is called "history." And it is helpful to separate the material dealing with the historical aspect of life from the part dealing with life generally. This corresponds to the fact that the symbol "Kingdom of God" is independent of the trinitarian structure which determines the central parts. This part of the system must give an analysis of man's historical existence (in unity with the nature of the historical generally) and of the questions implied in the ambiguities of history; and it must give an answer which is the Kingdom of God. This part is called "History and the Kingdom of God."

It would be most advantageous to begin with "Being and God," because this part outlines the basic structure of being and gives the answer to the questions implied in this structure—an answer which determines all other answers—for theology is first of all doctrine of God. But several considerations make it necessary to begin with the epistemological part, "Reason and Revelation." First, every theologian is asked, "On what do you base your assertions; what criteria, what verification, do you have?" This necessitates an epistemological answer from the very start. Second, the concept of reason (and Reason) must be clarified before statements can be made in which there is the assumption that reason transcends itself. Third, the doctrine of revelation must be dealt with at the very beginning, because revelation is presupposed in all parts of the system as the ultimate source of the contents of the Christian faith. For these reasons "Reason and Revelation" must open the system, just as for obvious reasons "History and the Kingdom of God" must close it. One cannot avoid the fact that in each part elements of the other parts are anticipated or repeated. In a way each part contains the whole from a different perspective, for the present system is by no means deductive. The very fact that in each part the question is developed anew makes any possible continuity of deduction impossible. Revelation is not given as a system. But revelation is not inconsistent either. The systematic theologian, therefore, can interpret that which transcends all possible systems, the self-manifestation of the divine mystery, in a systematic form.

PART I
REASON AND REVELATION

I

REASON AND THE QUEST FOR REVELATION

A. THE STRUCTURE OF REASON

1. THE TWO CONCEPTS OF REASON

Epistemology, the "knowledge" of knowing, is a part of ontology, the knowledge of being, for knowing is an event within the totality of events. Every epistemological assertion is implicitly ontological. Therefore, it is more adequate to begin an analysis of existence with the question of being rather than with the problem of knowledge. Moreover, it is in line with the predominant classical tradition. But there are situations in which the opposite order ought to be followed, namely, when an ontological tradition has become doubtful and the question arises whether the tools used in the creation of this tradition are responsible for its failure. This was the situation of ancient probabilism and skepticism in relation to the struggle between the philosophical schools. It was the situation of Descartes in the face of the disintegrating medieval traditions. It was the situation of Hume and Kant with respect to the traditional metaphysics. It is the perennial situation of theology, which always must give an account of its paths to knowledge because they seem to deviate radically from all ordinary ways. Although epistemology precedes ontology in these instances, it is an error to assume that epistemology is able to provide the foundation of the philosophical or theological system. Even if it precedes the other parts of the system, it is dependent on them in such a way that it can be elaborated only by anticipating them explicitly and implicitly. Recent Neo-Kantian philosophers recognized the dependence of epistemology on ontology and contributed to the fall of the epistemological tidal wave which arose in the second half of the nineteenth century. Classical theology always has been aware that a doctrine of revelation presupposes doctrines of God, man, Christ, etc. It has known that the epistemological "preamble" is dependent on the whole of the theological system. Recent attempts to make epistemological and methodological considerations an independent basis for theological

71

work have been futile.[1] Therefore, it is necessary that the systematic theologian, when he begins with the epistemological part (the doctrine of Reason and Revelation), should indicate clearly the anticipations he makes both with respect to Reason and with respect to Revelation.

One of the greatest weaknesss of much theological writing and of much religious talk is that the word "reason" is used in a loose and vague way, which is sometimes appreciative but usually depreciatory. While popular talk can be excused for such unpreciseness (although it has religious dangers), it is inexcusable if a theologian uses terms without having defined or exactly circumscribed them. Therefore, it is necessary to define from the very beginning the sense in which the term "reason" will be used.

We can distinguish between an ontological and a technical concept of reason. The former is predominant in the classical tradition from Parmenides to Hegel; the latter, though always present in pre-philosophical and philosophical thought, has become predominant since the breakdown of German classical idealism and in the wake of English empiricism.[2] According to the classical philosophical tradition, reason is the structure of the mind which enables the mind to grasp and to transform reality. It is effective in the cognitive, aesthetic, practical, and technical functions of the human mind. Even emotional life is not irrational in itself. *Erōs* drives the mind toward the true (Plato). Love for the perfect form moves all things (Aristotle). In the "apathy" of the soul the *logos* manifests its presence (Stoics). The longing for its origin elevates soul and mind toward the ineffable source of all meaning (Plotinus). The *appetitus* of everything finite drives it toward the good-itself (Aquinas). "Intellectual love" unites intellect and emotion in the most rational state of the mind (Spinoza). Philosophy is "service of God"; it is a thinking which is at the same time life and joy in the "absolute truth" (Hegel), etc. Classical reason is Logos, whether it is understood in a more intuitive or in a more critical way. Its cognitive nature is one element in addition to others; it is cognitive and aesthetic, theoretical and practical, detached and passionate, subjective and objective. The denial of reason in the classical sense is antihuman because it is antidivine.

But this ontological concept of reason always is accompanied and sometimes replaced by the technical concept of reason. Reason is reduced

---

1. See the Introduction.
2. See Max Horkheimer, *The Eclipse of Reason* (New York and Oxford: Oxford University Press, 1947).

to the capacity for "reasoning." Only the cognitive side of the classical concept of reason remains, and within the cognitive realm only those cognitive acts which deal with the discovery of means for ends. While reason in the sense of Logos determines the ends and only in the second place the means, reason in the technical sense determines the means while accepting the ends from "somewhere else." There is no danger in this situation as long as technical reason is the companion of ontological reason and "reasoning" is used to fulfil the demands of reason. This situation prevailed in most pre-philosophical as well as philosophical periods of human history, although there always was the threat that "reasoning" might separate itself from reason. Since the middle of the nineteenth century this threat has become a dominating reality. The consequence is that the ends are provided by nonrational forces, either by positive traditions or by arbitrary decisions serving the will to power. Critical reason has ceased to exercise its controlling function over norms and ends. At the same time the noncognitive sides of reason have been consigned to the irrelevance of pure subjectivity. In some forms of logical positivism the philosopher even refuses to "understand" anything that transcends technical reason, thus making his philosophy completely irrelevant for questions of existential concern. Technical reason, however refined in logical and methodological respects, dehumanizes man if it is separated from ontological reason. And, beyond this, technical reason itself is impoverished and corrupted if it is not continually nourished by ontological reason. Even in the means-ends structure of "reasoning" assertions about the nature of things are presupposed which themselves are not based on technical reason. Neither structures, Gestalt processes, values, nor meanings can be grasped without ontological reason. Technical reason can reduce them to something less than their true reality. But, by reducing them to this status, it has deprived itself of insights which are decisive for the means-ends relationship. Of course one knows many *aspects* of human nature by analyzing physiological and psychological processes and by using the elements provided by this analysis for physicotechnical or psychotechnical purposes. But if one claims to know man in this way, one misses not only the nature of man but even decisive truths about man within a means-ends relationship. This is true of every realm of reality. Technical reason always has an important function, even in systematic theology. But technical reason is adequate and meaningful only as an expression of ontological reason and as its companion. Theology need not make a decision for or against one of these two concepts of reason. It uses the methods of technical reason, the means-ends relation, in establishing a consistent, logical, and correctly derived organism of thought. It accepts the refinements of the cognitive methods applied by technical reason. But it rejects the confusion of technical with ontological reason. For instance, theology cannot accept the support of technical reason in "reasoning" the existence of a God. Such a God would belong to the means-ends relationship. He would be less than God. On the other hand, theology is not perturbed by the attack on the Christian message made by technical reason, for these attacks do not reach the level on which religion stands. They may destroy superstitions, but they do not even touch faith. Theology is (or should be) grateful for the critical function of the type of technical reason which shows that there is no such "thing" as a God within the context of means-ends relationships. Religious objects, seen in terms of the universe of discourse constituted by technical reason, are objects of superstition subject to destructive criticism. Wherever technical reason dominates, religion is superstition and is either foolishly supported by reason or rightly removed by it.

Although theology invariably uses technical reason in its systematic work, it cannot escape the question of its relation to ontological reason. The traditional question of the relation of reason to revelation should not be discussed on the level of technical reason, where it constitutes no genuine problem, but on the level of ontological reason, of reason in the sense of *logos*. Technical reason is an instrument, and, like every instrument, it can be more or less perfect and can be used more or less skilfully. But no existential problem is involved in its use. The situation is quite different with respect to ontological reason. It was the mistake of idealistic philosophy that it identified revelation with ontological reason while rejecting the claims of technical reason. This is the very essence of the idealistic philosophy of religion. In opposition to idealism, theology must show that, although the essence of ontological reason, the universal *logos* of being, is identical with the content of revelation, still reason, if actualized in self and world, is dependent on the destructive structures of existence and the saving structures of life (Parts III and IV); it is subjected to finitude and separation, and it can participate in the "New Being." Its actualization is not a matter of technique but of "fall" and "salvation." It follows that the theologian must consider reason from several different perspectives. In theology one must distinguish not only ontological from technical reason but also ontological reason in its essen-

tial perfection from its predicament in the different stages of its actualization in existence, life, and history. The religious judgment that reason
is "blind," for instance, neither refers to technical reason, which can see
most things in its own realm quite well, nor to ontological reason in its
essential perfection, namely, in unity with being-itself.[3] The judgment
that reason is blind refers to reason under the conditions of existence; and
the judgment that reason is weak—partly liberated from blindness, partly held in it—refers to reason within life and history. If these distinctions
are not made, every statement about reason is incorrect or dangerously
ambiguous.

2. SUBJECTIVE AND OBJECTIVE REASON

Ontological reason can be defined as the structure of the mind
which enables it to grasp and to shape reality. From the time of
Parmenides it has been a common assumption of all philosophers that
the *logos,* the word which grasps and shapes reality, can do so only
because reality itself has a *logos* character. There have been widely dif-
fering explanations of the relation between the *logos* structure of the
grasping-and-shaping-self and the *logos* structure of the grasped-and-
shaped-world. But the necessity of an explanation has been acknowledged almost unanimously. In the classical descriptions of the way in
which subjective reason and objective reason—the rational structure of
the mind and the rational structure of reality—are related, four main
types appear. The first type considers subjective reason as an effect of the
whole of reality on a part of it, namely, on the mind. It presupposes that
reality has the power of producing a reasonable mind through which it
can grasp and shape itself. Realism, whether naïve, critical, or dogmatic
(materialism), takes this stand, often without recognizing its basic presupposition. The second type considers objective reason as a creation of
subjective reason on the basis of an unstructured matter in which it
actualizes itself. Idealism, whether in the restricted forms of ancient
philosophy or in the unrestricted forms of modern philosophy, makes
this assertion, often without any explanation of the fact that matter is
receptive to the structural power of reason. The third type affirms the
ontological independence and the functional interdependence of subjective and objective reason, pointing to the mutual fulfilment of the one
in the other. Dualism or pluralism, whether metaphysical or epistemological, takes this position, often without asking the question of an

3. Cf. Plato's myth of the soul in its original state seeing the "ideas" or eternal essences.

underlying unity of subjective and objective reason. The fourth type affirms an underlying identity which expresses itself in the rational structure of reality. Monism, whether it describes the identity in terms of being or in terms of experience (pragmatism), takes this position, often without explaining the difference between subjective and objective reason.

The theologian is not obligated to make a decision about the degree of truth of these four types. However, he must consider their common presuppositions when he uses the concept of reason. Implicitly theologians always have done this. They have spoken of creation through the Logos or of the spiritual presence of God in everything real. They have called man the image of God because of his rational structure and have charged him with the task of grasping and shaping the world.

Subjective reason is the structure of the mind which enables it to grasp and to shape reality on the basis of a corresponding structure of reality (in whatever way this correspondence may be explained). The description of "grasping" and "shaping" in this definition is based on the fact that subjective reason always is actualized in an individual self which is related to its environment and to its world in terms of reception and reaction. The mind receives and reacts. In receiving reasonably, the mind grasps its world; in reacting reasonably, the mind shapes its world. "Grasping," in this context, has the connotation of penetrating into the depth, into the essential nature of a thing or an event, of understanding and expressing it. "Shaping," in this context, has the connotation of transforming a given material into a Gestalt, a living structure which has the power of being.

The division between the grasping and the shaping character of reason is not exclusive. In every act of reasonable reception an act of shaping is involved, and in every act of reasonable reaction an act of grasping is involved. We transform reality according to the way we see it, and we see reality according to the way we transform it. Grasping and shaping the world are interdependent. In the cognitive realm this has been clearly expressed in the Fourth Gospel, which speaks of knowing the truth by doing the truth.[4] Only in the active realization of the true does truth become manifest. In a similar way Karl Marx called every theory which is not based on the will to transform reality an "ideology," that is, an attempt to preserve existing evils by a theoretical construction which justifies them. Some of the impact of instrumentalist thinking on

4. John 3:21.

our contemporaries stems from its emphasis on the unity of action and knowledge.

While the cognitive side of "receiving rationality" demands special discussion, what has been said makes it possible to survey the entire field of ontological reason. In both types of rational acts, the grasping and the shaping, a basic polarity is visible. This is due to the fact that an emotional element is present in every rational act. On the receptive side of reason we find a polarity between the cognitive and the aesthetic elements. On the reactive side of reason we find a polarity between the organizational and the organic elements. But this description of the "field of reason" is only preliminary. Each of the four functions mentioned includes transitional stages on the path to its opposite pole. Music is further removed from the cognitive function than the novel, and technical science is further removed from the aesthetic realm than biography or ontology. Personal communion is further removed from organization than national community, and commercial law is further removed from the organic realm than government. One should not try to construe a static system of the rational functions of the human mind. There are no sharp limits between them, and there is much historical change in their growth and in their relationships. But all of them are functions of ontological reason, and the fact that in some of them the emotional element is more decisive than in others does not make them less rational. Music is no less rational than mathematics. The emotional element in music opens a dimension of reality which is closed to mathematics. Communion is no less rational than law. The emotional element in communion opens a dimension of reality which is closed to law. There is, of course, an implicit mathematical quality in music and a potential legal quality in all communal relations. But this is not their essence. They have their own rational structures. This is the meaning of Pascal's sentence about the "reasons of the heart which reason cannot comprehend."[5] Here "reason" is used in a double sense. The "reasons of the heart" are the structures of aesthetic and communal experience (beauty and love); the reason "which cannot comprehend them" is technical reason.

Subjective reason is the rational structure of the mind, while objective reason is the rational structure of reality which the mind can grasp and according to which it can shape reality. Reason in the philosopher grasps the reason in nature. Reason in the artist grasps the meaning of things. Reason in the legislator shapes society according to the structures of

5. Blaise Pascal, *Pensées*, Selection 277.

social balance. Reason in the leaders of a community shapes communal life according to the structure of organic interdependence. Subjective reason is rational if, in the twofold process of reception and reaction, it expresses the rational structure of reality. This relation, whether it is described in ontological or epistemological terms, is not static. Like being itself, reason unites a dynamic with a static element in an indissoluble amalgamation. This refers not only to subjective but also to objective reason. Both the rational structure of reality and the rational structure of the mind possess duration within change and change in duration. The problem of actual reason, therefore, is not only to avoid errors and failures in the grasping and shaping of reality but also to make the dynamics of reason effective in every act of subjective reason and in every moment of objective reason. The danger involved in this situation is that the dynamics of rational creativity may be confused with the distortions of reason in existence. The dynamic element of reason forces the mind to take this risk. In every rational act three elements inhere: the static element of reason, the dynamic element of reason, and the existential distortion of both of them. Therefore, it is possible for the mind to defend something as a static element of reason which is a distortion of it or for the mind to attack something as distorted which is a dynamic element of reason. Academic art defends the static element of aesthetic reason, but in much academic art there is a distortion of something which was creative and new when it first arose and which was attacked at its inception as a distortion of former academic ideals. Social conservatism is a distortion of something which once was a dynamic creation, attacked at the time of its appearance as a distortion of former conservative ideals. These risks are unavoidable in all processes of actual reason, in mind as well as in reality.

One must ask what the dynamic element in objective reason means. It is a problem whether one can speak about a changing element within the structure of reality. Nobody doubts that reality changes, but many people believe that change is possible only because the structure of reality is unchangeable. If this were so, the rational structure of the mind itself would be unchangeable, and the rational process would have only two elements—the static element and the failure to grasp and to shape it adequately. One would have to dismiss the dynamic element of reason altogether if subjective reason alone were dynamic. Reality itself creates structural possibilities within itself. Life, as well as mind, is creative. Only those things can live which embody a rational structure. Living beings are successful attempts of nature to actualize itself in accordance with the demands of objective reason. If nature does not follow these demands, its products are unsuccessful trials. The same is true of legal forms and social relations. New products of the historical process are attempts which can succeed only if they follow the demands of objective reason. Neither nature nor history can create anything that contradicts reason. The new and the old in history and nature are bound together in an overwhelming rational unity which is static and dynamic at the same time. The new does not break this unity; it cannot because objective reason is the structural possibility, the *logos* of being.

3. The Depth of Reason

The depth of reason is the expression of something that is not reason but which precedes reason and is manifest through it. Reason in both its objective and its subjective structures points to something which appears in these structures but which transcends them in power and meaning. This is not another field of reason which could progressively be discovered and expressed, but it is that which is expressed through every rational expression. It could be called the "substance" which appears in the rational structure, or "being-itself" which is manifest in the *logos* of being, or the "ground" which is creative in every rational creation, or the "abyss" which cannot be exhausted by any creation or by any totality of them, or the "infinite potentiality of being and meaning" which pours into the rational structures of mind and reality, actualizing and transforming them. All these terms which point to that which "precedes" reason have a metaphorical character. "Preceding" is itself metaphorical. This is necessarily so, because if the terms were used in their proper sense, they would belong to reason and would not precede it.

While only a metaphorical description of the depth of reason is possible, the metaphors may be applied to the various fields in which reason is actualized. In the cognitive realm the depth of reason is its quality of pointing to truth-itself, namely, to the infinite power of being and of the ultimately real, through the relative truths in every field of knowledge. In the aesthetic realm the depth of reason is its quality of pointing to "beauty-itself," namely, to an infinite meaning and an ultimate significance, through the creations in every field of aesthetic intuition. In the legal realm the depth of reason is its quality of pointing to "justice-itself," namely, to an infinite seriousness and an ultimate dignity, through every structure of actualized justice. In the communal realm the depth of reason is its quality of pointing to "love-itself," namely, to an infinite richness and an ultimate unity, through every form of actualized love. This dimension of reason, the dimension of depth, is an essential quality of all rational functions. It is their own depth, making them inexhaustible and giving them greatness.

The depth of reason is that characteristic of reason which explains two functions of the human mind, the rational character of which can neither be affirmed nor denied because they demonstrate an independent structure which can neither be reduced to other functions of reason nor be derived from prerational psychological or sociological elements. Myth is not primitive science, nor is cult primitive morality. Their content, as well as the attitude of people toward them, disclose elements which transcend science as well as morality—elements of infinity which express ultimate concern. These elements are essentially implicit in every rational act and process, so that in principle they do not require separate expression. In every act of grasping truth, truth-itself is grasped implicitly, and in every act of transforming love, love-itself transforms implicitly, etc. The depth of reason is essentially manifest in reason. But it is hidden in reason under the conditions of existence. Because of these conditions reason in existence expresses itself in myth and cult as well as in its proper functions. There should be neither myth nor cult. They contradict essential reason; they betray by their very existence the "fallen" state of a reason which has lost immediate unity with its own depth. It has become "superficial," cutting itself off from its ground and abyss. Christianity and the Enlightenment agree in the judgment that there should be neither myth nor cult, but from different presuppositions. Christianity envisages a state without myth and cult, potentially in the "beginning," actually in the "end," fragmentarily and by anticipation in the flux of time. Enlightenment sees the end of myth and cult in a new future when rational knowledge has vanquished myth and rational morals have conquered cult. Enlightenment and rationalism confuse the essential nature of reason with the predicament of reason in existence. Essentially reason is transparent toward its depth in each of its acts and processes. In existence this transparency is opaque and is replaced by myth and cult. Therefore, both of these are utterly ambiguous from the point of view of existential reason. Innumerable theories defining them, explaining them, and explaining them away are a token of this situation. If we ignore the merely negative theories, most of which are based on psychological and sociological explanations and which are consequences

of the rationalistic understanding of reason, we are driven to the following alternative: either myth and cult are special realms of reason along
with the others, or they represent the depth of reason in symbolic form.
If they are considered to be special rational functions in addition to the
others, they are in a never ending and insoluble conflict with the other
functions. They are swallowed by them, placed into the category of irrational feelings, or maintained as strange bodies, heteronomous and destructive, within the structure of reason. If, however, myth and cult are
considered to be the expressions of the depth of reason in symbolic form,
they lie in a dimension where no interference with the proper functions
of reason is possible. Wherever the ontological concept of reason is
accepted and the depth of reason is understood no conflicts between myth
and knowledge, between cult and morals, are necessary. Revelation does
not destroy reason, but reason raises the question of revelation.[6]

B. REASON IN EXISTENCE

4. The Finitude and the Ambiguities of Actual Reason

Reason as the structure of mind and reality is actual in the processes of
being, existence, and life. Being is finite, existence is self-contradictory,
and life is ambiguous (see Parts II–IV). Actual reason participates in
these characteristics of reality. Actual reason moves through finite categories, through self-destructive conflicts, through ambiguities, and through
the quest for what is unambiguous, beyond conflict, and beyond bondage
to the categories.

The nature of finite reason is described in classical form by Nicolaus
Cusanus and Immanuel Kant. The former speaks of the *docta ignorantia*, the "learned ignorance," which acknowledges the finitude of
man's cognitive reason and its inability to grasp its own infinite ground.
But, in recognizing this situation, man is at the same time aware of the
infinite which is present in everything finite, though infinitely transcending it. This presence of the inexhaustible ground in all beings is called by
Cusanus the "coincidence of the opposites." In spite of its finitude,
reason is aware of its infinite depth. It cannot express it in terms of rational knowledge (ignorance), but the knowledge that this is impossible is
real knowledge (learned). The finitude of reason does not lie in the fact
that it lacks perfection in grasping and shaping reality. Such imperfec-
tion is accidental to reason. Finitude is essential for reason, as it is for

6. For extensive discussion of symbolic forms see pp. 238–47.

everything that participates in being. The structure of this finitude is described in the most profound and comprehensive way in Kant's "critiques."[7] The categories of experience are categories of finitude. They do not enable human reason to grasp reality-in-itself; but they do enable man to grasp his world, the totality of the phenomena which appear to him and which constitute his actual experience. The main category of finitude is time. Being finite means being temporal. Reason cannot break through the limits of temporality and reach the eternal, just as it cannot break through the limits of causality, space, substance, in order to reach the first cause, absolute space, universal substance. At this point the situation is exactly the same as it is in Nicolaus Cusanus: by analyzing the categorical structure of reason, man discovers the finitude in which he is imprisoned. He also discovers that his reason does not accept this bondage and tries to grasp the infinite with the categories of finitude, the really real with the categories of experience, and that it necessarily fails. The only point at which the prison of finitude is open is the realm of moral experience, because in it something unconditional breaks into the whole of temporal and causal conditions. But this point which Kant reaches is nothing more than a point, an unconditional command, a mere awareness of the depth of reason.

Kant's "critical ignorance" describes the finitude of reason as clearly as the "learned ignorance" of Nicolaus Cusanus. The difference, however, is that, in Cusanus, Catholic mysticism points to an intuitive union with the ground and abyss of reason, while, in Kant, Protestant criticism restricts reason to the acceptance of the unconditional imperative as the only approach to reality-itself. In post-Kantian metaphysics reason forgot its bondage to the categories of finitude. But this self-elevation to divine dignity brought on dethronement and contempt of reason and made the victory of one of its functions over all the others possible. The fall of a deified reason after Hegel contributed decisively to the enthronement of technical reason in our time and to the loss of the universality and the depth of ontological reason.

But reason is not merely finite. It is true that reason, along with all things and events, is subject to the conditions of existence. It contradicts

7. It is unfortunate that Kant often is interpreted only as an epistemological idealist and an ethical formalist—and consequently rejected. Kant is more than this. His doctrine of the categories is a doctrine of human finitude. His doctrine of the categorical imperative is a doctrine of the unconditional element in the depth of practical reason. His doctrine of the teleological principle in art and nature enlarges the concept of reason beyond its cognitive-technical sense toward what we have called "ontological reason."

itself and is threatened with disruption and self-destruction. Its elements move against each other. But this is only the one side of the picture. In the actual life of reason its basic structure is never completely lost. If it were lost, mind as well as reality would have been destroyed in the very moment of their coming into existence. In the actual life of reason essential and existential forces, forces of creation and forces of destruction, are united and disunited at the same time. These conflicts in actual reason supply the content for a justifiable theological criticism of reason. But an accusation of reason *as such* is a symptom either of theological ignorance or of theological arrogance. On the other hand, an attack on theology *as such* in the name of reason is a symptom of rationalistic shallowness or rationalistic *hybris*. An adequate description of the inner conflicts of ontological reason should replace the popular religious and half-popular theological lamentations about reason as such. And it should, at the same time, force reason to acknowledge its own existential predicament out of which the quest for revelation arises.

5. The Conflict within Actual Reason and the Quest for Revelation

a) Autonomy against heteronomy.—Under the conditions of existence the structural elements of reason move against each other. Although never completely separated, they fall into self-destructive conflicts which cannot be solved on the basis of actual reason. A description of these conflicts must replace the popular religious or theological attacks on the weakness or blindness of reason. The self-criticism of reason in the light of revelation penetrates much deeper and is considerably more rational than these inarticulate and often merely emotional attacks. The polarity of structure and depth within reason produces a conflict between autonomous and heteronomous reason under the conditions of existence. Out of this conflict arises the quest for theonomy. The polarity of the static and the dynamic elements of reason produces a conflict between absolutism and relativism of reason under the conditions of existence. This conflict leads to the quest for the concrete-absolute. The polarity of the formal and the emotional elements of reason produces the conflict between formalism and irrationalism of reason under the conditions of existence. Out of this conflict arises the quest for the union of form and mystery. In all three cases reason is driven to the quest for revelation.

Reason which affirms and actualizes its structure without regarding its depth is autonomous. Autonomy does not mean the freedom of the individual to be a law to himself, as theological writers often have asserted, establishing in this way an easy scapegoat for their attacks on an independent culture. Autonomy means the obedience of the individual to the law of reason, which he finds in himself as a rational being. The *nomos* ("law") of *autos* ("self") is not the law of one's personality structure. It is the law of subjective-objective reason; it is the law implied in the *logos* structure of mind and reality. Autonomous reason, in affirming itself in its different functions and their structural demands, uses or rejects that which is merely an expression of an individual's situation within him and around him. It resists the danger of being conditioned by the situation of self and world in existence. It considers these conditions as the material which reason has to grasp and to shape according to its structural laws. Therefore, autonomous reason tries to keep itself free from "ungrasped impressions" and "unshaped strivings." Its independence is the opposite of wilfulness; it is obedience to its own essential structure, the law of reason which is the law of nature within mind and reality, and which is divine law, rooted in the ground of being itself. This is true of all functions of ontological reason.

Historically, autonomous reason has liberated and maintained itself in a never ending fight with heteronomy. Heteronomy imposes a strange (*heteros*) law (*nomos*) on one or all of the functions of reason. It issues commands from "outside" on how reason should grasp and shape reality. But this "outside" is not merely outside. It represents, at the same time, an element in reason itself, namely, the depth of reason. This makes the fight between autonomy and heteronomy dangerous and tragic. It is, finally, a conflict in reason itself. As long as reason is prerational, a confusing mass of sense impressions, a chaotic mass of instincts, strivings, compulsions, no genuine heteronomy has appeared. All this is outside reason, but it is not a law to which reason is asked to subject itself; it is not law in any rational sense. The problem of heteronomy is the problem of an authority which claims to represent reason, namely, the depth of reason, against its autonomous actualization. The basis of such a claim is not the superiority in rational power which many traditions, institutions, or personalities obviously have. The basis of a genuine heteronomy is the claim to speak in the name of the ground of being and therefore in an unconditional and ultimate way. A heteronomous authority usually expresses itself in terms of myth and cult because these are the direct and intentional expressions of the depth of reason. It is also possible for nonmythical and nonritual forms to gain power over the mind (e.g., political ideas). Heteronomy in this sense is usually a reaction against an autonomy which has lost its depth and has become empty and powerless. But as a reaction it is destructive, denying to reason the right of autonomy and destroying its structural laws from outside.

Autonomy and heteronomy are rooted in theonomy, and each goes astray when their theonomous unity is broken. Theonomy does not mean the acceptance of a divine law imposed on reason by a highest authority; it means autonomous reason united with its own depth. In a theonomous situation reason actualizes itself in obedience to its structural laws and in the power of its own inexhaustible ground. Since God (*theos*) is the law (*nomos*) for both the structure and the ground of reason, they are united in him, and their unity is manifest in a theonomous situation. But there is no complete theonomy under the conditions of existence. Both elements which essentially are united in it struggle with each other under the conditions of existence and try to destroy each other. In this struggle they tend to destroy reason itself. Therefore, the quest for a reunion of what is always split in time and space arises *out* of reason and not in opposition to reason. This quest is the quest for revelation.

Seen in a world historical perspective the conflict between autonomy and heteronomy is the key to any theological understanding of the Greek as well as of the modern development and of many other problems of the spiritual history of mankind. The history of Greek philosophy, for example, can be written as a curve which starts with the still theonomous pre-philosophical period (mythology and cosmology), the slow elaboration of the autonomous structures of reason (pre-Socratic), the classical synthesis of structure and depth (Plato), the rationalization of this synthesis in the different schools (after Aristotle), the despair of reason in trying autonomously to create a world to live in (skepticism), the mystical transcending of reason (Neo-Platonism), the questioning of authorities in past and present (philosophical schools and religious sects), the creation of a new theonomy under Christian influence (Clement and Origen), and the intrusion of heteronomous elements (Athanasius and Augustine). During the high Middle Ages a theonomy (Bonaventura) was realized under the preponderance of heteronomous elements (Thomas). Toward the end of the medieval period heteronomy became all-powerful (Inquisition), partly as a reaction against autonomous tendencies in culture and religion (nominalism), and destroyed the medieval theonomy. In the period of Renaissance and Reformation the conflict grew to new intensity. The Renaissance, which showed a theonomous character in its Neo-Platonic beginnings (Cusanus, Ficino), became increasingly autonomous in its later development (Erasmus, Galileo). Conversely, the Reformation, which in its early years united a religious with a cultural emphasis on autonomy (Luther's reliance on his conscience, and Luther and Zwingli's connection with the humanists), very soon developed a heteronomy which surpassed even that of the later Middle Ages in some respects (Protestant orthodoxy). In the eighteenth and nineteenth centuries, in spite of some heteronomous remnants and reactions, autonomy won an almost complete victory. Orthodoxy and fundamentalism were pushed into the corners of cultural life, sterile and ineffective. Classical and Romantic attempts to re-establish theonomy with autonomous means (Hegel, Schelling) did not succeed, producing radical autonomous reactions (post-Hegelians), on the one hand, and strong heteronomous reactions (revivalism), on the other hand. Under the guidance of technical reason autonomy conquered all reactions but completely lost the dimension of depth. It became shallow, empty, without ultimate meaning, and produced conscious or unconscious despair. In this situation powerful heteronomies of a quasi-political character entered the vacuum created by an autonomy which lacked the dimension of depth. The double fight against an empty autonomy and a destructive heteronomy makes the quest for a new theonomy as urgent today as it was at the end of the ancient world. The catastrophe of autonomous reason is complete. Neither autonomy nor heteronomy, isolated and in conflict, can give the answer.

b) Relativism against absolutism.—Essentially, reason unites a static and a dynamic element. The static element preserves reason from losing its identity within the life-process. The dynamic element is the power of reason to actualize itself rationally in the process of life, while without the static element reason could not be the structure of life. Under the conditions of existence the two elements are torn from each other and move against each other.

The static element of reason appears in two forms of absolutism—the absolutism of tradition and the absolutism of revolution. The dynamic element of reason appears in two forms of relativism—positivistic relativism and cynical relativism. The absolutism of tradition identifies the static element of reason with special traditions, such as socially accepted morals, established political forms, "academic" aesthetics, and unquestioned philosophical principles. This attitude is usually called "conservative." But conservatism can mean two things. It can mean the readiness to defend the static side of reason against an exclusive emphasis on the dynamic side, and it can mean the fanaticism which considers dynamic structures of reason as static and elevates them to absolute validity. However, in any special case it is impossible to separate the static from the dynamic element, and every attempt to do so leads finally to a destruction of the absolutized forms through the attack of other forms which emerge in the process of actual reason. Such attacks are made in the power of another type of absolutism, the revolutionary. But after one absolutism is destroyed by a revolutionary attack, the victor establishes itself in equally absolute terms. This is almost unavoidable, because the attack was victorious through the strength of an absolute claim, often of a utopian character. Revolutionary reason believes just as deeply as traditionalism that it represents unchangeable truth, but it is being more inconsistent in this belief. The absolutism of tradition can point to past ages, with the claim that it is saying what always has been said. Revolutionary absolutism, however, has experienced at least in one case the breakdown of such a claim, namely, the breaching of tradition involved in its own victory; and it should envisage the possibility of its own end. But it does not.[8] This shows that the two types of absolutism are not exclusive; they elicit each other.

Both are contradicted by different forms of relativism. Relativism denies a static element in the structure of reason or emphasizes the dynamic element so much that no definite place is left for actual reason. Relativism can be positivistic or cynical, the former parallel to the absolutism of tradition, the second to the absolutism of revolution. Positivistic relativism takes what is "given" (posited) without applying absolute criteria to its valuation. In practice, therefore, it can become as conservative as any kind of absolutism of tradition, but on another basis and with other implications. For instance, the positivism of law in the middle of the nineteenth century was a reaction against the revolutionary abso-

8. Protestant orthodox absolutism is less consistent than Catholic ecclesiastical absolutism. Schleiermacher's statement that "the Reformation continues" is the only consistent Protestant attitude. It is an astonishing, though anthropologically rather revealing, fact that in America groups representing a most radical absolutism of tradition call themselves "Daughters" or "Sons" of the American Revolution. Russian communism not only has maintained the absolutism of its revolutionary attack but has developed partially into an absolutism of tradition by relating itself consciously to the traditions of the pre-revolutionary past. Marx himself in his emphasis on the transitory character of every stage of the revolutionary process was much more consistent in this respect. He could have said: "The revolution continues."

lutism of the eighteenth century. But it was not absolutistic itself. It accepted the positive law of different nations and periods as "merely given," but it did not allow critical attacks from the side of the natural law, nor did it establish current positive law as eternal law. Similarly, the aesthetic relativism of this period placed all previous styles on the same level without giving any of them preference in terms of a classical ideal. In the sphere of social relations local traditions were praised and their divergent developments were accepted without a critical norm. More important than all these is philosophical positivism. From the time of David Hume it has developed in many directions and has replaced absolute norms and criteria in all realms of life by pragmatic tests. Truth is relative to a group, to a concrete situation, or to an existential predicament. In this respect the recent forms of existentialism agree with the principles of pragmatic relativism and with some forms of the European *Lebensphilosophie* ("philosophy of life") to a surprising degree. It is the tragedy of this positivism that it either transforms itself into a conservative absolutism or into the cynical type of relativism. Only in countries where the remnants of former absolutisms are still powerful enough to delay such developments are the self-destructive implications of positivism hidden (England, the United States).

Cynical relativism usually is a result of a disappointment over utopian absolutism. It employs skeptical arguments against absolute principles, but it does not draw either of the two possible consequences of radical skepticism. It neither turns to revelation nor leaves the realm of thought and action altogether as ancient skepticism often did. Cynicism is an attitude of superiority over, or indifference toward, any rational structure, whether static or dynamic. Cynical relativism uses reason only for the sake of denying reason—a self-contradiction which is "cynically" accepted. Rational criticism, which presupposes some valid structures, is not the basis of cynical relativism. Its basis is disbelief in the validity of any rational act, even if it is merely critical. Cynical relativism is not wrecked by its self-contradictions. Its nemesis is the empty space it produces, the complete vacuum into which new absolutisms pour.

"Criticism" is an attempt to overcome the conflict between absolutism and relativism. It is an attitude which is not restricted to so-called critical philosophy. It is present in the whole history of philosophy, nor is it restricted to philosophy. It is effective in all spheres of ontological reason. It is the attempt to unite the static and the dynamic elements of reason by depriving the static element of content and by reducing it to a pure form. An example is the "categorical imperative," which denies special demands and which surrenders concrete details to the contingencies of the situation. Criticism combines a positivistic with a revolutionary element, excluding traditionalism as well as cynicism. Socrates and Kant are representative of the critical attitude in philosophy. But the development of their schools proves that the critical attitude is more a demand than a possibility. In both schools either the static or the dynamic element prevailed, frustrating the critical attempt. Although Plato's earlier dialogues were critical, Platonism grew in the direction of absolutism. In spite of their acceptance of the rationalism of Socrates, hedonism and cynicism grew in the direction of absolutism. Kant's classical followers became pure absolutists, while the Neo-Kantian school emphasized the relativism of an infinite process. This is not accidental. The critical attitude, by establishing absolute though assumedly empty criteria, deceived itself about their emptiness. These criteria always mirrored a special situation, for example, the situation of Athens in the Peloponnesian War, or the victory of the bourgeois mind in western Europe. The principles established by critical philosophy were too concrete and consequently too relative for their absolute claim. But their application was too absolutistic; it represented a special form of life which claimed more than relative validity. Therefore, in the ancient as well as in the modern world, criticism was unable to overcome the conflict between absolutism and relativism. Only that which is absolute and concrete at the same time can overcome this conflict. Only revelation can do it.

c) Formalism against emotionalism.—In its essential structure reason unites formal and emotional elements. There is a predominance of the formal element in the cognitive and the legal functions of reason and of the emotional element in its aesthetic and communal functions. But in all its activities essential reason unites both elements. Under the conditions of existence the unity is disrupted. The elements move against each other and produce conflicts as deep and destructive as are the conflicts already discussed.

Formalism appears in the exclusive emphasis on the formal side of every rational function and in the separation of the functions from each other. Controlling knowledge and the corresponding formalized logic, if taken as the pattern of all knowledge, represent formalism in the cognitive realm. Controlling knowledge is one side of cognitive reason and an essential element in every cognitive act. But its attempt to monopolize the whole cognitive function and to deny that any other avenue is knowledge and can attain truth shows its existential disruption. It keeps cognitive reason from digging into those strata of things and events which can be grasped only with *amor intellectualis* ("intellectual love"). Formalism in the cognitive realm is intellectualism, the use of the cognitive intellect without *erōs*. Emotional reactions against intellectualism forget the obligation of strict, serious, and technically correct thinking in all matters of knowledge. But they are right in demanding a knowledge which not only controls but also unites.[9]

In the aesthetic realm formalism is an attitude, expressed in the phrase "art for art's sake," which disregards the content and meaning of artistic creations for the sake of their form. Aestheticism deprives art of its existential character by substituting detached judgments of taste and a refined connoisseurship for emotional union. No artistic expression is possible without the creative rational form, but the form, even in its greatest refinement, is empty if it does not express a spiritual substance. Even the richest and most profound artistic creation can be destructive for spiritual life if it is received in terms of formalism and aestheticism.[10] The emotional reactions of most people against aestheticism are wrong in their aesthetic judgment but right in their fundamental intention.

Formalism in the realm of legal reason places exclusive emphasis on the structural necessities of justice without asking the question of the adequacy of a legal form to the human reality which it is supposed to shape. The tragic alienation between law and life which is a subject of complaint in all periods is not caused by bad will on the part of those who make and enforce the law; it is a consequence of the separation of form from emotional participation. Legalism in the sense of legal formalism can become, like certain types of logic, a kind of play with pure forms, consistent in itself, detached from life. If applied to life, this play can turn into a destructive reality. Form armed with power can become a terrible organ of suppression in a social group. From our point of view, legal formalism and totalitarian suppression are intimately related. Emotional reactions against legal formalism misunderstand the structural necessities of law, but they realize instinctively the inadequacy of legal formalism for meeting the demands of life.

In the communal function of reason, formalism preserves, applies, and defends the conventional forms which have shaped social and personal

---

9. See the following sections.

10. Every public performance of Bach's *Passion of St. Matthew* carries with it the risk of making the gospel story more meaningless for people who admire the great art of Bach's music without being grasped by its infinite meaning.

life. Conventionalism, as this attitude can be called, must not be confused with traditionalism. The latter makes an absolute claim for special traditions or conventions because of their content and meaning. Conventionalism makes no absolute claim for the conventions it defends, nor does it value them because of their content and meaning. Conventionalism affirms the social and personal forms as forms. Automatic obedience to the accepted ways of behavior is demanded by conventional formalism. Its tremendous power in social relations, in education, and in self-discipline makes it a tragic force in all human history. It tends to destroy the inborn vitality and creativity of every new being and of every new generation. It cripples life and replaces love by rule. It shapes personalities and communities by suppressing the spiritual and emotional substance which it is supposed to shape. The form destroys the meaning. Emotional reactions against conventional formalism are especially explosive and catastrophic. They have a "blind spot" with regard to the supporting, preserving, and directing power of convention and habit; but they are right in opposing its formalistic distortion with passion and sacrifice.

Formalism appears not only in every function of ontological reason but also in the relation of the functions to each other. The unity of reason is disrupted by its division into departments each of which is controlled by a special set of structural forms. This refers to the grasping and to the shaping functions of reason as well as to their interrelationship. The cognitive function, deprived of its aesthetic element, is separated from the aesthetic function, deprived of its cognitive element. In essential reason these two elements are united in various degrees, as reflected in functions like historical and ontological intuition, on the one hand, psychological novels and metaphysical poetry, on the other hand. The union of the cognitive and aesthetic functions is fully expressed in mythology, the womb out of which both of them were born and came to independence and to which they tend to return. The Romanticists of the early nineteenth century, philosophers and artists, tried to re-establish the unity of the cognitive and the aesthetic functions (this attempt has been continued by many recent artists and philosophers—expressionism, new realism, existentialism). They turned away from cognitive and aesthetic formalism and consequently from the separation of the two functions. They even tried to unite both in a new myth. But in this they failed. No myth can be created, no unity of the rational functions can be reached, on the basis of reason in conflict. A new myth is the expression of the reuniting power of a new revelation, not a product of formalized reason.

The shaping functions of reason also are separated from each other by the formalization of reason and its separation from emotion. The organizational function, deprived of an organic basis, is separated from the organic function, deprived of an organizational structure. In essential reason these two elements are united in various degrees and with various transitions, in a way analogous to the life of free organizations within an embracing legal structure. The union of legal and communal functions is fully expressed in the cult community which is the mother of both of them and to which they try to return. Old and new romanticists long for a state which represents the Christian "body" of the idealized Middle Ages, or, if this cannot be re-established, national or racial bodies, or the "body" of mankind. They look for an organism which can become the bearer of a nonformalized law.[11] But neither mankind as an organism nor a common cult as the function of a religious world community can unite in itself law and communion. This unity can be created neither by a formalized constitution nor by unorganized sympathies, desires, and movements. The quest for a new and universal communion, in which organization and organism are united, is the quest for revelation.

Finally, the formalization of reason separates its grasping from its shaping functions. This conflict is usually described as the conflict between theory and practice. A grasping which has lost the element of shaping and a shaping which has lost the element of grasping are in conflict with each other. In essential reason the two elements are united. The much-abused word "experience" has *one* connotation which points to this unity: experience unites insight with action. In the relation of myth and cult no separation is even imaginable. Cult includes the myth on the basis of which it acts out the divine-human drama, and myth includes the cult of which it is the imaginary expression. It is, therefore, understandable that there is a continuous struggle for the reunion of theory and practice. In his description of the "poverty of philosophy" Marx challenged a philosophy which interprets the world without changing it. Nietzsche in his attack on historism challenged a historiography which is not related to our historical existence. Religious socialism took over the insight of the Fourth Gospel that truth must be done,

---

11. This is the real problem of the world organization toward which mankind is striving today and which is prematurely anticipated by the movement for a world government.

and it took over the insight of the whole biblical tradition that without active participation in the "new reality" its nature cannot be known. Instrumentalism points to the intimate relation between action and knowledge, though it remains predominantly on the level of technical reason. Nevertheless, the conflicts remain. Practice resists theory, which it considers inferior to itself; it demands an activism which cuts off every theoretical investigation before it has come to its end. In practice one cannot do otherwise, for one must act before one has finished thinking. On the other hand, the infinite horizons of thinking cannot supply the basis for any concrete decision with certainty. Except in the technical realm where an existential decision is not involved, one must make decisions on the basis of limited or distorted or incomplete insights. Neither theory nor practice in isolation can solve the problem of their conflict with each other. Only a truth which is present in spite of the infinity of theoretical possibilities and only a good which is present in spite of the infinite risk implied in every action can overcome the disruption between the grasping and the shaping functions of reason. The quest for such a truth and such a good is the quest for revelation.

The functional splits of reason are consequences of the formalization of reason, of the conflict between formalism and emotionalism. The consequences of the formalization of reason are manifest. Emotion reacts against them and against formal reason in all realms. But this reaction is futile because it is merely "emotional," that is, minus structural elements. Emotion is powerless against intellectualism and aestheticism, against legalism and conventionalism, if it remains mere emotion. But, although powerless over reason, it can have great power of destruction over the mind, personally and socially. Emotion without rational structure (in the sense, of course, of ontological reason) becomes irrationalism. And irrationalism is destructive in two respects. If it attacks formalized reason, it must have some rational content. This content, however, is not subjected to rational criticism and gets its power from the strength of the emotion which carries it. It is still reason, but irrationally promoted reason, and therefore blind and fanatical. It has all the qualities of the demonic, whether it is expressed in religious or secular terms. If, on the other hand, irrationalism empties itself of any content and becomes mere subjective feeling, a vacuum is produced, into which distorted reason can break without a rational check.[12] If reason sacrifices its formal structures, and with them its critical power, the re-

12. The empty irrationalism of the German youth movement was fertile soil for the rational irrationalism of the Nazis.

sult is not an empty sentimentality but the demonic rise of antirational forces, which often are supported by all the tools of technical reason. This experience drives men to the quest for the reunion of form and emotion. This is a quest for revelation. Reason does not resist revelation. It asks for revelation, for revelation means the reintegration of reason.

C. THE COGNITIVE FUNCTION OF REASON
AND THE QUEST FOR REVELATION

6. The Ontological Structure of Knowledge

Systematic theology must give special consideration to the cognitive function of ontological reason in developing the concept of revelation, for revelation is the manifestation of the ground of being for human knowledge. While theology as such cannot produce an epistemology of its own, it must refer to those characteristics of cognitive reason which are relevant for the cognitive character of revelation. In particular, theology must give a description of cognitive reason under the conditions of existence. But a description of the conflicts of existential cognition presupposes an understanding of its ontological structure, for it is the polar structure of cognitive reason which makes its existential conflicts possible and drives it to the quest for revelation.

Knowing is a form of union. In every act of knowledge the knower and that which is known are united; the gap between subject and object is overcome. The subject "grasps" the object, adapts it to itself, and, at the same time, adapts itself to the object. But the union of knowledge is a peculiar one; it is a union through separation. Detachment is the condition of cognitive union. In order to know, one must "look" at a thing, and, in order to look at a thing, one must be "at a distance." Cognitive distance is the presupposition of cognitive union. Most philosophers have seen both sides. The old dispute whether the equal recognizes the equal or whether the unequal recognizes the unequal is a classical expression of the insight that union (which presupposes some equality) and distance (which presupposes some inequality) are polar elements in the process of cognition. The unity of distance and union is the ontological problem of knowledge. It drove Plato to the myth of an original union of the soul with the essences (ideas), of the separation of soul from the truly real in temporal existence, of the recollection of the essences, and of reunion with them through the different degrees of cognitive elevation. The unity is never completely destroyed; but there is also estrangement. The particular object is strange as such, but it contains essential structures with which the cognitive subject is essentially united and which it can remember when looking at things. This motif runs through the whole history of philosophy. It explains the titanic attempts of human thought in all periods to make the cognitive relation understandable—the strangeness of subject and object and, in spite of it, their cognitive union. While skepticism despaired of the possibility of uniting the object with the subject, criticism removed the object as a thing-in-itself from the realm of actual knowledge without explaining how knowledge can grasp reality and not only appearance. While positivism completely removed the difference between subject and object, and idealism decreed their identity, both of them failed to explain the estrangement of subject and object and the possibility of error. Dualism postulated a transcendent unity of subject and object in a divine mind or substance, without explaining man's participation in it. Yet each of these attempts was aware of the ontological problem of knowledge: the unity of separation and union.

The epistemological situation is confirmed existentially by certain aspects of personal and social life as they are related to knowledge. The passion of knowing for the sake of knowing, which frequently can be found in primitive as well as in refined forms, indicates that a want, a vacuum, is filled by successful cognition. Something which was strange, but which nevertheless belongs to us, has become familiar, a part of us. According to Plato, the cognitive *erōs* is born out of poverty and abundance. It drives us toward reunion with that to which we belong and which belongs to us. In every act of knowledge want and estrangement are conquered.

But knowledge is more than a fulfilling; it also transforms and heals; this would be impossible if the knowing subject were only a mirror of the object, remaining in unconquered distance from it. Socrates was aware of this situation when he made the assertion that out of the knowing of the good the doing of the good follows. It is, of course, as easy as it is cheap to state that one may know the good without doing it, without being able to do it. One should not confront Socrates with Paul in order to show how much more realistic Paul was. It is at least probable that Socrates knew what every schoolboy knows—that some people act against their better knowledge. But he also knew something of which even philosophers and theologians are ignorant—that true knowledge includes union and, therefore, openness to receive that with which one unites. This is the knowledge of which Paul also speaks, the *gnosis* which in New Testament Greek means cognitive, sexual, and mystical union at the same time. In this respect there is no contrast between Socrates and Paul. He who knows God or the Christ in the sense of being grasped by him and being united with him does the good. He who knows the essential structure of things in the sense of having received their meaning and power acts according to them; he does the good, even if he has to die for it.

Recently the term "insight" has been given connotations of *gnosis*, namely, of a knowledge which transforms and heals. Depth psychology attributes healing powers to insight, meaning not a detached knowledge of psychoanalytic theory or of one's own past in the light of this theory but a repetition of one's actual experiences with all the pains and horrors of such a return. Insight in this sense is a reunion with one's own past and especially with those moments in it which influence the present destructively. Such a cognitive union produces a transformation just as radical and as difficult as that presupposed and demanded by Socrates and Paul. For most of the Asiatic philosophies and religions the uniting, healing, and transforming power of knowledge is a matter of course. Their problem—never completely solved—is the element of distance, not that of union.

Another existential confirmation of the interpretation of knowledge as a unity between distance and union is the social valuation of knowledge in all integrated human groups. Insight into the principles on which the life of the group is based, and acceptance of them, is considered an absolute precondition for the life of the group. There is no difference in this respect between religious or secular, democratic or totalitarian, groups. It is impossible to understand the emphasis in all social groups on the knowledge of the dominating principles, if the uniting character of knowledge is not recognized. Much criticism of so-called dogmatism, often made by people who are unaware of their own dogmatic assumptions, is rooted in the misinterpretation of knowledge as a detached cognizance of objects separated from the subject. Dogmatism with respect to such knowledge is indeed meaningless. But if knowledge unites, much depends on the object with which it unites. Error becomes dangerous if it means union with distorted and deceiving elements of reality, with that which is not really real but which only claims to be. Anxiety about falling into error or about the error into which others might fall or have fallen, the tremendous reactions against error in all cohesive social groups, the interpretation of error as demonic possession—all this is understandable only if knowledge includes union. Liberalism, the protest against dogmatism, is based on the authentic element of detachment which belongs to knowledge and which demands openness for questions, inquiries, and new answers, even to the point of the possible disintegration of a social group. Under the conditions of existence no final solution for this conflict can be found. As reason generally is drawn into the conflict between absolutism and relativism, so cognitive reason is subject to the conflict between union and detachment in every act of knowledge. Out of this conflict the quest arises for a knowledge which unites the certainty of existential union with the openness of cognitive detachment. This quest is the quest for the knowledge of revelation.

7. COGNITIVE RELATIONS

The element of union and the element of detachment appear in different proportions in the different realms of knowledge. But there is no knowledge without the presence of both elements. Statistical indexes are material for physical or sociological knowledge, but they are not themselves knowledge. Devotional meditations imply cognitive elements, but they are not themselves knowledge.

The type of knowledge which is predominantly determined by the element of detachment can be called "controlling knowledge."[13] Controlling knowledge is the outstanding, though not the only, example of technical reason. It unites subject and object for the sake of the control of the object by the subject. It transforms the object into a completely conditioned and calculable "thing." It deprives it of any subjective quality. Controlling knowledge looks upon its object as something which cannot return its look. Certainly, in every type of knowledge subject and object are logically distinguished. There is always an object, even in our knowledge of God. But controlling knowledge "objectifies" not only logically (which is unavoidable) but also ontologically and ethically. No thing, however, is merely a thing. Since everything that is participates in the self-world structure of being, elements of self-relatedness are universal. This makes union with everything possible. Nothing is absolutely strange. Speaking in a metaphorical manner, one could say that as we look at things so things looks at us with the expectation of being received and the offer of enriching us in cognitive union. Things indicate that they might be "interesting" if we enter their deeper levels and ex-

13. Cf. Max Scheler, *Versuche zu einer Soziologie des Wissens* (Munich, 1924).

perience their special power of being.[14] At the same time, this does not exclude the fact that they are objects in the technical sense, things to be used and formed, means for ends which are strange to their inner meaning (*telos*). A metal is "interesting"; it has elements of subjectivity and self-relatedness. It is, on the other hand, material for innumerable tools and purposes. While the nature of metals admits of an overwhelming amount of objectifying knowledge and technical use, the nature of man does not. Man resists objectification, and if his resistance to it is broken, man himself is broken. A truly objective relation to man is determined by the element of union; the element of detachment is secondary. It is not absent; there are levels in man's bodily, psychic, and mental constitution which can and must be grasped by controlling knowledge. But this is neither the way of knowing human nature nor is it the way of knowing any individual personality in past or present, including one's self. Without union there is no cognitive approach to man. In contrast to controlling knowledge this cognitive attitude can be called "receiving knowledge." Neither actually nor potentially is it determined by the means-ends relationship. Receiving knowledge takes the object into itself, into union with the subject. This includes the emotional element, from which controlling knowledge tries to detach itself as much as possible. Emotion is the vehicle for receiving cognition. But the vehicle is far from making the content itself emotional. The content is rational, something to be verified, to be looked at with critical caution. Nevertheless, nothing can be received cognitively without emotion. No union of subject and object is possible without emotional participation.

The unity of union and detachment is precisely described by the term "understanding." Its literal meaning, to stand under the place where the object of knowledge stands, implies intimate participation. In ordinary use it points to the ability to grasp the logical meaning of something. Understanding another person or a historical figure, the life of an animal or a religious text, involves an amalgamation of controlling and receiving knowledge, of union and detachment, of participation and analysis.

Most cognitive distortions are rooted in a disregard of the polarity which is in cognitive reason. This disregard is not simply an avoidable mistake; it is a genuine conflict under the conditions of existence. One side of this conflict is the tension between dogmatism and criticism

14. Goethe asks us to consider how "being" (*seiend*) things are, pointing to the unique structure which is their power of being.

within social groups. But there are other sides to it. Controlling knowledge claims control of every level of reality. Life, spirit, personality, community, meanings, values, even one's ultimate concern, should be treated in terms of detachment, analysis, calculation, technical use. The power behind this claim is the preciseness, verifiability, the public approachability of controlling knowledge, and, above all, the tremendous success of its application to certain levels of reality. It is impossible to disregard or even to restrain this claim. The public mind is so impregnated with its methodological demands and its astonishing results that every cognitive attempt in which reception and union are presupposed encounters utter distrust. A consequence of this attitude is a rapid decay of spiritual (not only of the Spiritual) life, an estrangement from nature, and, most dangerous of all, a dealing with human beings as with things. In psychology and sociology, in medicine and philosophy, man has been dissolved into elements out of which he is composed and which determine him. Treasures of empirical knowledge have been produced in this way, and new research projects augment those treasures daily. But man has been lost in this enterprise. That which can be known only by participation and union, that which is the object of receiving knowledge, is disregarded. Man actually has become what controlling knowledge considers him to be, a thing among things, a cog in the dominating machine of production and consumption, a dehumanized object of tyranny or a normalized object of public communications. Cognitive dehumanization has produced actual dehumanization.

Three main movements have tried to resist the tidal wave of controlling knowledge: romanticism, philosophy of life, and existentialism. They all have had instantaneous success, but they have lost out in the long run because they could not solve the problem of the criterion of the false and the true. The Romantic philosophy of nature confused poetry and symbolic intuition with knowledge. It ignored the strangeness of the world of objects, the strangeness not only of the lower but also of the higher levels of nature toward man. If Hegel called nature "estranged spirit," his emphasis was not on "estranged" but on "spirit," which gave him the possibility of approaching nature with receiving knowledge, with attempts to participate in it and to unite with it. But Hegel's philosophy of nature was a failure of world-wide significance. A Romantic philosophy of nature cannot escape this defeat. Neither can a philosophy of life which tries to create cognitive union with the dynamic process of life. Such a philosophy recognizes that life is not an object of controlling knowledge; that life must be killed in order to be subjected to the means-ends structure; that life in its dynamic creativity, in its *élan vital* (Bergson), is open only to receiving knowledge, to intuitive participation and mystical union. This, however, raises the question which life-philosophy never was able to answer: How can the intuitive union in which life is aware of itself be verified? If it is unexpressible, it is not knowledge. If it can be expressed, it falls under the criterion of cognitive reason, and its application demands detachment, analysis, and objectification. The relation between receiving and controlling knowledge is not explained by Bergson or by any other of the life-philosophers. Existentialism tries to save the freedom of the individual self from the domination of controlling knowledge. But this freedom is described in terms which not only lack any criterion but also any content. Existentialism is the most desperate attempt to escape the power of controlling knowledge and of the objectified world which technical reason has produced. It says "No" to this world, but, in order to say "Yes" to something else, it has either to use controlling knowledge or to turn to revelation. Existentialism, like romanticism and philosophy of life, must either surrender to technical reason or ask the question of revelation. Revelation claims to create complete union with that which appears in revelation. It is receiving knowledge in its fulfilment. But, at the same time, it claims to satisfy the demands of controlling knowledge, of detachment and analysis.

8. TRUTH AND VERIFICATION

Every cognitive act strives for truth. Since theology claims to be true, it must discuss the meaning of the term "truth," the nature of revealed truth, and its relation to other forms of truth. In the absence of such a discussion the theological claim can be dismissed by a simple semantic device, often used by naturalists and positivists. According to them, the use of the term "truth" is restricted to empirically verifiable statements. The predicate "true" should be reserved either for analytic sentences or for experimentally confirmed propositions. Such a terminological limitation of the terms "true" and "truth" is possible and is a matter of convention. But, whenever it is accepted, it means a break with the whole Western tradition and necessitates the creation of another term for what has been called *alēthēs* or *verum* in classical, ancient, medieval, and modern literature. Is such a break necessary? The answer ultimately depends not on reasons of expediency but on the nature of cognitive reason.

Modern philosophy usually speaks of true and false as qualities of judgments. Judgments can grasp or fail to grasp reality and can, accordingly, be true or false. But reality in itself is what it is, and it can neither be true nor false. This certainly is a possible line of arguing, but it is also possible to go beyond it. If the question is asked, "What makes a judgment true?" something must be said about reality itself. There must be an explanation of the fact that reality can give itself to the cognitive act in such a way that a false judgment can occur and in such a way that many processes of observation and thought are necessary in order to reach true judgments. The reason is that things hide their true being; it must be discovered under the surface of sense impressions, changing appearances, and unfounded opinions. This discovery is made through a process of preliminary affirmations, consequent negations, and final affirmations. It is made through "yes and no" or dialectically. The surface must be penetrated, the appearance undercut, the "depth" must be reached, namely, the *ousia*, the "essence" of things, that which gives them the power of being. This is their truth, the "really real" in difference from the seemingly real. It would not be called "true," however, if it were not true for someone, namely, for the mind which in the power of the rational word, the *logos*, grasps the level of reality in which the really real "dwells." This notion of truth is not bound to its Socratic-Platonic birthplace. In whatever way the terminology may be changed, in whatever way the relation between true and seeming reality may be described, in whatever way the relation of mind and reality may be understood, the problem of the "truly real" cannot be avoided. The seemingly real is not unreal, but it is deceptive if it is taken to be really real.

One could say that the concept of true being is the result of disappointed expectations in our encounter with reality. For instance, we meet a person, and the impressions we receive of him produce expectations in us about his future behavior. Some of these expectations will be deceptive and will provoke the desire for a "deeper" understanding of his personality, in comparison with which the first understanding was "superficial." New expectations arise and prove again to be partially deceptive, driving us to the question of a still deeper level of his personality. Finally we may succeed in discovering his real, true personality structure, the essence and power of his being, and we will not be deceived any longer. We may still be surprised; but such surprises are to be expected if a personality is the object of knowledge. The truth of something is that level of its being the knowledge of which prevents wrong expectations and consequent disappointments. Truth, therefore, is the essence of things as well as the cognitive act in which their essence is grasped. The term "truth" is, like the term "reason," subjective-objective. A judgment is true because it grasps and expresses true being; and the really real becomes truth if it is grasped and expressed in a true judgment.

The resistance of recent philosophy against the ontological use of the term has been aroused by the assumption that truth can be verified only within the realm of empirical science. Statements which cannot be verified by experiment are considered tautologies, emotional self-expressions, or meaningless propositions. There is an important truth in this attitude. Statements which have neither intrinsic evidence nor a way of being verified have no cognitive value. "Verification" means a method of deciding the truth or falsehood of a judgment. Without such a method, judgments are expressions of the subjective state of a person but not acts of cognitive reason. The verifying test belongs to the nature of truth; in this positivism is right. Every cognitive assumption (hypothesis) must be tested. The safest test is the repeatable experiment. A cognitive realm in which it can be used has the advantage of methodological strictness and the possibility of testing an assertion in every moment. But it is not permissible to make the experimental method of verification the exclusive pattern of all verification. Verification can occur within the life-process itself. Verification of this type (experiential in contradistinction to experimental) has the advantage that it need not halt and disrupt the totality of a life-process in order to distil calculable elements out of it (which experimental verification must do). The verifying experiences of a nonexperimental character are truer to life, though less exact and definite. By far the largest part of all cognitive verification is experiential. In some cases experimental and experiential verification work together. In other cases the experimental element is completely absent.

It is obvious that these two methods of verification correspond to the two cognitive attitudes, the controlling and the receiving. Controlling knowledge is verified by the success of controlling actions. The technical use of scientific knowledge is its greatest and most impressive verification. Every working machine is a continuously repeated test of the truth of the scientific assumptions on the basis of which it has been constructed.

Receiving knowledge is verified by the creative union of two natures, that of knowing and that of the known. This test, of course, is neither repeatable, precise, nor final at any particular moment. The life-process itself makes the test. Therefore, the test is indefinite and preliminary; there is an element of risk connected with it. Future stages of the same life-process may prove that what seemed to be a bad risk was a good one and vice versa. Nevertheless, the risk must be taken, receiving knowledge must be applied, experiential verification must go on continually, whether it is supported by experimental tests or not.

Life-processes are the object of biological, psychological, and sociological research. A large amount of controlling knowledge and experimental verification is possible and actual in these disciplines; and, in dealing with life-processes, scientists are justified in striving to extend the experimental method as far as possible. But there are limits to these attempts which are imposed not by impotence but by definition. Life-processes have the character of totality, spontaneity, and individuality. Experiments presuppose isolation, regularity, generality. Therefore, only separable elements of life-processes are open to experimental verification, while the processes themselves must be received in a creative union in order to be known. Physicians, psychotherapists, educators, social reformers, and political leaders deal with that side of a life-process which is individual, spontaneous, and total. They can work only on the basis of a knowledge which unites controlling and receiving elements. The truth of their knowledge is verified partly by experimental test, partly by a participation in the individual life with which they deal. If this "knowledge by participation" is called "intuition," the cognitive approach to every individual life-process is intuitive. Intuition in this sense is not irrational, and neither does it by-pass a full consciousness of experimentally verified knowledge.

Verification in the realm of historical knowledge also unites an experimental with an experiential element. The factual side of historical research is based on sources, traditions, and documents which test one another in a way comparable to experimental methods (although no historical event can be repeated). The selective and interpretative side, however, without which no historiography ever has been written, is based on participation in terms of understanding and explanation. Without a union of the nature of the historian with that of his object, no significant history is possible. But *with* this union the same period and the same historical figure have received many different historically significant interpretations on the basis of the same verified material. Verification in this respect means to illuminate, to make understandable, to give a meaningful and consistent picture. The historian's task is to "make alive" what has "passed away." The test of his cognitive success, of the truth of his picture, is whether or not he is able to do this. This test is not final, and every historical work is a risk. But it is a test, an experiential, though not an experimental, verification.

Principles and norms, which constitute the structure of subjective and objective reason, are the cognitive object of philosophy. Rationalism and pragmatism discuss the question of their verification in such a way that both of them by-pass the element of cognitive union and receiving knowledge. Rationalism tries to develop principles and norms in terms of self-evidence, universality, and necessity. Categories of being and thinking, principles of aesthetic expression, norms of law and communion, are open to critical analysis and to a priori knowledge. The analogy of mathematical evidence, which needs neither the tests of controlling nor those of receiving knowedge, is used for the derivation of the rational principles, categories, and norms. Analytic thought can make decisions about the rational structure of mind and reality.

Pragmatism asserts just the opposite. It takes the so-called principles of reason, the categories and norms, to be results of accumulated and tested experience, open for radical changes by future experience and subject to ever repeated tests. They must prove their power of explaining and judging a given material of empirical knowledge, of aesthetic expression, of legal structures and communal forms. If they are able to do this, they are pragmatically verified.

Neither rationalism nor pragmatism sees the element of participation in knowledge. Neither of them distinguishes receiving from controlling knowledge. Both are largely determined by the attitude of controlling knowledge and tied up with the alternatives implied in it. Against both of them it must be said that the verification of the principles of ontological reason has the character neither of rational self-evidence nor of a pragmatic test. Rational self-evidence cannot be attributed to a principle which contains more than the mere form of rationality, as, for instance, Kant's categorical imperative. Every concrete principle, every category and norm, which expresses more than pure rationality is subject to experimental or experiential verification. It is not self-evident, even if it contains a self-evident element (which, however, cannot be abstracted from it). Pragmatism is in no better position. It lacks a criterion. If the successful working of the principles is called the "criterion," the question arises, "What is the criterion of success?" This question cannot be answered again in terms of success, that is, pragmatically. Neither can it be answered rationally except in a completely formalistic way.

The way in which philosophical systems have been accepted, experienced, and verified points to a method of verification beyond rationalism and pragmatism. These systems have forced themselves upon the mind of many human beings in terms of receptive knowledge and cognitive union. In terms of controlling knowledge, rational criticism, or pragmatic tests, they have been refuted innumerable times. But they live. Their verification is their efficacy in the life-process of mankind. They prove to be inexhaustible in meaning and creative in power. This method of verification is certainly not precise and not definite, but it is permanent and effective. It throws out of the historical process what is exhausted and powerless and what cannot stand in the light of pure rationality. Somehow it combines the pragmatic and the rational elements without falling into the fallacies of either pragmatism or rationalism. Nevertheless, even this way of verification is threatened by the possibility of final meaninglessness. It is more true to life than the competing methods. But it carries with it the radical risk of life. It is significant in what it tries to verify, but it is not secure in its verification.

This situation mirrors a basic conflict in cognitive reason. Knowledge stands in a dilemma; controlling knowledge is safe but not ultimately significant, while receiving knowledge can be ultimately significant, but it cannot give certainty. The threatening character of this dilemma is rarely recognized and understood. But if it is realized and not covered up by preliminary and incomplete verifications, it must lead either to a desperate resignation of truth or to the quest for revelation, for revelation claims to give a truth which is both certain and of ultimate concern—a truth which includes and accepts the risk and uncertainty of every significant cognitive act, yet transcends it in accepting it.

II

THE REALITY OF REVELATION

A. THE MEANING OF REVELATION

1. THE MARKS OF REVELATION

a) *Methodological remarks.*—It is the aim of the so-called phenomenological method to describe "meanings," disregarding, for the time being, the question of the reality to which they refer.[1] The significance of this methodological approach lies in its demand that the meaning of a notion must be clarified and circumscribed before its validity can be determined, before it can be approved or rejected. In too many cases, especially in the realm of religion, an idea has been taken in its undistilled, vague, or popular sense and made the victim of an easy and unfair rejection. Theology must apply the phenomenological approach to all its basic concepts, forcing its critics first of all to see what the criticized concepts mean and also forcing itself to make careful descriptions of its concepts and to use them with logical consistency, thus avoiding the danger of trying to fill in logical gaps with devotional material. The present system, therefore, begins each of its five parts with a description of the meaning of the determining ideas, before asserting and discussing their truth and actuality.

The test of a phenomenological description is that the picture given by it is convincing, that it can be seen by anyone who is willing to look in the same direction, that the description illuminates other related ideas, and that it makes the reality which these ideas are supposed to reflect understandable. Phenomenology is a way of pointing to phenomena as they "give themselves," without the interference of negative or positive prejudices and explanations.

However, the phenomenological method leaves one question unanswered which is decisive for its validity. Where, and to whom, is an idea revealed? The phenomenologist answers: Take as an example a typical revelatory event and see within it and through it the universal meaning of revelation. This answer proves insufficient as soon as different and

1. Cf. Edmund Husserl, *Ideas*, trans. Boyce Gibson (New York: Macmillan Co., 1931).

perhaps contradictory examples of revelation are encountered by phenomenological intuition. What criterion is to govern the choice of an example? Phenomenology cannot answer this question. This points to the fact that while phenomenology is competent in the realm of logical meanings, which was the object of the original inquiries made by Husserl, the inventor of the phenomenological method, it is only partially competent in the realm of spiritual realities like religion.[2]

The question of the choice of an example can be answered only if a critical element is introduced into "pure" phenomenology. The decision about the example cannot be left to accident. If the example were nothing more than an exemplar of a species, as is the case in the realm of nature, there would be no problem. But spiritual life creates more than exemplars; it creates unique embodiments of something universal. Therefore, the decision about the example to be used for a phenomenological description of the meaning of a concept like revelation is of the utmost importance. Such a decision is critical in form, existential in matter. Actually, it is dependent on a revelation which has been received and which is considered final, and it is critical with respect to other revelations. Nevertheless, the phenomenological approach is preserved. This is "critical phenomenology," uniting an intuitive-descriptive element with an existential-critical element.

The existential-critical element is the criterion according to which the example is selected; the intuitive-descriptive element is the technique by means of which the meaning which is manifest in the example is portrayed. The concrete and unique character of the example (e.g., the revelatory vision of Isaiah) is in tension with the universal claim of the phenomenological description of the meaning of this example to be valid for every example. This tension is unavoidable. It can be reduced in two ways: either by a comparison of different examples or by the choice of an example in which absolute concreteness and absolute universality are united. The first way, however, leads to the method of abstraction, which deprives the examples of their concreteness and reduces their meaning to an empty generality (e.g., a revelation which is neither Jewish nor Christian, neither prophetic nor mystical). This is precisely what phenomenology is designed to overcome. The second way is dependent on the conviction that a special revelation (e.g., the reception of Jesus as

2. Cf. Max Scheler's phenomenological justification of the whole Roman Catholic system in his book, *Vom Ewigen im Menschen* (Leipzig: Neue Geist, 1923). Husserl rightly rejected this attempt.

the Christ by Peter) is the final revelation and that it is, consequently, universally valid. The meaning of revelation is derived from the "classical" example, but the idea derived in this way is valid of every revelation, however imperfect and distorted the revelatory event actually may be. Each example of revelation is judged in terms of this phenomenological concept, and this concept can be employed as a criterion because it expresses the essential nature of every revelation.

Critical phenomenology is the method best fitted to supply a normative description of spiritual (and also Spiritual) meanings. Theology must use it in dealing with each of its basic concepts.

b) Revelation and mystery.—The word "revelation" ("removing the veil") has been used traditionally to mean the manifestation of something hidden which cannot be approached through ordinary ways of gaining knowledge. There is a wider use of the word in the language of everyday life which is quite vague: someone reveals a hidden thought to a friend, a witness reveals the circumstances of a crime, a scientist reveals a new method which he has been testing for a long time, an insight comes to someone "like a revelation." In all these cases, however, the strength of the words "reveal" or "revelation" is derived from their proper and narrower sense. A revelation is a special and extraordinary manifestation which removes the veil from something which is hidden in a special and extraordinary way. This hiddenness is often called "mystery," a word which also has a narrower and a wider sense. In the wider sense it covers mystery stories as well as the mystery of higher mathematics and the mystery of success. In the narrower sense, from which the incisiveness of these phrases is derived, it points to something which is essentially a mystery, something which would lose its very nature if it lost its mysterious character. "Mystery," in this proper sense, is derived from *muein*, "closing the eyes" or "closing the mouth." In gaining ordinary knowledge it is necessary to open one's eyes in order to grasp the object and to open one's mouth in order to communicate with other persons and to have one's insights tested. A genuine mystery, however, is experienced in an attitude which contradicts the attitude of ordinary cognition. The eyes are "closed" because the genuine mystery transcends the act of seeing, of confronting objects whose structures and relations present themselves to a subject for his knowledge. Mystery characterizes a dimension which "precedes" the subject-object relationship. The same dimension is indicated in the "closing of the mouth." It is impossible to express the experience of mystery in ordinary language, because this language has grown out of, and is bound to, the subject-object scheme. If mystery is expressed in ordinary language, it necessarily is misunderstood, reduced to another dimension, desecrated. This is the reason why betrayal of the content of the mystery cults was a blasphemy which had to be expiated by death.

Whatever is essentially mysterious cannot lose its mysteriousness even when it is revealed. Otherwise something which only seemed to be mysterious would be revealed, and not that which is essentially mysterious. But is it not a contradiction in terms to speak of the revelation of something which remains a mystery in its very revelation? It is just this seeming paradox which is asserted by religion and theology. Wherever the two propositions are maintained, that God has revealed himself and that God is an infinite mystery for those to whom he has revealed himself, the paradox is stated implicitly. But this is not a real paradox, for revelation includes cognitive elements. Revelation of that which is essentially and necessarily mysterious means the manifestation of something within the context of ordinary experience which transcends the ordinary context of experience. Something more is known of the mystery after it has become manifest in revelation. First, its reality has become a matter of experience. Second, our relation to it has become a matter of experience. Both of these are cognitive elements. But revelation does not dissolve the mystery into knowledge. Nor does it add anything directly to the totality of our ordinary knowledge, namely, to our knowledge about the subject-object structure of reality.

In order to safeguard the proper use of the word "mystery," uses which are wrong or confusing must be avoided. "Mystery" should not be applied to something which ceases to be a mystery after it has been revealed. Nothing which can be discovered by a methodical cognitive approach should be called a "mystery." What is not known today, but which might possibly be known tomorrow, is not a mystery. Another inaccurate and confusing use of the word is connected with the difference between controlling and receiving knowledge. Those elements of reality which cannot be reached by controlling knowledge, like qualities, *Gestalten,* meanings, ideas, values, are called "mysterious." But the fact that they involve a different cognitive approach does not make them mysterious. The quality of a color, or the meaning of an idea, or the nature of a living being is a mystery only if the method of quantitative analysis is the pattern of all knowledge. There is no justification for such a reduction of the cognitive power of reason. The knowledge of these elements of reality is rational, although it is not controlling knowledge.

The genuine mystery appears when reason is driven beyond itself to its "ground and abyss," to that which "precedes" reason, to the fact that "being is and nonbeing is not" (Parmenides), to the original fact (*Ur-Tatsache*) that there is *something* and not *nothing*. We can call this the "negative side" of the mystery. This side of the mystery is present in all the functions of reason; it becomes manifest in subjective as well as in objective reason. The "stigma" of finitude (see pp. 189 ff.) which appears in all things and in the whole of reality and the "shock" which grasps the mind when it encounters the threat of nonbeing (see pp. 186 ff.) reveal the negative side of the mystery, the abysmal element in the ground of being. This negative side is always potentially present, and it can be realized in cognitive as well as in communal experiences. It is a necessary element in revelation. Without it the mystery would not be mystery. Without the "I am undone" of Isaiah in his vocational vision, God cannot be experienced (Isa. 6:5). Without the "dark night of the soul," the mystic cannot experience the mystery of the ground.

The positive side of the mystery—which includes the negative side—becomes manifest in actual revelation. Here the mystery appears as ground and not only as abyss. It appears as the power of being, conquering nonbeing. It appears as our ultimate concern. And it expresses itself in symbols and myths which point to the depth of reason and its mystery.

Revelation is the manifestation of what concerns us ultimately. The mystery which is revealed is of ultimate concern to us because it is the ground of our being. In the history of religion revelatory events always have been described as shaking, transforming, demanding, significant in an ultimate way. They derive from divine sources, from the power of that which is holy and which therefore has an unconditional claim on us. Only that mystery which is of ultimate concern for us appears in revelation. A large proportion of the ideas which are derived from assumed revelations concerning objects and events within the subject-object structure of reality neither are genuine mysteries nor are they based on genuine revelation. Knowledge about nature and history, about individuals, their future and their past, about hidden things and happenings—all this is not a matter of revelation but of observations, intuitions, and conclusions. If such knowledge pretends to come from revelation, it must be subjected to the verifying tests of scholarly methods and accepted or rejected on the basis of these tests. It lies outside revelation because it is a matter neither of ultimate concern nor of essential mystery.

Revelation, as revelation of the mystery which is our ultimate concern, is invariably revelation for someone in a concrete situation of concern. This is clearly indicated in all events which traditionally have been characterized as revelatory. There is no revelation "in general" (*Offenbarung ueberhaupt*). Revelation grasps an individual or a group, usually a group through an individual; it has revealing power only in this correlation. Revelations received outside the concrete situation can be apprehended only as reports about revelations which other groups assert that they have received. The knowledge of such reports, and even a keen understanding of them, does not make them revelatory for anyone who does not belong to the group which is grasped by the revelation. There is no revelation if there is no one who receives it as his ultimate concern.

Revelation always is a subjective and an objective event in strict interdependence. Someone is grasped by the manifestation of the mystery; this is the subjective side of the event. Something occurs through which the mystery of revelation grasps someone; this is the objective side. These two sides cannot be separated. If nothing happens objectively, nothing is revealed. If no one receives what happens subjectively, the event fails to reveal anything. The objective occurrence and the subjective reception belong to the whole event of revelation. Revelation is not real without the receiving side, and it is not real without the giving side. The mystery appears objectively in terms of what traditionally has been called "miracle." It appears subjectively in terms of what has sometimes been called "ecstasy." Both terms must be given a radical reinterpretation.

c) *Revelation and ecstasy.*—The use of the word "ecstasy" in a theological explanation involves an even greater risk than the use of the word "mystery," for, in spite of many distortions of the meaning of mystery, very few people would hesitate to speak of the divine mystery—if they speak of God at all. It is different with "ecstasy." The so-called "ecstatic" movements have saddled this term with unfortunate connotations, in spite of the fact that prophets and apostles have spoken of their own ecstatic experiences again and again, using a variety of terms. "Ecstasy" must be rescued from its distorted connotations and restored to a sober theological function. If this proves to be impossible, the reality which is described by the word will disappear from our sight unless another word can be found.

"Ecstasy" ("standing outside one's self") points to a state of mind which is extraordinary in the sense that the mind transcends its ordinary situation. Ecstasy is not a negation of reason; it is the state of mind in which reason is beyond itself, that is, beyond its subject-object structure. In being beyond itself reason does not deny itself. "Ecstatic reason" remains reason; it does not receive anything irrational or antirational—which it could not do without self-destruction—but it transcends the basic condition of finite rationality, the subject-object structure. This is the state mystics try to reach by ascetic and meditative activities. But mystics know that these activities are only preparations and that the experience of ecstasy is due exclusively to the manifestation of the mystery in a revelatory situation. Ecstasy occurs only if the mind is grasped by the mystery, namely, by the ground of being and meaning. And, conversely, there is no revelation without ecstasy. At best there is information which can be tested scientifically. The "prophet's ecstasy," of which the hymn sings and of which the prophetic literature is full, indicates that the experience of ecstasy has universal significance.

The term "ecstasy" often is confused with enthusiasm. This confusion is easily understood. The word "enthusiasm" means the state of having the god within one's self or of being within the god. In both senses the enthusiastic state of mind has ecstatic qualities, and there is no basic difference in the original meaning of the two words.[3] But "enthusiasm" has lost these religious connotations and has been applied to the passionate support of an idea, a value, a tendency, a human being, etc. "Enthusiasm" no longer carries the connotation of a relation to the divine, while "ecstasy," at least to some degree, still has this connotation.

Today the meaning of "ecstasy" is determined largely by those religious groups who claim to have special religious experiences, personal inspirations, extraordinary Spiritual gifts, individual revelations, knowledge of esoteric mysteries. Such claims are as old as religion and always have been an object of astonishment and of critical evaluation. It would be wrong to reject these claims a priori and to deny that genuine ecstasy has been experienced in these groups. But one should not allow them to usurp this term. "Ecstasy" has a legitimate use in theology, especially in apologetic theology.

The so-called ecstatic movements are in continuous danger—to which they succumb more often than not—of confusing overexcitement with the presence of the divine Spirit or with the occurrence of revelation.

3. During the Reformation period those groups who claimed to be guided by special Spiritual revelations were called "Enthusiasts."

Something happens objectively as well as subjectively in every genuine manifestation of the mystery. Only something subjective happens in a state of religious overexcitement, often artificially produced. Therefore, it has no revelatory power. No new practical or theoretical interpretation of what concerns us ultimately can be derived from such subjective experiences. Overexcitement is a state of mind which can be comprised completely in psychological terms. Ecstasy transcends the psychological level, although it has a psychological side. It reveals something valid about the relation between the mystery of our being and ourselves. Ecstasy is the form in which that which concerns us unconditionally manifests itself within the whole of our psychological conditions. It appears through them. But it cannot be derived from them.

The threat of nonbeing, grasping the mind, produces the "ontological shock" in which the negative side of the mystery of being—its abysmal element—is experienced. "Shock" points to a state of mind in which the mind is thrown out of its normal balance, shaken in its structure. Reason reaches its boundary line, is thrown back upon itself, and then is driven again to its extreme situation. This experience of ontological shock is expressed in the cognitive function by the basic philosophical question, the question of being and nonbeing. It is, of course, misleading if one asks with some philosophers: "Why is there something? Why not nothing?" For this form of the question points to something that precedes being, from which being can be derived. But being can only be derived from being. The meaning of this question can be expressed in the statement that being is the original fact which cannot be derived from anything else. Taken in this sense, the question is a paradoxical expression of the ontological shock and, as such, the beginning of all genuine philosophy.

In revelation and in the ecstatic experience in which it is received, the ontological shock is preserved and overcome at the same time. It is preserved in the annihilating power of the divine presence (*mysterium tremendum*) and is overcome in the elevating power of the divine presence (*mysterium fascinosum*). Ecstasy unites the experience of the abyss to which reason in all its functions is driven with the experience of the ground in which reason is grasped by the mystery of its own depth and of the depth of being generally.

The ecstatic state in which revelation occurs does not destroy the rational structure of the mind. The reports about ecstatic experiences in the classical literature of the great religions agree on this point—that, while demonic possession destroys the rational structure of the mind, divine ecstacy preserves and elevates it, although transcending it. Demonic possession destroys the ethical and logical principles of reason; divine ecstasy affirms them. Demonic "revelations" are exposed and rejected in many religious sources, especially in the Old Testament. An assumed revelation in which justice as the principle of practical reason is violated is antidivine, and it is therefore judged a lie. The demonic blinds; it does not reveal. In the state of demonic possession the mind is not really "beside itself," but rather it is in the power of elements of itself which aspire to be the whole mind which grasp the center of the rational self and destroy it. There is, however, a point of identity between ecstasy and possession. In both cases the ordinary subject-object structure of the mind is put out of action. But divine ecstasy does not violate the wholeness of the rational mind, while demonic possession weakens or destroys it. This indicates that, although ecstasy is not a product of reason, it does not destroy reason.

It is obvious that ecstasy has a strong emotional side. But it would be a mistake to reduce ecstasy to emotion. In every ecstatic experience all the grasping and shaping functions of reason are driven beyond themselves, and so is emotion. Feeling is no nearer to the mystery of revelation and its ecstatic reception than are the cognitive and the ethical functions.

With respect to its cognitive element, ecstasy is often called "inspiration." This word, which is derived from *spirare,* "to breathe," emphasizes the pure receptivity of cognitive reason in an ecstatic experience. Confusions and distortions have made the term "inspiration" almost as useless as "ecstasy" and "miracle." The vague use of the word in describing nonreflective acts of cognition is partly responsible for this situation. In this use of the word, being inspired means being in a creative mood, or being grasped by an idea, or reaching an understanding of something through a sudden intuition. The opposite abuse of the term is connected with certain forms of the doctrine of the inspiration of the biblical writings. Inspiration is described as a mechanical act of dictation or, in a more refined way, as an act of imparting information. In such ideas of inspiration reason is invaded by a strange body of knowledge with which it cannot unite, a body which would destroy the rational structure of the mind if it were to remain within it. In the last analysis, a mechanical or any other form of nonecstatic doctrine of inspiration is demonic. It destroys the rational structure which is supposed to receive inspiration. It is obvious that inspiration, if it is the name for the cognitive quality of the ecstatic experience, cannot mediate knowledge of finite objects or relations. It does not add anything to the complex of knowledge which is determined by the subject-object structure of reason. Inspiration opens a new dimension of knowledge, the dimension of understanding in relation to our ultimate concern and to the mystery of being.

d) *Revelation and miracle.*—The word "miracle," according to the ordinary definition, designates a happening that contradicts the laws of nature. This definition and the innumerable unverified miracle stories in all religions have rendered the term misleading and dangerous for theological use. But a word which expresses a genuine experience can only be dropped if a substitute is at hand, and it does not seem that such a substitute has been found. The New Testament often uses the Greek work *sēmeion,* "sign," pointing to the religious meaning of the miracles. But the word "sign" without a qualifying addition cannot express this religious meaning. It would be more accurate to add the word "event" to "sign" and to speak of *sign-events.* The original meaning of miracle, "that which produces astonishment," is quite adequate for describing the "giving side" of a revelatory experience. But this connotation has been swallowed by the bad connotation of a supranatural interference which destroys the natural structure of events. The bad connotation is avoided in the word "sign" and the phrase "sign-event."

While the original naïve religious consciousness accepts astounding stories in connection with divine manifestations without elaborating a supranaturalistic theory of miracles, rationalistic periods make the negation of natural laws the main point in miracle stories. A kind of irrationalist rationalism develops in which the degree of absurdity in a miracle story becomes the measure of its religious value. The more impossible, the more revelatory! Already in the New Testament one can observe that, the later the tradition, the more the antinatural element is emphasized over against the sign element. In the post-apostolic period, when the apocryphal Gospels were produced, there were no checks against absurdity. Pagans and Christians alike were not so much interested in the presence of the divine in shaking and sign-giving events as they were in the sensation produced in their rationalistic minds by antirational happenings. This rationalistic antirationalism infected later Christianity, and it is still a burden for the life of the church and for theology.

The manifestation of the mystery of being does not destroy the structure of being in which it becomes manifest. The ecstasy in which the mystery is received does not destroy the rational structure of the mind by which it is received. The sign-event which gives the mystery of revelation does not destroy the rational structure of the reality in which it appears. If these criteria are applied, a meaningful doctrine of sign-events or miracles can be stated.

One should not use the word "miracle" for events which create astonishment for a certain time, such as scientific discoveries, technical creations, impressive works of art or politics, personal achievements, etc. These cease to produce astonishment after one has become accustomed to them, although a profound admiration of them may remain and even increase. Nor are the structures of reality, the *Gestalten,* the qualities, the inner *teloi* of things miracles, although they always will be objects of admiration. There is an element of astonishment in admiration, but it is not a numinous astonishment; it does not point to a miracle.

As ecstasy presupposes the shock of nonbeing in the mind, so sign-events presuppose the stigma of nonbeing in the reality. In shock and stigma, which are strictly correlated, the negative side of the mystery of being appears. The word "stigma" points to marks of disgrace, for example, in the case of a criminal, and to marks of grace, for example, in the case of a saint; in both instances, however, it indicates something negative. There is a stigma that appears on everything, the stigma of finitude, or implicit and inescapable nonbeing. It is striking that in many miracle stories there is a description of the "numinous" dread which grasps those who participate in the miraculous events. There is the feeling that the solid ground of ordinary reality is taken "out from under" their feet. The correlative experience of the stigma of nonbeing in the reality and the shock of nonbeing in the mind produces this feeling, which, although not revelatory in itself, accompanies every genuine revelatory experience.

Miracles cannot be interpreted in terms of a supranatural interference in natural processes. If such an interpretation were true, the manifestation of the ground of being would destroy the structure of being; God would be split within himself, as religious dualism has asserted. It would be more adequate to call such a miracle "demonic," not because it is produced by "demons," but because it discloses a "structure of destruction" (see Part IV, Sec. I). It corresponds with the state of "being possessed" in the mind and could be called "sorcery." The supranaturalistic theory of miracles makes God a sorcerer and a cause of "possession"; it confuses God with demonic structures in the mind and in reality. There are such structures, based on a distortion of genuine manifestations of the mystery of being. A supranaturalistic theology which employs patterns derived from the structure of possession and sorcery for the sake of describing the nature of revelation in terms of the destruction of the subjective as well as of objective reason is certainly intolerable.

The sign-events in which the mystery of being gives itself consist in special constellations of elements of reality in correlation with special constellations of elements of the mind. A genuine miracle is first of all an event which is astonishing, unusual, shaking, without contradicting the rational structure of reality. In the second place, it is an event which points to the mystery of being, expressing its relation to us in a definite way. In the third place, it is an occurrence which is received as a sign-event in an ecstatic experience. Only if these three conditions are fulfilled can one speak of a genuine miracle. That which does not shake one by its astonishing character has no revelatory power. That which shakes one without pointing to the mystery of being is not miracle but sorcery. That which is not received in ecstasy is a report about the belief in a miracle, not an actual miracle. This is emphasized in the synoptic records of the miracles of Jesus. Miracles are given only to those for whom they are sign-events, to those who receive them in faith. Jesus refuses to perform "objective" miracles. They are a contradiction in terms. This strict correlation makes it possible to exchange the words describing miracles and those describing ecstasy. One can say that ecstasy is the miracle of the mind and that miracle is the ecstasy of reality.

Since neither ecstasy nor miracle destroys the structure of cognitive reason, scientific analysis, psychological and physical, as well as historical investigation are possible and necessary. Research can and must proceed without restriction. It can undercut the superstitions and demonic interpretations of revelation, ecstasy, and miracle. Science, psychology, and history are allies of theology in the fight against the supranaturalistic distortions of genuine revelation. Scientific explanation and historical criticism protect revelation; they cannot dissolve it, for revelation belongs to a dimension of reality for which scientific and historical analysis are inadequate. Revelation is the manifestation of the depth of reason and the ground of being. It points to the mystery of existence and to our ultimate concern. It is independent of what science and history say about the conditions in which it appears; and it cannot make science and history dependent on itself. No conflict between different dimensions of reality is possible. Reason receives revelation in ecstasy and miracles; but reason is not destroyed by revelation, just as revelation is not emptied by reason.

2. THE MEDIUMS OF REVELATION

a) Nature as a medium of revelation.—There is no reality, thing, or event which cannot become a bearer of the mystery of being and enter into a revelatory correlation. Nothing is excluded from revelation in principle because nothing is included in it on the basis of special qualities. No person and no thing is worthy in itself to represent our ultimate concern. On the other hand, every person and every thing participates in being-itself, that is, in the ground and meaning of being. Without such participation it would not have the power of being. This is the reason why almost every type of reality has become a medium of revelation somewhere.

Although nothing has become the bearer of revelation by its outstanding qualities, these qualities determine the direction in which a thing or event expresses our ultimate concern and our relation to the mystery of being. There is no difference between a stone and a person in their potentiality of becoming bearers of revelation by entering a revelatory constellation. But there is a great difference between them with respect to the significance and truth of the revelations mediated through them. The stone represents a rather limited number of qualities which are able to point to the ground of being and meaning. The person represents the central qualities, and by implication all qualities, which can point to the mystery of existence. There are, however, qualities in the stone for which the person is not explicitly representative (the power of enduring, resisting, etc.). Such qualities can make the stone a supporting element in the revelation through a person, for instance, the metaphor "rock of ages" applied to God. Sacramental elements (water, wine, oil, etc.) must be seen in this light. Their original character as independent bearers of revelation has been transformed into a supporting function. But even in this function their original independent power is still noticeable.

The mediums of revelation taken from nature are as innumerable as natural objects. Ocean and stars, plants and animals, human bodies and souls, are natural mediums of revelation. Equally numerous are natural events which can enter a constellation of revelatory character: the movements of the sky, the change of day and night, growth and decay, birth and death, natural catastrophes, psychosomatic experiences, such as maturing, illness, sex, danger. In all these cases it is not the thing or the event as such which has revelatory character; they reveal that which uses them as a medium and bearer of revelation.[4]

While everyday life is an ambiguous mixture of the regular and the irregular, in revelatory constellations the one or the other is experienced in its radical form. If the "extraordinarily regular" is the medium of revelation, the mystery of being becomes manifest in its relation to the rational character of mind and reality; the divine discloses its *logos* quality without ceasing to be the divine *mystery*. If the "extraordinarily irregular" is the medium of revelation, the mystery of being becomes manifest in its relation to the prerational character of mind and reality, the divine shows its *abyss* character without ceasing to be the *divine* mystery. The extraordinarily regular as a medium of revelation determines the social and ethical type of religion. Kant's co-ordination of the moral law with the starry sky as expressions of the unconditionally sublime is the classical formulation of the mutual interdependence of the experience of the social and the natural law and the relation of both to the ultimate meaning of existence. The extraordinarily irregular as a medium of revelation determines the individualistic and paradoxical type of religion. Kierkegaard's symbol of his continual suspension as a swimmer over the depth of the ocean and his emphasis on the "leap" which leaves everything regular and rational behind are classical expressions of this type of religion. The same difference underlies the present conflict between Ritschlian and neo-orthodox theology.

Revelation through natural mediums is not natural revelation. "Natural revelation," if distinguished from revelation through nature, is a contradiction in terms, for if it is natural knowledge it is not revelation, and if it is revelation it makes nature ecstatic and miraculous. Natural knowledge about self and world cannot lead to the revelation of the ground of being. It can lead to the question of the ground of being, and that is what so-called natural theology can do and must do. But this

4. In judging the sexual rites and symbols of many religions, one should remember that it is not the sexual in itself which is revealing but the mystery of being which through the medium of the sexual manifests its relation to us in a special way. This explains and justifies the rich use of sexual symbols in classical Christianity. Protestantism, rightly aware of the danger of a demonization of these symbols, has developed an extreme distrust of them, often forgetting the mediating character of sex in revelatory experiences. But the goddesses of love are in the first place goddesses, displaying divine power and dignity, and only in the second place do they represent the sexual realm in its ultimate meaning. Protestantism, in rejecting sexual symbolism, is in danger not only of losing much symbolic wealth but also of cutting off the sexual realm from the ground of being and meaning in which it is rooted and from which it gets its consecration.

question is asked neither by natural revelation nor by natural theology. It is the question of reason about its own ground and abyss. It is asked by reason, but reason cannot answer it. Revelation can answer it. And this answer is based neither on a so-called natural revelation nor on a so-called natural theology. It is based on real revelation, on ecstasy and sign-events. Natural theology and, even more definitely, natural revelation are misnomers for the negative side of the revelation of the mystery, for an interpretation of the shock and stigma of nonbeing.

Cognitive reason can go as far as this. It can develop the question of the mystery in the ground of reason. But every step beyond the analysis of this situation is either inconclusive arguing or a remnant of traditional beliefs or both. When Paul speaks of the idolatrous perversion of a potential knowledge of God through nature, he does not challenge the nations because of their questionable arguing but because of their distortion of revelations through nature. Nature in special sections or nature as a whole can be a medium of revelation in an ecstatic experience. But nature cannot be an argumentative basis for conclusions about the mystery of being. Even if it could be this, it should not be called natural theology and, even less, natural revelation.

b) History, groups, and individuals as mediums of revelation.— Historical events, groups, or individuals as such are not mediums of revelation. It is the revelatory constellation into which they enter under special conditions that make them revelatory, not their historical significance or their social or personal greatness. If history points beyond itself in a correlation of ecstasy and sign-event, revelation occurs. If groups of persons become transparent for the ground of being and meaning, revelation occurs. But its occurrence cannot be foreseen or derived from the qualities of persons, groups, and events. It is historical, social, and personal destiny. It stands under the "directing creativity" of the divine life (see below, pp. 263 ff.).

Historical revelation is not revelation *in* history but *through* history. Since man is essentially historical, every revelation, even if it is mediated through a rock or a tree, occurs *in* history. But history itself is revelatory only if a special event or a series of events is experienced ecstatically as miracle. Such experiences can be connected with great creative or destructive events in a national history. The political events then are interpreted as divine gifts, judgments, promises, and therefore as a matter of ultimate concern and a manifestation of the mystery of being.

History is the history of groups, represented and interpreted by personalities. Both groups and personalities can become mediums of revelation in connection with historical events of a revelatory character. The group which has an ecstatic experience in relation to its historical destiny can become a medium of revelation for other groups. That is what Jewish prophetism anticipated when it included all nations in the blessing of Abraham and foresaw all nations coming to Mount Zion to adore the God of Israel. The Christian church always has been conscious of its vocation to be the bearer of revelation for nations and individuals. In the same way, personalities connected with revelatory events can become mediums of revelation themselves, either as representatives or as interpreters of these events, and sometimes as both. Moses, David, and Peter are described as representatives as well as interpreters of revelatory events. Cyrus represents a revelatory happening, but Second Isaiah interprets it. Paul the missionary represents, while Paul the theologian interprets, a revelatory event. In both functions all these men are mediums of historical revelation. And all of them, as well as the events themselves, point to something that transcends them infinitely, to the self-manifestation of that which concerns us ultimately.

Revelation through personalities is not restricted to those who represent or interpret history. Revelation can occur through every personality which is transparent for the ground of being. The prophet, although a medium of historical revelation, does not exclude other personal mediums of revelation. The priest who administers the sphere of the holy, the saint who embodies holiness himself, the ordinary believer who is grasped by the divine Spirit, can be mediums of revelation for others and for a whole group. It is not the priestly function as such, however, which has revelatory character. A mechanized administration of religious rites can exclude any revelatory presence of the holy reality which it claims to mediate. Only under special conditions does the priestly function reveal the mystery of being. The same is true of the saint. The term "saint" has been misunderstood and distorted; saintliness has been identified with religious or moral perfection. Protestantism, for these reasons, has finally removed the concept of sainthood from theology and the reality of the saint from religion. But sainthood is not personal perfection. Saints are persons who are transparent for the ground of being which is revealed through them and who are able to enter a revelatory constellation as mediums. Their being can become a sign-event for others. This is the truth behind the Catholic practice of demanding miracles from every saint. Protestantism does not allow a difference between the saint and the ordinary believer. Every believer is a saint in so far as he belongs to the communion of saints, the new reality which is holy in its foundation; and every saint is an ordinary believer, in so far as he belongs to those who need forgiveness of sins. On this basis, however, the believer can become a medium of revelation for others and in *this* sense a saint. His faith and his love can become sign-events for those who are grasped by their power and creativity. A rethinking of the problem of sainthood by Protestant theology is certainly needed.

Historical revelation can be, and usually is, accompanied and supported by revelation through nature, since nature is the basis on which history moves and without which history would have no reality. Therefore, myth and holy legend report the participation of natural constellations of revelatory character in historical revelation. The Synoptic Gospels are full of stories in which the presence of the Kingdom of God in Jesus as the Christ is witnessed to by natural events which enter the correlation of revelation.

c) *The word as a medium of revelation and the question of the inner word.*—The importance of the "word," not only for the idea of revelation, but for almost every theological doctrine, is so great that a "theological semantics" is urgently needed. Within the theological system there are several places where semantic questions must be asked and answered. Man's rational structure cannot be understood without the word in which he grasps the rational structure of reality. Revelation cannot be understood without the word as a medium of revelation. The knowledge of God cannot be described except through a semantic analysis of the symbolic word. The symbols "Word of God" and "Logos" cannot be understood in their various meanings without an insight into the general nature of the word. The biblical message cannot be interpreted without semantic and hermeneutic principles. The preaching of the church presupposes an understanding of the expressive and denotative functions of the word in addition to its communicative function. Under these circumstances it is not surprising that an attempt has been made to reduce the whole of theology to an enlarged doctrine of the "Word of God" (Barth). But if this is done, "word" must either be identified with revelation and the term "word" must be used with such a wide meaning that every divine self-manifestation can be subsumed under it, or revelation must be restricted to the spoken word and the "Word of God" taken literally instead of symbolically. In the first case the specific sense of the term "word" is lost; in the second case the specific sense is preserved, but God is prevented from any nonvocal self-manifestation. This, however, contradicts not only the meaning of God's power but also the religious symbolism inside and outside the biblical literature, which uses seeing, feeling, and tasting as often as hearing in describing the experience of the divine presence. Therefore, "word" can only be made the all-embracing symbol of the divine self-manifestation if the divine "Word" can be seen and tasted as well as heard. The Christian doctrine of the Incarnation of the Logos includes the paradox that the Word has become an object of vision and touch (see below, pp. 157 ff.).

Revelation through words must not be confused with "revealed words." Human words, whether in sacred or in secular language, are produced in the process of human history and are based on the experiential correlation between mind and reality. The ecstatic experience of revelation, like any other experience, can contribute to the formation and transformation of a language. But it cannot create a language of its own which must be learned as in the case of a foreign language. Revelation uses ordinary language, just as it uses nature and history, man's psychic and spiritual life, as mediums of revelation. Ordinary language, which expresses and denotes the ordinary experience of mind and reality in their categorical structure, is made a vehicle for expressing and denoting the extraordinary experience of mind and reality in ecstasy and sign-event.

The word communicates the self-related and unapproachable experience of an ego-self to another ego-self in two ways: by expression and by denotation. These two ways are largely united, but there is a pole of expression at which denotation is almost absent, and there is a pole of denotation where expression is almost absent. The denotative power of language is its ability to grasp and communicate general meanings. The expressive power of language is its ability to disclose and to communicate personal states. An algebraic equation has an almost exclusively denotative character, an outcry has an almost exclusively expressive character. But even in the case of an outcry a definite content of feeling is indicated, and even in the case of a mathematical equation a satisfaction about the evidence of the result and the adequacy of the method can be expressed. Most speaking moves between these two poles: the more scientific and technical, the nearer the denotative pole; the more poetic and communal, the nearer the expressive pole.

The word as a medium of revelation points beyond its ordinary sense both in denotation and in expression. In the situation of revelation, language has a denotative power which points through the ordinary meanings of the words to their relation to us. In the situation of revelation, language has an expressive power which points through the ordinary expressive possibilities of language to the unexpressible and its relation to us. This does not mean that the logical structure of ordinary language is destroyed if the word becomes a medium of revelation. Nonsensical combinations of words do not indicate the presence of the divine, although they may have an expressive power without any denotative function. Ordinary language, on the other hand, even when dealing with matters of ultimate concern, is not a medium of revelation. It does not possess the "sound" and "voice" which makes the ultimate perceivable. When speaking of the ultimate, of being and meaning, ordinary language brings it down to the level of the preliminary, the conditioned, the finite, thus muffling its revelatory power. Language as a medium of revelation, on the contrary, has the "sound" and "voice" of the divine mystery in and through the sound and voice of human expression and denotation. Language with this power is the "Word of God." If it is possible to use an optical metaphor for the characterization of language, one could say that the Word of God as the word of revelation is transparent language. Something shines (more precisely, sounds) through ordinary language which is the self-manifestation of the depth of being and meaning.

It is obvious that the word as a medium of revelation, the "Word of God," is not a word of information about otherwise hidden truth. If it were this, if revelation were information, no "transparency" of language would be needed. Ordinary language, transmitting no "sound" of ultimacy, could give information about "divine matters." Such information would be of cognitive and perhaps of ethical interest, but it would lack all the characteristics of revelation. It would not have the power of grasping, shaking, and transforming, the power which is attributed to the "Word of God."

If the word as a medium of revelation is not information, it cannot be spoken apart from revelatory events in nature, history, and man. The word is not a medium of revelation in addition to the other mediums; it is a necessary element in all forms of revelation. Since man is man through the power of the word, nothing really human can be so without the word, whether it be spoken or silent. When the prophets spoke, they spoke about the "great deeds of God," the revelatory events in the history of Israel. When the apostles spoke, they spoke about the one great deed of God, the revelatory event which is called Jesus, the Christ. When the priests and seers and mystics in paganism gave holy oracles and created sacred writings, they were giving interpretations of a Spiritual reality which they had entered after having left ordinary reality. Being precedes speaking, and the revelatory reality precedes and determines the revelatory word. A collection of assumed divine revelations concerning "faith and morals" without a revelatory event which they interpret is a lawbook with divine authorization, but it is not the Word of God, and it has no revelatory power. Neither the Ten Commandments nor the great commandment is revelatory if separated from the divine covenant with Israel or from the presence of the Kingdom of God in the Christ. These commandments were meant and should be taken as interpretations of a new reality, not as orders directed against the old reality. They are descriptions and not laws. The same is true of the doctrines. There are no revealed doctrines, but there are revelatory events and situations which can be described in doctrinal terms. Ecclesiastical doctrines are meaningless if separated from the revelatory situation out of which they have grown. The "Word of God" contains neither revealed commandments nor revealed doctrines; it accompanies and interprets revelatory situations.

The phrase "inner word" is unfortunate. Words are means of communication. The "inner word" would be a kind of self-communication, a monologue of the soul with itself. But "inner word" is used in order to describe the speaking of God in the depth of the individual soul. Something is said to the soul, but it is said neither in spoken nor in silent words. It is not said in words at all. It is a movement of the soul in itself. The "inner word" is an expression of the negation of the word as a medium of revelation. A word is spoken *to* someone; the "inner word" is the awareness of what is already present and does not need to be said. The same is true of the phrase "inner revelation." An inner revelation must reveal something which is not yet a part of the inner man. Otherwise it would not be revelation but recollection; something potentially present would become actual and conscious. This, in fact, is the position of mystics, idealists, and spiritualists,[5] whether they notice it or not. But man in the state of existential separation cannot attain the message of

5. The word "spiritualists," which has received the connotation of occultists, should be used for the so-called Enthusiasts of the Reformation period and the early eighteenth century. Their characteristic was the belief in the inner word or the inner revelation within the soul of the individual Christian.

the New Being by recollection. It must come to him, it must be said to him; it is a matter of revelation. This criticism of the doctrine of the inner word is historically confirmed by the easy transition from spiritualism to rationalism. The inner word was more and more identified with the logical and ethical norms which constitute the rational structure of mind and reality. The voice of revelation was replaced by the voice of our moral conscience, reminding us of what we essentially know. Against the doctrine of the inner word Christian theology must maintain the doctrine of the word as a medium of revelation, symbolically the doctrine of the Word of God.

3. The Dynamics of Revelation: Original
   and Dependent Revelation

The history of revelation indicates that there is a difference between original and dependent revelations. This is a consequence of the correlative character of revelation. An original revelation is a revelation which occurs in a constellation that did not exist before. This miracle and this ecstasy are joined for the first time. Both sides are original. In a dependent revelation the miracle and its original reception together form the giving side, while the receiving side changes as new individuals and groups enter the same correlation of revelation. Jesus is the Christ, both because he could become the Christ and because he was received as the Christ. Without both these sides he would not have been the Christ. Not only was this true of those who first received him, but it is true of all the following generations which have entered into a revelatory correlation with him. There is, however, a difference between original and dependent revelation through him. While Peter encountered the man Jesus whom he called the Christ in an original revelatory ecstasy, following generations met the Jesus who had been received as the Christ by Peter and the other apostles. There is continuous revelation in the history of the church, but it is dependent revelation. The original miracle, together with its original reception, is the permanent point of reference, while the Spiritual reception by following generations changes continuously. But if one side of a correlation is changed, the whole correlation is transformed. It is true that "Jesus Christ . . . the same yesterday, today, and forever" is the immovable point of reference in all periods of church history. But the act of referring is never the same, since new generations with new potentialities of reception enter the correlation and transform it. No ecclesiastical traditionalism and no orthodox biblicism can escape this situation of "dependent revelation." This answers the much-discussed question whether the history of the church has revelatory power. The history of the church is not a locus of original revelations in addition to the one on which it is based (cf. the section on experience, pp. 40 ff.). Rather, it is the locus of continuous dependent revelations which are one side of the work of the divine Spirit in the church. This side often is called "illumination," referring to the church as a whole as well as to its individual members. The term "illumination" points to the cognitive element in the process of actualizing the New Being. It is the cognitive side of ecstasy. While "inspiration" traditionally has been used to designate an original revelation, "illumination" has been used to express what we call "dependent revelation." The divine Spirit, illuminating believers individually and as a group, brings their cognitive reason into revelatory correlation with the event on which Christianity is based.

This leads to a broader view of revelation in the life of the Christian. A dependent revelatory situation exists in every moment in which the divine Spirit grasps, shakes, and moves the human spirit. Every prayer and meditation, if it fulfils its meaning, namely, to reunite the creature with its creative ground, is revelatory in this sense. The marks of revelation—mystery, miracle, and ecstasy—are present in every true prayer. Speaking to God and receiving an answer is an ecstatic and miraculous experience; it transcends all ordinary structures of subjective and objective reason. It is the presence of the mystery of being and an actualization of our ultimate concern. If it is brought down to the level of a conversation between two beings, it is blasphemous and ridiculous. If, however, it is understood as the "elevation of the heart," namely, the center of the personality, to God, it is a revelatory event.

This consideration radically excludes a nonexistential concept of revelation. Propositions about a past revelation give theoretical information; they have no revelatory power. Only through an autonomous use of the intellect or through a heteronomous subjection of the will could they be accepted as truth. Such acceptance would be a human work, a meritorious deed of the type against which the Reformation fought a life-and-death struggle. Revelation, whether it is original or dependent, has revelatory power only for those who participate in it, who enter into the revelatory correlation.

Original revelation is given to a group through an individual. Revelation can be received originally only in the depth of a personal life, in its struggles, decisions, and self-surrender. No individual receives revelation for himself. He receives it for his group, and implicitly for all groups, for mankind as a whole. This is obvious in prophetic revelation, which always is vocational. The prophet is the mediator of revelation for the group which follows him—often after it first has rejected him. Nor is this restricted to classical prophetism. We find the same situation in most religions, and even in mystical groups. A seer, a religious founder, a priest, a mystic—these are the individuals from whom original revelation is derived by groups which enter into the same correlation of revelation in a dependent way.

Since the correlation of revelation is transformed by every new group, and in an infinitesimal way by every new individual who enters it, the question must be asked whether this transformation can reach a point where the original revelation is exhausted and superseded. It is the question of the possible end of a revelatory correlation, either by a complete disappearance of the unchanging point of reference, or by a complete loss of its power to create new correlations. Both possibilities have been actualized innumerable times in the history of religion. Sectarian and Protestant movements in all the great religions have attacked given religious institutions as a complete betrayal of the meaning of the original revelation, although they still have kept it as their point of reference. On the other hand, most of the gods of the past have lost even this power; they have become poetic symbols and have ceased to create a revelatory situation. Apollo has no revelatory significance for Christians; the Virgin Mother Mary reveals nothing to Protestants. Revelation through these two figures has come to an end. Yet one might ask how a real revelation can come to an end. If it is God who stands behind every revelation, how can something divine come to an end? If it is not God who reveals himself, why should one use the term "revelation"? But this alternative does not exist! Every revelation is mediated by one or several of the mediums of revelation. None of these mediums possesses revelatory power in itself; but under the conditions of existence these mediums claim to have it. This claim makes them idols, and the breakdown of this claim deprives them of their power. The revelatory side is not lost if a revelation comes to an end; but its idolatrous side is destroyed. That which was revelatory in it is preserved as an element in more embracing and more purified revelations, and everything revelatory is potentially present in the final revelation, which cannot come to an end because the bearer of it does not claim anything for himself.

4. THE KNOWLEDGE OF REVELATION

Revelation is the manifestation of the mystery of being for the cognitive function of human reason. It mediates knowledge—a knowledge, however, which can be received only in a revelatory situation, through ecstasy and miracle. This correlation indicates the special character of the "knowledge of revelation."[6] Since the knowledge of revelation cannot be separated from the situation of revelation, it cannot be introduced into the context of ordinary knowledge as an addition, provided in a peculiar way, yet independent of this way once it has been received. Knowledge of revelation does not increase our knowledge about the structures of nature, history, and man. Whenever a claim to knowledge is made on this level, it must be subjected to the experimental tests through which truth is established. If such a claim is made in the name of revelation or of any other authority, it must be disregarded, and the ordinary methods of research and verification must be applied. For the physicist the revelatory knowledge of creation neither adds to nor subtracts from his scientific description of the natural structure of things. For the historian the revelatory interpretation of history as the history of revelation neither confirms nor negates any of his statements about documents, traditions, and the interdependence of historical events. For the psychologist no revelatory truth about the destiny of man can influence his analysis of the dynamics of the human soul. If revealed knowledge did interfere with ordinary knowledge, it would destroy scientific honesty and methodological humility. It would exhibit demonic possession, not divine revelation. Knowledge of revelation is knowledge about the revelation of the mystery of being to us, not information about the nature of beings and their relation to one another. Therefore, the knowledge of revelation can be received only in the situation of revelation, and it can be communicated—in contrast to ordinary knowledge—only to those who participate in this situation. For those outside this situation the same words have a different sound. A reader of the New Testament, for example, a philologist for whom its contents are not a matter of ultimate concern, may be able to interpret the text exactly and

6. One should not speak of revealed knowledge because this term gives the impression that ordinary contents of knowledge are communicated in an extraordinary way, thus separating revealed knowledge from the revelatory situation. This is the basic fallacy in most of the popular and many of the theological interpretations of revelation and the knowledge mediated through it. The term "knowledge of revelation" (or revelatory knowledge) emphasizes the inseparable unity of knowledge and situation.

correctly; but he will miss the ecstatic-revelatory significance of the words and sentences. He may speak with scientific preciseness about them as reports concerning an assumed revelation, but he cannot speak of them as witnesses to an actual revelation. His knowledge of the documents of revelation is nonexistential. As such it may contribute much to the historical-philosophical understanding of the documents. It cannot contribute anything to the knowledge of revelation mediated through the documents.

Knowledge of revelation cannot interfere with ordinary knowledge. Likewise, ordinary knowledge cannot interfere with knowledge of revelation. There is no scientific theory which is more favorable to the truth of revelation than any other theory. It is disastrous for theology if theologians prefer one scientific view to others on theological grounds. And it was humiliating for theology when theologians were afraid of new theories for religious reasons, trying to resist them as long as possible, and finally giving in when resistance had become impossible. This ill-conceived resistance of theologians from the time of Galileo to the time of Darwin was one of the causes of the split between religion and secular culture in the past centuries.

The same situation prevails with regard to historical research. Theologians need not be afraid of any historical conjecture, for revealed truth lies in a dimension where it can neither be confirmed nor negated by historiography. Therefore, theologians should not prefer some results of historical research to others on theological grounds, and they should not resist results which finally have to be accepted if scientific honesty is not to be destroyed, even if they seem to undermine the knowledge of revelation. Historical investigations should neither comfort nor worry theologians. Knowledge of revelation, although it is mediated primarily through historical events, does not imply factual assertions, and it is therefore not exposed to critical analysis by historical research. Its truth is to be judged by criteria which lie within the dimension of revelatory knowledge.

Psychology, including depth psychology, psychosomatics, and social psychology, is equally unable to interfere with knowledge of revelation. There are many insights into the nature of man in revelation. But all of them refer to the relation of man to what concerns him ultimately, to the ground and meaning of his being. There is no revealed psychology just as there is no revealed historiography or revealed physics. It is not the task of theology to protect the truth of revelation by attacking Freudian doctrines of libido, repression, and sublimation on religious grounds or by defending a Jungian doctrine of man in the name of revelatory knowledge.

There is, however, one limit to the indifference of the knowledge of revelation toward all forms of ordinary knowledge, namely, the presence of revelatory elements within assertions of ordinary knowledge. If, under the cover of ordinary knowledge, matters of ultimate concern are discussed, theology must protect the truth of revelation against attacks from distorted revelations, whether they appear as genuine religions or as metaphysically transformed ideas. This, however, is a religious struggle in the dimension of revelatory knowledge and not a conflict between knowledge of revelation and ordinary knowledge.

The truth of revelation is not dependent on criteria which are not themselves revelatory. Knowledge of revelation, like ordinary knowledge, must be judged by its own implicit criteria. It is the task of the doctrine of the final revelation to make these criteria explicit (see the following sections).

The knowledge of revelation, directly or indirectly, is knowledge of God, and therefore it is analogous or symbolic. The nature of this kind of knowing is dependent on the nature of the relation between God and the world and can be discussed only in the context of the doctrine of God. But two possible misunderstandings must be mentioned and removed. If the knowledge of revelation is called "analogous," this certainly refers to the classical doctrine of the *analogia entis* between the finite and the infinite. Without such an analogy nothing could be said about God. But the *analogia entis* is in no way able to create a natural theology. It is not a method of discovering truth about God; it is the form in which every knowledge of revelation must be expressed. In this sense *analogia entis*, like "religious symbol," points to the necessity of using material taken from finite reality in order to give content to the cognitive function in revelation. This necessity, however, does not diminish the cognitive value of revelatory knowledge. The phrase "only a symbol" should be avoided, because nonanalogous or nonsymbolic knowledge of God has *less* truth than analogous or symbolic knowledge. The use of finite materials in their ordinary sense for the knowledge of revelation destroys the meaning of revelation and deprives God of his divinity.

B. ACTUAL REVELATION

5. ACTUAL AND FINAL REVELATION

We have described the meaning of revelation in the light of the criteria of what Christianity considers to be revelation. The description of the meaning of revelation was supposed to cover all possible and actual revelations, but the criterion of revelation has not yet been developed. We now turn to the Christian affirmation, no longer indirectly as in the preceding chapters, but directly and dogmatically, in the genuine sense of dogma as the doctrinal basis of a special philosophical school or religious community.

From the point of view of the theological circle, actual revelation is necessarily final revelation, for the person who is grasped by a revelatory experience believes it to be the truth concerning the mystery of being and his relation to it. If he is open for other original revelations, he already has left the revelatory situation and looks at it in a detached way. His point of reference has ceased to be the original revelation by means of which he had entered an original correlation, or, more frequently, a dependent correlation. There is also the possibility that a person may believe that no concrete revelation concerns him ultimately, that the real ultimate is beyond all concreteness. In Hinduism the ecstatic experience of the Brahman power is the ultimate; in humanism it is heroic subjection to the moral principle. In both cases a concrete revelation, for example, a manifestation of Vishnu in Hinduism or the picture of Jesus as the moral ideal in Protestantism, has no finality. For the Hindu the final revelation is the mystical experience, and for the humanist there is neither actual nor final revelation but only moral autonomy, supported by the impression of the synoptic Jesus.

Christianity claims to be based on the revelation in Jesus as the Christ as the final revelation. This claim establishes a Christian church, and, where this claim is absent, Christianity has ceased to exist—at least manifestly though not always latently (see Part IV, Sec. II). The word "final" in the phrase "final revelation" means more than *last*. Christianity often has affirmed, and certainly should affirm, that there is continuous revelation in the history of the church. In this sense the final revelation is not the last. Only if *last* means the last *genuine* revelation can final revelation be interpreted as the last revelation. There can be no revelation in the history of the church whose point of reference is not Jesus as the Christ. If another point of reference is sought or accepted, the Christian church has lost its foundation. But final revelation means more than the last genuine revelation. It means the decisive, fulfilling, unsurpassable revelation, that which is the criterion of all the others. This is the Christian claim, and this is the basis of a Christian theology.

The question, however, is how such a claim can be justified, whether there are criteria within the revelation in Jesus as the Christ which make it final. Such criteria cannot be derived from anything outside the revelatory situation. But it is possible to discover them within this situation. And this is just what theology must do.

The first and basic answer theology must give to the question of the finality of the revelation in Jesus as the Christ is the following: a revelation is final if it has the power of negating itself without losing itself. This paradox is based on the fact that every revelation is conditioned by the medium in and through which it appears. The question of the final revelation is the question of a medium of revelation which overcomes its own finite conditions by sacrificing them, and itself with them. He who is the bearer of the final revelation must surrender his finitude —not only his life but also his finite power and knowledge and perfection. In doing so, he affirms that he is the bearer of final revelation (the "Son of God" in classical terms). He becomes completely transparent to the mystery he reveals. But, in order to be able to surrender himself completely, he must possess himself completely. And only he can possess— and therefore surrender—himself completely who is united with the ground of his being and meaning without separation and disruption. In the picture of Jesus as the Christ we have the picture of a man who possesses these qualities, a man who, therefore, can be called the medium of final revelation.

In the biblical records of Jesus as the Christ (there are no records besides the New Testament) Jesus became the Christ by conquering the demonic forces which tried to make him demonic by tempting him to claim ultimacy for his finite nature. These forces, often represented by his own disciples, tried to induce him to avoid sacrificing of himself as a medium of revelation. They wanted him to avoid the cross (cf. Matthew, chap. 16). They tried to make him an object of idolatry. Idolatry is the perversion of a genuine revelation; it is the elevation of the medium of revelation to the dignity of the revelation itself. The true prophets in Israel fought continuously against this idolatry, which was defended by the false prophets and their priestly supporters. This fight is the dynamic power in the history of revelation. Its classical document is the Old

Testament, and it is just for this reason that the Old Testament is an inseparable part of the revelation of Jesus as the Christ. But the New Testament and the history of the church show the same conflict. In the Reformation the prophetic spirit attacked a demonically perverted priestly system and produced the deepest split which has occurred in the development of Christianity.

According to Paul, the demonic-idolatrous powers which rule the world and distort religion have been conquered in the cross of Christ. In his cross Jesus sacrificed that medium of revelation which impressed itself on his followers as messianic in power and significance. For us this means that in following him we are liberated from the authority of everything finite in him, from his special traditions, from his individual piety, from his rather conditioned world view, from any legalistic understanding of his ethics. Only as the crucified is he "grace and truth" and not law. Only as he who has sacrificed his flesh, that is, his historical existence, is he Spirit or New Creature. These are the *paradoxa* in which the criterion of final revelation becomes manifest. Even the Christ is Christ only because he did not insist on his equality with God but renounced it as a personal possession (Philippians, chap. 2). Christian theology can affirm the finality of the revelation in Jesus as the Christ only on this basis. The claim of anything finite to be final in its own right is demonic. Jesus rejected this possibility as a satanic temptation, and in the words of the Fourth Gospel he emphasized that he had nothing himself but that he had received everything from his father. He remained transparent to the divine mystery until his death, which was the final manifestation of his transparency. This condemns a Jesus-centered religion and theology. Jesus is the religious and theological object as the Christ and only as the Christ. And he is the Christ as the one who sacrifices what is merely "Jesus" in him. The decisive trait in his picture is the continuous self-surrender of Jesus who is Jesus to Jesus who is the Christ.

Therefore, the final revelation is universal without being heteronomous. No finite being imposes itself in the name of God on other finite beings. The unconditional and universal claim of Christianity is not based on its own superiority over other religions. Christianity, without being final itself, witnesses to the final revelation. Christianity as Christianity is neither final nor universal. But that to which it witnesses is final and universal. This profound dialectics of Christianity must not be forgotten in favor of ecclesiastical or orthodox self-affirmations. Against them the so-called liberal theology is right in denying that one religion can claim finality, or even superiority. A Christianity which does not assert that Jesus of Nazareth is sacrificed to Jesus as the Christ is just one more religion among many others. It has no justifiable claim to finality.

6. The Final Revelation in Jesus as the Christ

In accord with the circular character of systematic theology, the criterion of final revelation is derived from what Christianity considers to be the final revelation, the appearance of Jesus as the Christ. Theologians should not be afraid to admit this circle. It is not a shortcoming; rather it is the necessary expression of the existential character of theology. It provides a description of final revelation in two ways, first in terms of an abstract principle which is the criterion of every assumed or real revelation and, second, in terms of a concrete picture which mirrors the occurrence of the final revelation. In the preceding chapter the abstract principle was elaborated with the concrete picture in view; the present chapter describes the actualization of the abstract principle in the concrete.

All reports and interpretations of the New Testament concerning Jesus as the Christ possess two outstanding characteristics: his maintenance of unity with God and his sacrifice of everything he could have gained for himself from this unity.

The first point is clear in the Gospel reports about the unbreakable unity of his being with that of the ground of all being, in spite of his participation in the ambiguities of human life. The being of Jesus as the Christ is determined in every moment by God. In all his utterances, words, deeds, and sufferings, he is transparent to that which he represents as the Christ, the divine mystery. While the Synoptic Gospels emphasize the active maintenance of this unity against demonic attacks, the Fourth Gospel emphasizes the basic unity between Jesus and the "Father." In the epistles the victory of the unity over against the powers of separation is presupposed, though sometimes the toil and burden of this battle is indicated. However, it is never a moral, intellectual, or emotional quality which makes him the bearer of the final revelation. According to the witness of the whole New Testament and, by anticipation, also of many passages of the Old Testament, it is the presence of God in him which makes him the Christ. His words, his deeds, and his sufferings are consequences of this presence; they are expressions of the New Being which is his being.

Jesus' maintenance of unity with God includes the second emphasis of the biblical writers, his victory over every temptation to exploit his unity with God as a means of advantage for himself. He does not give in to the temptation to which he is exposed as the designated Messiah, the success of which would have deprived him of his messianic function. The acceptance of the cross, both during his life and at the end of it, is the decisive test of his unity with God, of his complete transparency to the ground of being. Only in view of the crucifixion can the Fourth Gospel have him say that "he who believes in me does not believe in *me*" (John 12:44). Only through his continuous acceptance of the cross has he become the "Spirit" who has surrendered himself as flesh, namely, as a historical individual (II Corinthians). This sacrifice is the end of all attempts to impose him, as a finite being, on other finite beings. It is the end of Jesusology. Jesus of Nazareth is the medium of the final revelation because he sacrifices himself completely to Jesus as the Christ. He not only sacrifices his life, as many martyrs and many ordinary people have done, but he also sacrifices everything in him and of him which could bring people to him as an "overwhelming personality" instead of bringing them to that in him which is greater than he and they. This is the meaning of the symbol "Son of God" (see the christological part in Part III, Sec. II).

The final revelation, like every revelation, occurs in a correlation of ecstasy and miracle. The revelatory event is Jesus as the Christ. He is the miracle of the final revelation, and his reception is the ecstasy of the final revelation. His appearance is the decisive constellation of historical (and by participation, natural) forces. It is the ecstatic moment of human history and, therefore, its center, giving meaning to all possible and actual history. The Kairos (see Part V, Sec. II) which was fulfilled in him is the constellation of final revelation. But it is this only for those who received him as the final revelation, namely, as the Messiah, the Christ, the Man-from-above, the Son of God, the Spirit, the Logos-who-became-flesh—the New Being. All these terms are symbolic variations of the theme first enunciated by Peter when he said to Jesus, "Thou art the Christ." In these words Peter accepted him as the medium of the final revelation. This acceptance, however, is a part of the revelation itself. It is a miracle of the mind which corresponds with the ecstasy of history. Or, in the opposite terminology (the terms are interchangeable; see above, p. 117), it is an ecstasy of the mind which corresponds with the miracle of history. Jesus as the Christ, the miracle of the final revelation, and the church, receiving him as the Christ or the final revelation, belong to each other. The Christ is not the Christ without the church, and the church is not the church without the Christ. The final revelation, like every revelation, is correlative.

The final revelation, the revelation in Jesus as the Christ, is universally valid, because it includes the criterion of every revelation and is the *finis* or *telos* (intrinsic aim) of all of them. The final revelation is the criterion of every revelation which precedes or follows. It is the criterion of every religion and of every culture, not only of the culture and religion in and through which it has appeared. It is valid for the social existence of every human group and for the personal existence of every human individual. It is valid for mankind as such, and, in an indescribable way, it has meaning for the universe also. Nothing less than this should be asserted by Christian theology. If some element is cut off from the universal validity of the message of Jesus as the Christ, if he is put into the sphere of personal achievement only, or into the sphere of history only, he is less than the final revelation and is neither the Christ nor the New Being. But Christian theology affirms that he is all this because he stands the double test of finality: uninterrupted unity with the ground of his being and the continuous sacrifice of himself as Jesus to himself as the Christ.

7. THE HISTORY OF REVELATION

The event which is called "final revelation" was not an isolated event. It presupposed a revelatory history which was a preparation for it and in which it was received. It could not have occurred without having been expected, and it could not have been expected if it had not been preceded by other revelations which had become distorted. It would not have been the final revelation if it had not been received as such, and it would lose its character as final revelation if it were not able to make itself available to every group in every place. The history of the preparation and reception of the final revelation can be called the "history of revelation."

The history of revelation is not the history of religion, not even the history of the Jewish and Christian religions. There is revelation outside the religious sphere, and there is much in religion which is not revelation. Revelation judges religion and nonreligion equally. Nor is the history of revelation a history of all revelations which have taken place. There is no such history, for one can speak of a revelatory event only on the basis of an existential relation to it. The "historian of all revelations" would be merely a historian of all reports about revelations. The history of revelation is history interpreted in the light of the final revelation. The event of final revelation establishes itself as the center, aim, and origin of the revelatory events which occur in the period of preparation and in the period of reception. This, of course, is true only for the person who participates existentially in the final revelation. But for him it is a true and inescapable implication of his revelatory experience. While humanistic theology tends to identify the history of revelation with the history of religion and culture, thus removing the concept of final revelation, neo-orthodox theology and an allied liberal (e.g., Ritschlian) theology try to eliminate the history of revelation by identifying revelation with final revelation. The latter group says that there is only *one* revelation, namely, that in Jesus the Christ; to which the former group answers that there are revelations everywhere and that none of them is ultimate. Both contentions must be rejected. In the actual revelatory situation, a revelation which is not taken to be final is a detached reflection and not an involved experience. On the other hand, if a revelation whose historical preparation is denied as final, the necessity of its historical reception makes the unique revelatory event a strange body which has no relation whatsoever to human existence and history. Therefore, it cannot be assimilated by man's spiritual life. It either destroys this life or is thrown out by it. "The history of revelation" is a necessary correlate of final revelation. It should neither be leveled down to a history of religion nor be eliminated by a destructive supranaturalism.

The final revelation divides the history of revelation into a period of preparation and a period of reception. The revelation which occurs in the period of preparation is universal. "Universal" can be misunderstood in three ways. It can be confused with "general," in the sense of a general and necessary law abstracted from all special revelatory events. But there is no such general law. Revelation occurs or it does not occur; but it certainly does not occur "generally." It is not a structural element of reality. "Universal," as distinguished from "general," means (or can mean) a special event with an all-embracing claim. In this sense the Christian church is universal ("catholic" or *for* everyone) but not general (abstracted *from* everyone). The second misunderstanding of the term "universal revelation" is its confusion with natural revelation. As we have seen, there is no natural revelation. Only revelation *through* nature can be asserted. And revelation through nature is special and concrete. The third misunderstanding of the term "universal" is the assumption that revelation is occurring always and everywhere. Nothing like this can be said in view of the marks of revelation and its existential character. But it is equally impossible to exclude the universal possibility of revelation. This also would deny its existential character, and, even more, it would make the final revelation impossible.

Only on the wide basis of universal revelation could the final revelation occur and be received. Without the symbols created by universal revelation the final revelation would not be understandable. Without the religious experiences created by universal revelation no categories and forms would exist to receive the final revelation. The biblical terminology is full of words whose meaning and connotations would be completely strange to listeners and readers if there had been no preceding revelations in Judaism as well as in paganism. Missions could not have reached anyone if there had not been a preparation for the Christian message in universal revelation. The question of the final revelation would not have been asked; therefore, the answer could not have been received. If someone, for example, a neo-orthodox theologian, should assert that with God everything is possible and that God in his revelation is not dependent on the stages of human maturity, it must be emphasized that God acts through men according to their nature and receptiveness. He does not replace man with another kind of being, and he does not replace childhood with maturity in order to reveal himself. He reveals himself to man and saves man, and, in doing so, he does not replace man with something else created for this purpose. This would be the method of a demon and not of God. To assert that a revelation is final revelation without pointing to a history of revelation in which there has been a preparation for it dehumanizes man and demonizes God.

The preparation for the final revelation in the history of revelation is threefold. The preparation is carried through by conservation, by criticism, and by anticipation. Any revelatory experience transforms the medium of revelation into a sacramental object, whether it is an object of nature, a human being, a historical event, or a sacred text. It is the function of the priest to conserve the sacramental object and to keep alive the power of original revelation by making new individuals, new

groups, and new generations enter the revelatory situation. The symbolic material used, transformed, and increased by every later revelation,
and also by the final revelation, grows out of the priestly conservation
and continuation of revelatory events. No prophet could speak in the
power of a new revelation, no mystic could contemplate the depth of
the divine ground, no meaning could be given over to the appearance
of the Christ, if there were not this sacramental-priestly substance. But
the sacramental-priestly element of the universal revelation is subject
to a confusion between the medium and the content of revelation. It
tends to make the medium and its excellencies into the content. It tends
to become demonic, for the demonic is the elevation of something conditional to unconditional significance. Against this tendency the second
stage of the preparatory revelation is directed, the critical approach. It
has appeared in three forms: the mystical, the rational, and the prophetic.
Mysticism has criticized the demonically distorted sacramental-priestly
substance by devaluating every medium of revelation and by trying to
unite the soul directly with the ground of being, to make it enter the
mystery of existence without the help of a finite medium. Revelation
occurs in the depth of the soul; the objective side is accidental. The impact of the antidemonic fight of mysticism on large sections of humanity
has been, and still is, tremendous. But its power of preparing for the
final revelation is ambiguous. Mysticism liberates one from the concrete-
sacramental sphere and its demonic distortions, but it pays the price of
removing the concrete character of revelation and of making it irrelevant to the actual human situation. It elevates man above everything
that concerns him actually, and it implies an ultimate negation of his
existence in time and space. In spite of these ambiguities it is the permanent function of mysticism to point to the abysmal character of the
ground of being and to reject the demonic identification of anything
finite with that which transcends everything finite. It is unfortunate
that those in the Kant-Ritschl line and those in the neo-orthodox schools
in theology have pointed only to the possible and actual abuses of the
mystical approach without acknowledging its world historical function
of transcending the concrete mediums of revelation toward the mystery
which is mediated by them. Even the final revelation needs the corrective of mysticism in order to transcend its own finite symbols.

The rational approach seems to fall outside the revelatory situation
and to be without any revelatory function. Indeed, reason is not revelatory. But in every creation of reason the depth of reason is present and

makes itself felt, in form as well as in content. Elements which contribute to the history of revelation are implicitly or explicitly present
in the style of a cultural creation, in its basic principle, in its criticisms
and demands. They presuppose revelatory events by expressing them
either in terms of rational creations or in terms of rational criticisms
directed against distorted revelations. Xenophanes' and Heraclitus' criticism of the Homeric gods and Plato's philosophical interpretation of the
Apollonian-Dionysian substance of Greek culture are examples of the
influence of a rational creation on the revelatory situation. In men like
Plotinus, Eckhart, Cusanus, Spinoza, and Böhme, mystical and rational
elements were united which criticized and transformed sacramental traditions and which elicited the quest for new revelatory constellations.
But it is not only mystical elevation over the realm of concrete symbols
which can be united with rational criticism; the prophetic criticism of a
sacramental-priestly system also can ally itself with rational criticism.
The social and political elements in the prophets, the Reformers, and the
sectarian revolutionaries were amalgamated inseparably with the revelatory experience which drove them. And, conversely, the expectation of a
new revelatory situation is often the hidden driving power in secular
movements for political freedom and social justice. Universal revelation
includes not only mystical (and prophetic) reactions against distorted
sacramental forms and systems. It also includes rational reactions, separated from or united with mysticism and prophetism. In the light of
this situation, any theology which in terms of a general proposition excludes the creations of reason, that is, man's cultural life, from an indirect participation in the history of revelation, must be rejected.

Decisive, however, for the development of universal preparatory revelation is the prophetic attack on distorted sacramentalism. It is not justifiable to restrict prophetism to the Old Testament prophets or to the
prophetic Spirit which is present in most sections of the Old and New
Testament. Prophetic criticism and promise are active in the whole
history of the church, especially in the movements of monasticism, the
Reformation, and evangelical radicalism. They are active in religious
revolutions and foundations outside Christianity, as in the religion of
Zoroaster, in some of the Greek mysteries, in Islam, and in many smaller
reform movements. The common denominator in all of them, which
distinguishes them from mysticism, is the concrete foundation of their
attack on a given sacramental system. They do not devaluate it; they do
not elevate themselves above it; they do not demand union with the

ground of being. They subject the concrete mediums of revelation and the concrete sacramental symbols and priestly systems to the judgment of the divine law, to that which ought to be because it is the law of God. Prophetism tries to shape reality in the power of the divine form. It does not transcend reality for the sake of the divine abyss. It promises fulfil-ment in the future (however transcendent the future may be under-stood to be), and it does not point to an eternity which is equally near to every moment of time, as mysticism does.

There is, however, something unique in the prophets of Israel, from Moses, who is called the greatest of the prophets, to John the Baptist, who is called the greatest in the old eon. The revelation through the prophets of Israel is the direct concrete preparation of the final revelation, and it cannot be separated from it. The universal revelation as such is not the immediate preparation for the final revelation; only the universal revela-tion criticized and transformed by the prophetism of the Old Testament is such preparation. The universal revelation as such could not have prepared the final revelation. Since the latter is concrete, only *one* con-crete development could have been its immediate preparation. And since the final revelation is the criterion of every revelation, the criterion of finality must have been envisaged and applied, though fragmentarily and by anticipation. When the early church accepted Jesus as the Christ, it was guided by criteria such as those given by the Second Isaiah. With-out a group of people who were indoctrinated by the paradoxes of Jewish prophetism, the paradox of the Cross could not have been understood and accepted. It is, therefore, not surprising that those who separated the New from the Old Testament—from early gnosticism to recent naziism—lost the christological paradox, the center of the New Testa-ment. They considered the final revelation as one of the examples of universal revelation, and they denounced the religion of the Old Testa-ment as one of the lower forms of paganism. They understood it as an expression of the religious nationalism of the Jews. But this is a com-plete misunderstanding. The Old Testament certainly is full of Jewish nationalism, but it appears over and over as that against which the Old Testament fights. Religious nationalism is the mark of the false proph-ets. The true prophets threaten Israel in the name of the God of justice who is able to reject his nation because of its injustice without losing his power, which is not the case in polytheism. As the god of justice he is universal, and, if justice is violated, he rejects any claim on the basis of a special relation to his nation. The term "elected nation" is by no means an expression of national arrogance. To be elected includes the permanent threat of rejection and destruction and the demand to accept destruction in order to save the covenant of election. Election and destruction are bound together so that no finite being, group, or individual may consider himself as more than a medium of the mystery of being. If, however, a group or single individuals endure this tension, their destruction is their fulfilment. This is the meaning of the prophetic promise which transcends the prophetic threat. This promise is not a matter of a "happy ending." Empirically speaking, there is no happy ending for the elected nation—or for the elected one of the final revelation. But "empirically speaking" is not the prophetic form of speaking. Prophets speak in terms which express the "depth of reason" and its ecstatic experience.

In the process of the prophetic struggle with distorted sacramentalism, the revelatory elements of the universal revelation are received, developed, and transformed. Distorted expressions are either rejected or purified. This process occurs in all periods of the history of Israel and does not stop in the New Testament and in church history. It is the dynamic acceptance, rejection, and transformation of preparatory revelation by the final revelation. In the light of this process it is impossible to separate the Old Testament from universal revelation, as it is impossible and absurd to interpret the Old Testament not as the concrete and unique preparation of the final revelation but as a document of the final revelation itself, as a kind of anticipated New Testament. Reception, rejection, and transformation—that is the movement from the side of the Old Testament toward the universal revelation, and from the side of the New Testament toward the universal revelation *and* the Old Testament. The dynamics of the history of revelation exclude the mechanistic-supranatural theories of revelation and inspiration.

Neither the Jewish nation as a whole nor the small "remnant" groups to whom the prophets often referred were able to overcome the identification of the medium with the content of revelation. The history of Israel shows that no group can be the bearer of the final revelation, that it cannot perform a complete self-sacrifice. The breakthrough and the perfect self-surrender must happen in a personal life, or it cannot happen at all. Christianity claims that it has happened and that the moment in which it happened is the center of the history of revelation and indirectly the center of all history.

The center of the history of revelation divides the whole process into preparatory and receiving revelation. The bearer of the receiving revelation is the Christian church. The period of receiving revelation has begun with the beginning of the church. All religions and cultures outside the church, according to the Christian judgment, are still in the period of preparation. And, even more, there are many groups and individuals within the Christian nations and the Christian churches who are definitely in the stage of preparation. They have never received the message of the final revelation in its meaning and power. And the Christian churches themselves, in their institutions and actions, are in permanent danger of relapsing into the preparatory stage—a danger which has become a reality again and again. Nevertheless, the Christian church is based on the final revelation and is supposed to receive it in a continuous process of reception, interpretation, and actualization. This is a revelatory process with all the marks of revelation. The presence of the divine Spirit in the church is revelatory. But it is a dependent revelation, possessing all the marks of dependent revelations. It is dependent on the event of the final revelation from which it takes meaning and power in all generations, although the kind of reception, interpretation, and transformation creates new correlations in all periods, groups, and individuals. Receiving revelation is *revelation,* although the Spirit through whom the revelation occurs is always the Spirit of Jesus as the Christ. The Christian church takes the "risk of faith" in affirming practically and theoretically that this revelation cannot come to an end, that it has the power of reformation within itself, and that no new original revelation could surpass the event of final revelation. On the basis of this faith Christianity asserts that the history of original revelation is finished in principle, although it may still continue indefinitely in places where the center of the history of revelation has not yet been acknowledged. But if the final revelation has been accepted, the revelatory process has not stopped; it continues to the end of history.

8. REVELATION AND SALVATION

The history of revelation and the history of salvation are the same history. Revelation can be received only in the presence of salvation, and salvation can occur only within a correlation of revelation. These assertions can be contradicted on the basis of an intellectual, nonexistential concept of revelation or on the basis of an individualistic, nondynamic concept of salvation; but such concepts must be radically rejected by systematic theology, and with them any attempt to separate revelation and salvation also must be rejected.

If revelation is understood to mean information about "divine matters," which is supposed to be accepted partly through intellectual operations, partly through a subjection of the will to authorities, there can be revelation without salvation. Information is given which can be received without a transformation of the existence of the receiver. Neither ecstasy nor miracle belongs to this notion of a revelatory situation. The divine Spirit either is unnecessary or becomes a supranatural informer and teacher of objective, nonexistential truths. The biblical reports concerning revelatory situations directly contradict this notion; they give unambiguous support to the assertion that revelation and salvation cannot be separated. Moses must remove his shoes before he can walk on the holy ground of a revelatory situation; Isaiah must be touched by a burning coal for the sake of expiation before he can receive his vocational revelation; Peter must leave his environment and follow Jesus before he can make the ecstatic statement that Jesus is the Christ; Paul must experience a revolution of his whole being when he receives the revelation which makes him a Christian and an apostle.

But one might say that this is true only of great religious personalities who lead others into a revelatory situation after the breakthrough has occurred in them. For these other persons, revelation is a deposit of truths they take over which may or may not have saving consequences for them. If this interpretation is accepted, revelatory truth is independent of the receiving side, and the saving consequences for the individual are a matter of his personal destiny; they have no significance for the revelation itself. Obviously such an argument is very favorable to authoritarian systems, ecclesiastical or doctrinal, which handle the contents of revelation like property. In such systems revealed truths are administered by authorities and are presented to the people as ready-made commodities which they must accept. Authoritarian systems unavoidably intellectualize and voluntarize revelation; they dismember the existential correlation between the revelatory event and those who are asked to receive it. They are strongly opposed, therefore, to the identification of revelation and salvation, which implies an existential understanding of revelation, that is, a creative and transforming participation of every believer in the correlation of revelation.

Another argument against the identification of revelation and salvation is based on a concept of salvation which would separate salvation from revelation. If salvation is understood to mean the ultimate fulfilment of the individual beyond time and history, revelation which occurs in history cannot be identified with it. In this view salvation is either complete, or it is not salvation at all. Since the reception of revelation under the conditions of existence is always fragmentary, revelation has no saving quality in itself, although it may become an instrument of salvation. This concept of salvation must be rejected as unambiguously as the intellectualistic concept of revelation. Salvation is derived from *salvus,* "healthy" or "whole," and it can be applied to every act of heal- ing: to the healing of sickness, of demonic possession, and of servitude to sin and to the ultimate power of death. Salvation in this sense takes place in time and history, just as revelation takes place in time and his- tory. Revelation has an unshakable objective foundation in the event of Jesus as the Christ, and salvation is based on the same event, for this event unites the final power of salvation with the final truth of revelation. Revelation as it is received by man living under the conditions of exist- ence is always fragmentary; so is salvation. Revelation and salvation are final, complete, and unchangeable with respect to the revealing and saving event; they are preliminary, fragmentary, and changeable with respect to the persons who receive revelatory truth and saving power. In terms of classical theology one could say that no one can receive reve- lation except through the divine Spirit and that, if someone is grasped by the divine Spirit, the center of his personality is transformed; he has received saving power.

One further argument against this equation still remains to be dis- cussed. It may be asked whether a person who has lost the saving power of the New Being in Christ cannot, at the same time, still accept its rev- elatory truth. He may experience the revelation at his own condemna- tion. In such a situation salvation and revelation seem to be distinctly separated from each other. But this is not the case. As Luther frequently emphasized, the feeling of being rejected is the first and decisive step toward salvation; it is a basic part of the process of salvation. This ele- ment is never completely absent. Nor should it be absent, even in the moments when one experiences the strongest feeling of being saved. As long as the condemning function of revelation is experienced, saving power is effective. Neither sin nor despair, as such, proves the absence of saving power. The absence of saving power is expressed in flight from an ultimate concern and in the type of complacency which resists both the shaking experience of revelation and the transforming experience of salvation.

The identity of revelation and salvation leads to a further consideration. Salvation and revelation are ambiguous in the process of time and history. Therefore, the Christian message points to an ultimate salvation which cannot be lost because it is reunion with the ground of being. This ultimate salvation is also the ultimate revelation, often described as the "vision of God." The mystery of being is present without the *paradoxa* of every revelation in time and space and beyond anything fragmentary and preliminary. This does not refer to the individual in isolation. Fulfilment is universal. A limited fulfilment of separated individuals would not be fulfilment at all, not even for these individuals, for no person is separated from other persons and from the whole of reality in such a way that he could be saved apart from the salvation of everyone and everything. One can be saved only within the Kingdom of God which comprises the universe. But the Kingdom of God is also the place where there is complete transparency of everything for the divine to shine through it. In his fulfilled kingdom, God is everything for everything. This is the symbol of ultimate revelation and ultimate salvation in complete unity. The recognition or nonrecognition of this unity is a decisive test of the character of a theology.

C. REASON IN FINAL REVELATION

9. FINAL REVELATION OVERCOMING THE CONFLICT OF AUTONOMY AND HETERONOMY

Revelation is the answer to the questions implied in the existential conflicts of reason. After describing the meaning and actuality of revelation generally and of final revelation especially, we must show how final revelation answers the questions and overcomes the conflicts of reason in existence.

Revelation overcomes the conflict between autonomy and heteronomy by re-establishing their essential unity. We have discussed the meaning of the three concepts—autonomy, heteronomy, and theonomy. The question now is how theonomy is created by final revelation. Final revelation includes two elements which are decisive for the reunion of autonomy and heteronomy, the complete transparency of the ground of being in him who is the bearer of the final revelation, and the complete self-sacrifice of the medium to the content of revelation. The first element keeps autonomous reason from losing its depth and from becoming empty and open for demonic intrusions. The presence of the divine ground as it is manifest in Jesus as the Christ gives a spiritual substance to all forms of rational creativity. It gives them the dimension of depth, and it unites them under symbols expressing this depth in rites and myths. The other element of final revelation, the self-sacrifice of the finite medium, keeps heteronomous reason from establishing itself against rational autonomy. Heteronomy is the authority claimed or exercised by a finite being in the name of the infinite. Final revelation does not make such a claim and cannot exercise such a power. If it did, it would become demonic and cease to be final revelation. Far from being heteronomous and authoritarian, final revelation liberates. "He who believes in me does not believe in *me*," says Jesus in the Fourth Gospel,[7] destroying any heteronomous interpretation of his divine authority.

The church as the community of the New Being is the place where the new theonomy is actual. But from there it pours into the whole of man's cultural life and gives a Spiritual center to man's spiritual life. In the church as it should be, nothing is heteronomous in contrast to autonomous. And in man's spiritual life nothing is autonomous, in contrast to heteronomous, whenever spiritual life has an ultimate integration. Yet this is not the human situation. The church is not only the community of the New Being; it is also a sociological group immersed in the conflicts of existence. Therefore, it is subject to the almost irresistible temptation of becoming heteronomous and of suppressing autonomous criticism, eliciting just by this method autonomous reactions which often are strong enough to secularize not only culture but also the church itself. A heteronomous tide may then start the vicious circle again. But the church is never completely bereft of theonomous forces. There have been periods in the history of the church in which theonomy, though limited and destructible, was realized more than in other periods. This does not mean that these periods were morally better or intellectually more profound or in a more radical way ultimately concerned. It does mean that they were more aware of the "depth of reason," of the ground of autonomy, and of the uniting center without which spiritual life becomes shallow, disintegrates, and produces a vacuum into which demonic forces may enter.

Theonomous periods are periods in which rational autonomy is preserved in law and knowledge, in community and art. Where there is theonomy nothing which is considered true and just is sacrificed. Theonomous periods do not feel split, but whole and centered. Their center is neither their autonomous freedom nor their heteronomous authority but the depth of reason ecstatically experienced and symbolically ex-

7. John 12:44.

pressed. Myth and cult give them a unity in which all spiritual functions are centered. Culture is not controlled from outside by the church, nor is it left alone so that the community of the New Being stands beside it. Culture receives its substance and integrating power from the community of the New Being, from its symbols and its life.

Where theonomy determines a religious and cultural situation—however fragmentarily and ambiguously, as, for instance, in the early and high Middle Ages—reason is neither subject to revelation nor independent of it. Aesthetic reason does not obey ecclesiastical or political prescripts, nor does it produce secular art cut off from the depth of aesthetic reason; through its autonomous artistic forms it points to the New Being which has appeared in final revelation. In theonomy cognitive reason does not develop authoritatively enforced doctrines, nor does it pursue knowledge for the sake of knowledge; it seeks in everything true an expression of the truth which is of ultimate concern, the truth of being as being, the truth which is present in the final revelation. Legal reason does not establish a system of sacred and untouchable laws, nor does it interpret the meaning of the law in technical-utilitarian terms; it relates the special as well as the basic laws of a society to the "justice of the Kingdom of God" and to the Logos of being as manifest in the final revelation. Communal reason does not accept communal forms dictated by sacred ecclesiastical or political authorities, nor does it surrender human relations to their growth and decay through will to power and libido; it relates them to the ultimate and universal community, the community of love, transforming the will to power by creativity and the libido by *agapē*. In very general terms, this is the meaning of theonomy. It is the task of a constructive theology of culture to apply these principles to the concrete problems of our cultural existence. Systematic theology must restrict itself to a statement of principles.

There are numerous descriptions of theonomy in Romanticism, numerous attempts to re-establish a theonomy according to the pattern of an idealized Middle Ages. Catholicism, too, demands a new theonomy, but what it really wants is the re-establishment of ecclesiastical heteronomy. Protestantism cannot accept the medieval pattern either in Romantic or in Roman terms. It must look forward to a new theonomy. Yet, in order to do so, it must know what theonomy means, and this it can find in the Middle Ages. In contrast to Romanticism, however, Protestantism is aware that a new theonomy cannot be created intentionally by autonomous reason. Autonomous reason is one side in the conflict between autonomy and heteronomy and cannot overcome this conflict. Therefore, the Romantic quest for theonomy cannot be fulfilled except through final revelation and in unity with the church. The breakdown of Romantic art and philosophy, of Romantic ethics and politics (in an especially conspicuous way in the middle of the nineteenth century), shows that a new theonomy is not a matter of intention and good will but that it is a matter of historical destiny and grace. It is an effect of the final revelation which no autonomy can produce and which no heteronomy can prevent.

10. The Final Revelation Overcoming the Conflict
    of Absolutism and Relativism

Final revelation does not destroy reason; it fulfils reason. It liberates reason from the conflict between heteronomy and autonomy by giving the basis for a new theonomy, and it liberates reason from the conflict between absolutism and relativism by appearing in the form of a concrete absolute. In the New Being which is manifest in Jesus as the Christ, the most concrete of all possible forms of concreteness, a personal life, is the bearer of that which is absolute without condition and restriction. This concrete personal life has achieved what neither criticism nor pragmatism is able to accomplish, namely, to unite the conflicting poles of existential reason. As criticism, with its emphasis on the merely formal character of its principle, deceives itself about its assumed lack of absolutistic elements, so pragmatism, with its emphasis on complete openness for everything, deceives itself about *its* assumed lack of absolutistic elements. Neither of them faces the problem radically enough, because neither of them can give the solution. The solution can come only out of the depth of reason, not from its structure. It can come only from final revelation.

The logical form in which the perfectly concrete and the perfectly absolute are united is the paradox. All biblical and ecclesiastical assertions about the final revelation have a paradoxical character. They transcend ordinary opinion, not only preliminarily but definitively; they cannot be expressed in terms of the structure of reason but must be expressed in terms of the depth of reason. If they are expressed in ordinary terms, logically contradictory statements appear. But these contradictions are not the paradox, and no one is asked to "swallow" them as contradictions. This is not only impossible but destructive. The paradox is the reality to which the contradicting form points; it is the surprising, miraculous, and ecstatic way in which that which is the mystery of being universally is manifest in time, space, and under the conditions of existence, in complete historical concreteness. Final revelation is not logical nonsense; it is a concrete event which on the level of rationality must be expressed in contradictory terms.[8]

The concrete side of final revelation appears in the picture of Jesus as the Christ. The paradoxical Christian claim is that this picture has unconditional and universal validity, that it is not subject to the attacks of positivistic or cynical relativism, that it is not absolutistic, whether in the traditional or the revolutionary sense, and that it cannot be achieved either by the critical or by the pragmatic compromise. It is unique and beyond all these conflicting elements and methods of existential reason. This implies above all that no special trait of this picture can be used as an absolute law. The final revelation does not give us absolute ethics, absolute doctrines, or an absolute ideal of personal and communal life. It gives us examples which point to that which is absolute; but the examples are not absolute in themselves. It belongs to the tragic character of all life that the church, although it is based on the concrete absolute, continuously tends to distort its paradoxical meaning and to transform the paradox into absolutisms of a cognitive and moral character. This necessarily provokes relativistic reactions. If Jesus is understood as the divine teacher of absolute theoretical and practical truth, the paradoxical nature of his appearance is misunderstood. If, in opposition to this misunderstanding, he is understood as a religious founder, conditioned by the situation of his time and by the structure of his personality, he is equally misunderstood. In the first case the concreteness is sacrificed; in the second case, the absoluteness. In both cases the paradox has disappeared. The New Being in Jesus as the Christ is the paradox of the final revelation. The words of Jesus and the apostles point to this New Being; they make it visible through stories, legends, symbols, paradoxical descriptions, and theological interpretations. But none of these expressions of the experience of the final revelation is final and absolute in itself. They are all conditioned, relative, open to change and additions.

The absolute side of the final revelation, that in it which is unconditional and unchangeable, involves the complete transparency and the complete self-sacrifice of the medium in which it appears. Every con-

8. It is not only bad theology but also a kind of ascetic arrogance when some theologians —since Tertullian—indulge in nonsensical combinations of words, demanding of all true Christians that in an act of intellectual self-destruction they accept nonsense as "divine sense." The "foolishness" of the cross (Paul) has nothing to do with the assumedly good but actually demonic "work" of the sacrifice of reason.

crete occurrence in the event Jesus as the Christ discloses these qualities. No situation which Jesus faced and no act through which he met it establishes an absolutism of dogmatic or moral character. Both situation and act are transparent and not binding in themselves. Although potentially absolute, they are sacrificed in the moment they occur. Whoever makes Jesus the Christ into a giver of absolute laws for thinking and acting opens the dike for revolutionary revolt, on the one hand, and relativistic undercutting, on the other hand, both of them justifiable. There is, however, an absolute law which can stand under the criterion of finality because it is not denied in the act of self-sacrifice but rather fulfilled. The law of love is the ultimate law because it is the negation of law; it is absolute because it concerns everything concrete. The paradox of final revelation, overcoming the conflict between absolutism and relativism, is love. The love of Jesus as the Christ, which is the manifestation of the divine love—and only this—embraces everything concrete in self and world. Love is always love; that is its static and absolute side. But love is always dependent on that which is loved, and therefore it is unable to force finite elements on finite existence in the name of an assumed absolute. The absoluteness of love is its power to go into the concrete situation, to discover what is demanded by the predicament of the concrete to which it turns. Therefore, love can never become fanatical in a fight for an absolute, or cynical under the impact of the relative. This refers to all realms of rational creativity. Where the paradox of final revelation is present, neither cognitive nor aesthetic, neither legal nor communal, absolutes can stand. Love conquers them without producing cognitive skepticism or aesthetic chaos or lawlessness or estrangement.

The final revelation makes action possible. There is something paradoxical in every action; it always contains a conflict of absolutism and relativism. It is based on decision; but to decide for something as true or as good means excluding countless other possibilities. Every decision is, in some respect, absolutistic, resisting the skeptical temptation of *epoche* (not judging and not acting). It is a risk, rooted in the courage of being, threatened by the excluded possibilities, many of which might have been better and truer than the chosen one. These possibilities take their revenge, often in a very destructive way; and escape into non-action becomes very tempting. Final revelation conquers the conflict between the absolutistic character and the relativistic fate of every decision and action. It shows that the right decision must sacrifice its claim to be the right decision. There are no right decisions; there are trials and defeats and successes. But there *are* decisions which are rooted in love, which by resigning the absolute do not fall into the relative. They are not exposed to the revenge of the excluded possibilities because they were and still are open for them. No decision can be annihilated; no action can be undone. But love gives meaning even to those decisions and actions which prove to be failures. The failures of love do not lead to resignation but to new decisions beyond absolutism and relativism. The final revelation overcomes the conflict between absolutism and relativism in active decisions. Love conquers the revenge of the excluded possibilities. It is absolute as love and relative in every love relationship.

11. The Final Revelation Overcoming the Conflict between Formalism and Emotionalism

When the mystery of being appears in a revelatory experience, the whole of the person's life participates. This means that reason is present both structurally and emotionally and that there is no conflict between these two elements. That which is the mystery of being and meaning is, at the same time, the ground of its rational structure and the power of our emotional participation in it. This refers to all functions of reason. Here it will be applied to the cognitive function alone. The problem of cognitive reason lies in the conflict between the element of union and the element of detachment in every cognitive act. Technical reason has given a tremendous preponderance to the side of detachment. What cannot be grasped by analytic reasoning is relegated to emotion. All the relevant problems of existence are thrown out of the realm of knowledge into the formless realm of emotion. Assertions about the meaning of life and the depth of reason are denied any truth value. Not only myth and cult but also aesthetic intuitions and communal relations are excluded from reason and cognition. They are considered to be emotional effusions without validity and criteria. There are Protestant theologians who accept this separation of form and emotion; in terms of a misinterpretation of Schleiermacher they put religion into the realm of mere emotion. But, in doing so, they deny the power of final revelation to overcome the split between form and emotion, cognitive detachment and cognitive union.

Early classical theologians believed in the power of final revelation to overcome this split. They used the concept *gnosis,* which means cognitive as well as mystical and sexual union. *Gnosis* does not contradict *epistēmē,* detached scientific knowledge. There can be no conflict, because the same Logos who taught the philosophers and legislators is the source of final revelation and teaches the Christian theologians. This solution of the Alexandrian school appears again and again in the history of the Christian thought, either transformed or attacked. Whenever it is accepted, though in many variations, the final revelation is considered to be that which conquers the conflict between theological and scientific knowledge, and implicitly also the conflict between emotion and form. Whenever the Alexandrian solution is rejected, the conflict between the two sides is deepened and made permanent. This happened in the medieval development from Duns Scotus to Ockham, in some expressions of the Reformation theology, in Pascal and Kierkegaard, in the neo-orthodox theology, and—on the opposite side—in naturalism and empiricism. In a surprising alliance orthodox theologians and rationalists deny the reunion of form and emotion in the final revelation. They deny the healing power of revelation in the conflicts of cognitive reason. But if final revelation is unable to heal the splits of cognitive reason, how could it heal the splits of reason in any of its functions? There cannot simultaneously be a reunited "heart" and an eternally split mind. Either healing embraces the cognitive function or nothing is healed. It is one of the merits of "existential" philosophy that it endeavors to reunite union and detachment. Certainly the emphasis is on union and participation; but detachment is not excluded. Otherwise existentialism would not be a philosophy but only a set of emotional exclamations.

Emotion within the cognitive realm does not deform a given structure; it opens it up. Yet it must be admitted that emotional distortions of truth occur incessantly. Passion, libido, will to power, rationalization, and ideology are the most persistent enemies of truth. It is understandable that emotion as such has been denounced as the archenemy of knowledge. But this leads to the consequence that in order to protect knowledge itself relevant knowledge has to be eliminated. It is the claim of final revelation that ultimately relevant knowledge is beyond this alternative, that that which can be grasped only with "infinite passion" (Kierkegaard) is identical with that which appears as the criterion in every act of rational knowledge. If it could not make this claim, Christianity either would have to abdicate, or it would become an instrument of the suppression of truth. The ultimate concern about the final revelation is as radically rational as it is radically emotional, and neither side can be eliminated without destructive consequences.

The conquest of the conflicts of existential reason is what can be called "saved reason." Actual reason needs salvation, as do all the other sides of man's nature and of reality generally. Reason is not excluded from the healing power of the New Being in Jesus as the Christ. Theonomous reason, beyond the conflict of absolutism and relativism, of formalism and emotionalism—this is reason in revelation. Reason in revelation is neither confirmed in its state of conflict nor denied in its essential structure. But its essential structure is re-established under the conditions of existence, fragmentarily, yet really and in power. Religion and theology, therefore, should never attack reason as such, just as they should not attack the world as such or man as such. Undiscerning attacks of this kind drive Christianity into the Manichean camp, and much theological negativism about reason is more Manichean than Christian.

A final word about the nature of theology can be said on the basis of this description of reason in revelation and salvation. Theology obviously must use theonomous reason in order to explain the Christian message. This includes the fact that the conflict between the receiving and the shaping functions of reason is conquered in theological work. No one was more aware of this fact than the early Franciscan school, represented, for instance, by Alexander of Hales. They called theology a "practical" knowledge, pointing to what today, perhaps more adequately, is called "existential" knowledge. It is unfortunate that ever since the day of Thomas Aquinas this emphasis increasingly has been lost (together with the general loss of theonomy in all realms of life) and that the Reformers combined their rediscovery of the existential character of theology with a badly defined rejection of reason. If it is understood that reason receives revelation and that it is an object of salvation like every other element of reality, a theology which uses theonomous reason may again be possible.

D. THE GROUND OF REVELATION

12. God and the Mystery of Revelation

A consequence of the method used in apologetic theology is that the concept of revelation is approached from "below," from man in the situation of revelation, and not from "above," from the divine ground of revelation. But after the meaning and actuality of revelation have been discussed, the question of the ground of revelation arises.

The ground of revelation is not its "cause," in the categorical sense of the word "cause." It is the "ground of being" manifest in existence. The relation between the ground of being and its revelatory manifestations can be expressed only in terms of finite actions originating in a highest being and transforming the course of finite events. This is unavoidable. In the same way the relation of the ground of revelation to those who receive revelation can be conceived only in personal categories; for that which is the ultimate concern of a person cannot be less than a person, although it can be and must be more than personality. Under these circumstances, the theologian must emphasize the symbolic character of all concepts which are used to describe the divine act of self-revelation, and he must try to use terms which indicate that their meaning is not categorical. "Ground" is such a term. It oscillates between cause and substance and transcends both of them. It indicates that the ground of revelation is neither a cause which keeps itself at a distance from the revelatory effect nor a substance which effuses itself into the effect, but rather the mystery which appears in revelation and which remains a mystery in its appearance.

The religious word for what is called the ground of being is God. A major difficulty of any systematic theology is that it presupposes all other parts in each of its parts. A doctrine of God as the ground of revelation presupposes the doctrine of Being and God, which, on the other hand, is dependent on the doctrine of revelation. At this point, therefore, it is necessary to anticipate some concepts which can be explained fully only within the context of the doctrine of God.

If we use the symbol "divine life," as we certainly must, we imply that there is an analogy between the basic structure of experienced life and the ground of being in which life is rooted. This analogy leads to the recognition of three elements which appear in different ways in all sections of systematic theology and which are the basis for the trinitarian interpretation of the final revelation.

The divine life is the dynamic unity of depth and form. In mystical language the depth of the divine life, its inexhaustible and ineffable character, is called "Abyss." In philosophical language the form, the meaning and structure element of the divine life, is called "Logos." In religious language the dynamic unity of both elements is called "Spirit." Theologians must use all three terms in order to point to the ground of revelation. It is the abysmal character of the divine life which makes revelation mysterious; it is the logical character of the divine life which makes the revelation of the mystery possible; and it is the spiritual character of the divine life which creates the correlation of miracle and ecstasy in which revelation can be received. Each of these three concepts which point to the ground of revelation must be used. If the abysmal character of the divine life is neglected, a rationalistic deism transforms revelation into information. If the logical character of the divine life is neglected, an irrationalistic theism transforms revelation into heteronomous subjection. If the spiritual character of the divine life is neglected, a history of revelation is impossible. The doctrine of revelation is based on a trinitarian interpretation of the divine life and its self-manifestation.

Revelation and salvation are elements of God's directing creativity. God directs the processes of individual, social, and universal life toward their fulfilment in the Kingdom of God. Revelatory experiences are imbedded in general experience. They are distinguished from it but not separated from it. World history is the basis of the history of revelation, and in the history of revelation world history reveals its mystery.

13. Final Revelation and the Word of God

The doctrine of revelation has been developed traditionally as a doctrine of the "Word of God." This is possible if Word is interpreted as the *logos* element in the ground of being, which is the interpretation which the classical Logos doctrine gave it. But the Word of God often is understood—half-literally, half-symbolically—as a spoken word, and a "theology of the Word" is presented which is a theology of the spoken word. This intellectualization of revelation runs counter to the sense of the Logos Christology. The Logos Christology was not overintellectualistic; actually it was a weapon against this danger. If Jesus as the Christ is called the Logos, Logos points to a revelatory reality, not to revelatory words. Taken seriously, the doctrine of the Logos prevents the elaboration of a theology of the spoken or the written word, which is *the* Protestant pitfall.[9]

The term "Word of God" has six different meanings. The "Word" is first of all the principle of the divine self-manifestation in the ground of being itself. The ground is not only an abyss in which every form

9. This statement is a complete reversal of the doctrine of the Ritschlian school that the reception of Christianity by the Greek mind meant an intellectualization of Christianity. The Greek mind can be called "intellectualistic" only in its limited and distorted manifestations, but not as such. From the beginning to the end, knowledge means "union with the unchangeable," with the "really real." Metaphysical knowledge is existential; even in an empiricist and logician like Aristotle it has a mystical element. The reduction of knowledge to detached observation for the sake of control is not Greek but modern. This understanding of Greek philosophy demands a reorientation of that type of interpretation of the history of dogma of which Harnack was the classical representative.

disappears; it also is the source from which every form emerges. The ground of being has the character of self-manifestation; it has *logos* character. This is not something added to the divine life; it is the divine life itself. In spite of its abysmal character the ground of being is "logical"; it includes its own *logos*.

Second, the Word is the medium of creation, the dynamic spiritual word which mediates between the silent mystery of the abyss of being and the fulness of concrete, individualized, self-related beings. Creation through the Word, in contrast to a process of emanation as elaborated in Neo-Platonism, points symbolically both to the freedom of creation and to the freedom of the created. The manifestation of the ground of being is spiritual, not mechanical (as it is, for instance, in Spinoza).

Third, the Word is the manifestation of the divine life in the history of revelation. It is the word received by all those who are in a revelatory correlation. If revelation is called the Word of God, this emphasizes the fact that all revelation, however subpersonal the medium may be, addresses itself to the centered self and must have *logos* character to be received by it. The ecstasy of revelation is not *a-logos* (irrational), although it is not produced by human reason. It is inspired, spiritual; it unites the abyss and the *logos* elements in the manifestation of the mystery.

Fourth, the Word is the manifestation of the divine life in the final revelation. The Word is a name for Jesus as the Christ. The Logos, the principle of all divine manifestation, becomes a being in history under the conditions of existence, revealing in this form the basic and determinative relation of the ground of being to us, symbolically speaking, the "heart of the divine life." The Word is not the sum of the words spoken by Jesus. It is the being of the Christ, of which his words and his deeds are an expression. Here the impossibility of identifying the Word with speech is so obvious that it is hard to understand how theologians who accept the doctrines of the Incarnation can maintain this confusion.

Fifth, the term Word is applied to the document of the final revelation and its special preparation, namely, the Bible. But if the Bible is called the Word of God, theological confusion is almost unavoidable. Such consequences as the dictation theory of inspiration, dishonesty in dealing with the biblical text, a "monophysitic" dogma of the infallibility of a book, etc., follow from such an identification. The Bible is the Word of God in two senses. It is the document of the final revelation; and it participates in the final revelation of which it is the document. Probably nothing has contributed more to the misinterpretation of the biblical doctrine of the Word than the identification of the Word with the Bible.

Sixth, the message of the church as proclaimed in her preaching and teaching is called the Word. In so far as Word means the objective message which is given to the church and which should be spoken to her, it is the Word in the same sense in which the biblical revelation or any other revelation is the Word. But in so far as Word means the actual preaching of the church, it might be only words and not the Word at all, mere human speech without divine manifestation in it. The Word depends not only on the meaning of the words of preaching alone but also on the power with which they are spoken. And it depends not only on the understanding of the listener alone but also on his existential reception of the content. Nor does the Word depend on the preacher or the listener alone, but on both in correlation. These four factors and their interdependence constitute the "constellation" in which human words may become the Word, divine self-manifestation. They may and they may not become the Word. Therefore, no activity of the church can be carried through with the certainty that it expresses the Word. No minister should claim more than his intention to speak the Word when he preaches. He never should claim that he has spoken it or that he will be able to speak it in the future, for, since he has no power over the revelatory constellation, he possesses no power to preach the Word. He may speak mere words, theologically correct though they may be. And he may speak the Word, though his formulations are theologically incorrect. Finally, the mediator of revelation may not be a preacher or religious teacher at all but simply someone whom we meet and whose words become the Word for us in a special constellation.

The many different meanings of the term "Word" are all united in one meaning, namely, "God manifest"—manifest in himself, in creation, in the history of revelation, in the final revelation, in the Bible, in the words of the church and her members. "God manifest"—the mystery of the divine abyss expressing itself through the divine Logos—this is the meaning of the symbol, the "Word of God."

PART II
BEING AND GOD

1

I

BEING AND THE QUESTION OF GOD

INTRODUCTION: THE QUESTION OF BEING

The basic theological question is the question of God. God is the answer to the question implied in being. The problem of reason and revelation is secondary to that of being and God, although it was discussed first. Like everything else, reason has being, participates in being, and is logically subordinate to being. Therefore, in the analysis of reason and of the questions implied in its existential conflicts we have been forced to anticipate concepts which are derived from an analysis of being. In proceeding from the correlation of reason and revelation to that of being and God, we move to the more fundamental consideration; in traditional terms, we move from the epistemological to the ontological question. The ontological question is: What is being itself? What is that which is not a special being or a group of beings, not something concrete or something abstract, but rather something which is always thought implicitly, and sometimes explicitly, if something is said to *be*? Philosophy asks the question of being as being. It investigates the character of everything that is in so far as it is. This is its basic task, and the answer it provides determines the analysis of all special forms of being. It is "first philosophy," or, if the term still could be used, "metaphysics." Since the connotations of the term "metaphysics" make its use precarious, the word "ontology" is preferable. The ontological question, the question of being-itself, arises in something like a "metaphysical shock" —the shock of possible nonbeing. This shock often has been expressed in the question, "Why is there something; why not nothing?" But in this form the question is meaningless, for every possible answer would be subject to the same question in an infinite regression. Thought must start with being; it cannot go behind it, as the form of the question itself shows. If one asks why there *is* not nothing, one attributes being even to nothing. Thought is based on being, and it cannot leave this basis; but thought can imagine the negation of everything that *is*, and it can describe the nature and structure of being which give everything that is the power of resisting nonbeing. Mythology, cosmogony, and metaphysics have asked the question of being both implicitly and explicitly and have tried to answer it. It is the ultimate question, although fundamentally it is the expression of a state of existence rather than a formulated question. Whenever this state is experienced and this question is asked, everything disappears in the abyss of possible nonbeing; even a god would disappear if he were not being-itself. But if everything special and definite disappears in the light of the ultimate question, one must ask how an answer is possible. Does this not mean that ontology is reduced to the empty tautology that being is being? Is not the term "structure of being" a contradiction in terms, saying that that which is beyond every structure itself has a structure?

Ontology is possible because there are concepts which are less universal than being but more universal than any ontic concept, that is, more universal than any concept designating a realm of beings. Such concepts have been called "principles" or "categories" or "ultimate notions." The human mind has worked for thousands of years in their discovery, elaboration, and organization. But no agreement has been reached, although certain concepts reappear in almost every ontology. Systematic theology cannot, and should not, enter into the ontological discussion as such. Yet it can and must consider these central concepts from the point of view of their theological significance. Such consideration, demanded in every part of the theological system, may well influence the ontological analysis indirectly. But the arena of ontological discussion is not the theological arena, although the theologian must be familiar in it.

It is possible to distinguish four levels of ontological concepts: (1) the basic ontological structure which is the implicit condition of the ontological question; (2) the elements which constitute the ontological structure; (3) the characteristics of being which are the conditions of existence; and (4) the categories of being and knowing. Each of these levels demands a special analysis. Only a few remarks concerning their general ontological character are necessary at this point.

The ontological question presupposes an asking subject and an object about which the question is asked; it presupposes the subject-object structure of being, which in turn presupposes the self-world structure as the basic articulation of being. The self having a world to which it belongs —this highly dialectical structure—logically and experientially precedes all other structures. Its analysis should be the first step in every ontological task. The second level of ontological analysis deals with the elements which constitute the basic structure of being. They share the polar character of the basic structure, and it is just their polarity that makes them principles by preventing them from becoming highest generic concepts. One can imagine a realm of nature beside or outside the realm of history, but there is no realm of dynamics without form or of individuality without universality. The converse also is true. Each pole is meaningful only in so far as it refers by implication to the opposite pole. Three outstanding pairs of elements constitute the basic ontological structure: individuality and universality, dynamics and form, freedom and destiny. In these three polarities the first element expresses the self-relatedness of being, its power of being something for itself, while the second element expresses the belongingness of being, its character of being a part of a universe of being.

The third level of ontological concepts expresses the power of being to exist and the difference between essential and existential being. Both in experience and in analysis being manifests the duality of essential and existential being. There is no ontology which can disregard these two aspects, whether they are hypostasized into two realms (Plato), or combined in the polar relation of potentiality and actuality (Aristotle), or contrasted with each other (Schelling II, Kierkegaard, Heidegger), or derived from each other, either existence from essence (Spinoza, Hegel) or essence from existence (Dewey, Sartre). In all these ontologies the duality of essential and existential being is seen, and the question of their relation to one another and to being-itself is asked. The answer is prepared by the polarity of freedom and destiny on the second level of ontological analysis. However, freedom as such is not the basis of existence, but rather freedom in unity with finitude. Finite freedom is the turning point from being to existence. Therefore, it is the analysis of finitude in its polarity with infinity as well as in its relation to freedom and destiny, to being and nonbeing, to essence and existence, which is the task of ontology in the third level.

The fourth level deals with those concepts which traditionally have been called categories, that is, the basic forms of thought and being. They participate in the nature of finitude and can be called structures of finite being and thinking. To determine their number and organization is one of the infinite tasks of philosophy. From the theological point of view four main categories must be analyzed: time, space, causality, and substance.[1] Categories like quantity and quality have no direct theological significance and are not especially discussed. Other concepts which often have been called "categories," like movement and rest, or unity and manifoldness, are treated implicitly on the second level of analysis, movement and rest in connection with dynamics and form, unity and manifoldness in connection with individuality and universality. The polar character of these concepts puts them on the level of the elements of the basic ontological structure and not on the level of the categories. Finally, it must be stated that two of the *transcendentalia* of scholastic philosophy, the true and the good (*verum, bonum*), usually combined with being and oneness (*esse, unum*), do not belong to pure ontology, because they are meaningful only in relation to a judging subject. Their ontological foundation, however, is discussed in connection with the duality of essence and existence.

Since it is the purpose of this section of the theological system to develop the question of God as the question implied in being, the concept of finitude is the center of the following analysis, for it is the finitude of being which drives us to the question of God.

First, however, it is necessary to say something about the epistemological character of all ontological concepts. Ontological concepts are a priori in the strict sense of the word. They determine the nature of experience. They are present whenever something is experienced. A priori does not mean that ontological concepts are known prior to experience. They should not be attacked as if this were meant. On the contrary, they are products of a critical analysis of experience. Nor does a priori mean that the ontological concepts constitute a static and unchangeable structure which, once discovered, will always be valid. The structure of experience may have changed in the past and may change in the future, but, while such a possibility cannot be excluded, there is no reason for using it as an argument against the a priori character of ontological concepts.

Those concepts are a priori which are presupposed in every actual experience, since they constitute the very structure of experience itself. The conditions of experience are a priori. If these conditions change—and with them the structure of experience—another set of conditions must make it possible to have experience. This situation will persist

---

1. If time and space are called "categories," this is a deviation from the Kantian terminology which calls time and space forms of intuition. But the larger sense of category has been accepted generally, even in the post-Kantian schools.

as long as it is meaningful to speak of experience at all. As long as there is experience in any definite sense of the word, there is a structure of experience which can be recognized within the process of experiencing and which can be elaborated critically. Process philosophy is justified in its attempt to dissolve into processes everything which seems to be static. But it would become absurd if it tried to dissolve the structure of process into a process. This simply would mean that what we know as process has been superseded by something else, the nature of which is unknown at present. In the meantime, every philosophy of process has an explicit or implicit ontology which is aprioristic in character.

This also is the answer to historical relativism, which denies the possibility of an ontological or a theological doctrine of man by arguing as follows: since man's nature changes in the historical process, nothing ontologically definite or theologically relevant can be affirmed with regard to it; and since the doctrine of man (i.e., his freedom, his finitude, his existential predicament, his historical creativity), is the main entrance for ontology and the main point of reference for theology, neither ontology nor theology is really possible. Such a criticism would remain unanswerable if the ontological and the theological doctrines of man claimed to deal with an unchangeable structure called human nature. Although such a claim often has been attempted, it is not necessary. Human nature changes in history. Process philosophy is right in this. But human nature changes in *history*. The structure of a being *which has history* underlies all historical changes. This structure is the subject of an ontological and a theological doctrine of man. Historical man is a descendant of beings who had no history, and perhaps there will be beings who are descendants of historical man who have no history. This simply means that neither animals nor supermen are the objects of a doctrine of man. Ontology and theology deal with historical man as he is given in present experience and in historical memory. An anthropology which transcends these limits, empirically toward the past or speculatively toward the future, is not a doctrine of man. It is a doctrine of the biological preparation for, or the biological continuation of, what in a special stage of the universal development was and is and perhaps will be historical man. In this case, as in all others, ontology and theology establish a relatively but not absolutely static a priori, overcoming the alternatives of absolutism and relativism which threaten to destroy both of them.

This agrees with a powerful tradition in classical ontology and theology represented by voluntarism and nominalism. Even before Duns Scotus, theologians rejected the "realistic" attempts to fix God to a static structure of being. In Duns Scotus and all ontology and theology influenced by him—up to Bergson and Heidegger—an element of ultimate indeterminacy is seen in the ground of being. God's *potestas absoluta* is a perennial threat to any given structure of things. It undercuts any absolute apriorism, but it does not remove ontology and the relatively a priori structures with which ontology is concerned.

A. THE BASIC ONTOLOGICAL STRUCTURE
SELF AND WORLD

1. Man, Self, and World

Every being participates in the structure of being, but man alone is immediately aware of this structure. It belongs to the character of existence that man is estranged from nature, that he is unable to understand it in the way he can understand man. He can describe the behavior of all beings, but he does not know directly what their behavior means to them. This is the truth of the behaviorist method—ultimately a tragic truth. It expresses the strangeness of all beings to each other. We can approach other beings only in terms of analogy and, therefore, only indirectly and uncertainly. Myth and poetry have tried to overcome this limitation of our cognitive function. Knowledge either has resigned itself to failure or has transformed the world, aside from the knowing subject, into a vast machine of which all living beings, including man's body, are mere parts (Cartesians).

However, there is a third possibility, based on an understanding of man as that being in whom all levels of being are united and approachable. Consciously or unconsciously, ontology in all its forms has used this possibility. Man occupies a pre-eminent position in ontology, not as an outstanding object among other objects, but as that being who asks the ontological question and in whose self-awareness the ontological answer can be found. The old tradition—expressed equally by mythology and mysticism, by poetry and metaphysics—that the principles which constitute the universe must be sought in man is indirectly and involuntarily confirmed, even by the behavioristic self-restriction. "Philosophers of life" and "Existentialists" have reminded us in our time of this truth on which ontology depends. Characteristic in this respect is Heidegger's method in *Sein und Zeit*. He calls "Dasein" ("being there") the place where the structure of being is manifest. But "Dasein" is given to man within himself. Man is able to answer the ontological question himself because he experiences directly and immediately the structure of being and its elements.

This approach must, however, be protected against a fundamental misunderstanding. It in no way assumes that man is more easily accessible as an object of knowledge, physical or psychological, than are nonhuman objects. Just the contrary is asserted. Man is the most difficult object encountered in the cognitive process. The point is that man is aware of the structures which make cognition possible. He lives in them and acts through them. They are immediately present to him. They are he himself. Any confusion on this point has destructive consequences. The basic structure of being and all its elements and the conditions of existence lose their meaning and their truth if they are seen as objects among objects. If the self is considered to be a thing among things, its existence is questionable; if freedom is thought to be a thing among things, its existence is questionable; if freedom is thought to be a quality of will, it loses out to necessity; if finitude is understood in terms of measurement, it has no relation to the infinite. The truth of all ontological concepts is their power of expressing that which makes the subject-object structure possible. They constitute this structure; they are not controlled by it.

Man experiences himself as having a world to which he belongs. The basic ontological structure is derived from an analysis of this complex dialectical relationship. Self-relatedness is implied in every experience. There is something that "has" and something that is "had," and the two are one. The question is not whether selves exist. The question is whether we are aware of self-relatedness. And this awareness can only be denied in a statement in which self-relatedness is implicitly affirmed. for self-relatedness is experienced in acts of negation as well as in acts of affirmation. A self is not a thing that may or may not exist; it is an original phenomenon which logically precedes all questions of existence.

The term "self" is more embracing than the term "ego." It includes the subconscious and the unconscious "basis" of the self-conscious ego as well as self-consciousness (*cogitatio* in the Cartesian sense). Therefore, selfhood or self-centeredness must be attributed in some measure to all living beings and, in terms of analogy, to all individual *Gestalten* even in the inorganic realm. One can speak of self-centeredness in atoms as well as in animals, wherever the reaction to a stimulus is dependent on a structural whole. Man is a fully developed and completely centered self. He "possesses" himself in the form of self-consciousness. He has an ego-self.

Being a self means being separated in some way from everything else, having everything else opposite one's self, being able to look at it and to act upon it. At the same time, however, this self is aware that it belongs to that at which it looks. The self is "in" it. Every self has an environment in which it lives, and the ego-self has a world in which it lives. All beings have an environment which is *their* environment. Not everything that can be found in the space in which an animal lives belongs to its environment. Its environment consists in those things with which it has an active interrelation. Different beings within the same limited space have different environments. Each being *has* an environment, although it belongs *to* its environment. The mistake of all theories which explain the behavior of a being in terms of environment alone is that they fail to explain the special character of the environment in terms of the special character of the being which *has* such an environment. Self and environment determine each other.

Because man has an ego-self, he transcends every possible environment. Man has a world. Like environment, world is a correlative concept. Man *has* a world, although he is *in* it at the same time. "World" is not the sum total of all beings—an inconceivable concept. As the Greek *kosmos* and the Latin *universum* indicate, "world" is a structure or a unity of manifoldness. If we say that man has a world at which he looks, from which he is separated and to which he belongs, we think of a structured whole even though we may describe this world in pluralistic terms. The whole opposite man is *one* at least in this respect, that it is related to us perspectively, however discontinuous it may be in itself. Every pluralistic philosopher speaks of the pluralistic character of the *world*, thus implicitly rejecting an absolute pluralism. The world is the structural whole which includes and transcends all environments, not only those of beings which lack a fully developed self, but also the environments in which man partially lives. As long as he is human, that is, as long as he has not "fallen" from humanity (e.g., in intoxication or insanity), man never is bound completely to an environment. He always transcends it by grasping and shaping it according to universal norms and ideas. Even in the most limited environment man possesses the universe; he has a world. Language, as the power of universals, is the basic expression of man's transcending his environment, of having a world. The ego-self is that self which can speak and which by speaking trespasses the boundaries of any given situation.

When man looks at his world, he looks at himself as an infinitely small part of his world. Although he is the perspective-center, he becomes a particle of what is centered in him, a particle of the universe. This structure enables man to encounter himself. Without its world the self would be an empty form. Self-consciousness would have no content, for every content, psychic as well as bodily, lies within the universe. There is no self-consciousness without world-consciousness, but the converse also is true. World-consciousness is possible only on the basis of a fully developed self-consciousness. Man must be completely separated from his world in order to look at it as a world. Otherwise he would remain in the bondage of mere environment. The interdependence of ego-self and world is the basic ontological structure and implies all the others.

Both sides of the polarity are lost if either side is lost. The self without a world is empty; the world without a self is dead. The subjective idealism of philosophers like Fichte is unable to reach the world of contents unless the ego makes an irrational leap into its opposite, the non-ego. The objective realism of philosophers like Hobbes is unable to reach the form of self-relatedness without an irrational leap from the movement of things into the ego. Descartes tried desperately and unsuccessfully to reunite the empty *cogitatio* of the pure ego with the mechanical movement of dead bodies. Whenever the self-world correlation is cut, no reunion is possible. On the other hand, if the basic structure of self-world relatedness is affirmed, it is possible to show how this structure might disappear from *cognitive* view because of the subject-object structure of reason, which is rooted in the self-world correlation and which grows out of it.

2. The Logical and the Ontological Object

The self-world polarity is the basis of the subject-object structure of reason. It was not possible, except by anticipation, to discuss this structure in Part I before discussing the self-world polarity. The relation between the self-world polarity and the subject-object structure must now be explained.

We have described the world as a structured whole, and we have called its structure "objective reason." We have described the self as a structure of centeredness, and we have called this structure "subjective reason." And we have stated that these correspond to each other, without, however, giving any special interpretation of the correspondence.

Reason makes the self a self, namely, a centered structure; and reason makes the world a world, namely, a structured whole. Without reason, without the *logos* of being, being would be chaos, that is, it would not be being but only the possibility of it (*me on*). But where there is reason there are a self and a world in interdependence. The function of the self in which it actualizes its rational structure is the mind, the bearer of subjective reason. Looked at by the mind, the world is reality, the bearer of objective reason.

The terms "subject" and "object" have had a long history during which their meanings practically traded places. Originally subjective meant that which has independent being, a hypostasis of its own. Objective meant that which is in the mind as its content. Today, especially under the influence of the great British empiricists, that which is real is said to have objective being, while that which is in the mind is said to have subjective being. We must follow the present terminology, but we must go beyond it.

In the cognitive realm everything toward which the cognitive act is directed is considered an object, be it God or a stone, be it one's self or a mathematical definition. In the logical sense everything about which a predication is made is, by this very fact, an object. The theologian cannot escape making God an object in the logical sense of the word, just as the lover cannot escape making the beloved an object of knowledge and action. The danger of logical objectification is that it never is merely logical. It carries ontological presuppositions and implications. If God is brought into the subject-object structure of being, he ceases to be the ground of being and becomes one being among others (first of all, a being beside the subject who looks at him as an object). He ceases to be the God who is really God. Religion and theology are aware of the danger of religious objectification. They attempt to escape the unintentional blasphemy implied in this situation in several ways. Prophetic religion denies that one can "see" God, for sight is the most objectifying sense. If there is a knowledge of God, it is God who knows himself through man. God remains the subject, even if he becomes a logical object (cf. I Cor. 13:12). Mysticism tries to overcome the objectifying scheme by an ecstatic union of man and God, analogous to the erotic relation in which there is a drive toward a moment in which the difference between lover and beloved is extinguished. Theology always must remember that in speaking of God it makes an object of that which precedes the subject-object structure and that, therefore, it must include in its speaking of God the acknowledgment that it cannot make God an object.

But there is a third sense in which the objectifying scheme is used. Making an object can mean depriving it of its subjective elements, making it into something which is an object and *nothing but* an object. Such an object is a "thing," in German a *Ding,* something which is altogether *bedingt* ("conditioned"). The word "thing" does not necessarily have this connotation; it can stand for everything that is. But it is counter to our linguistic feeling to call human beings "things." They are more than things and more than mere objects. They are selves and therefore bearers of subjectivity. Metaphysical theories as well as social institutions in which selves are transformed into things contradict truth and justice, for they contradict the basic ontological structure of being, the self-world polarity in which every being participates in varying degrees of approximation to the one or the other pole. The fully developed human personality represents one pole, the mechanical tool the other. The term "thing" is most adequately applied to the tool. It is almost devoid of subjectivity. But not completely. Its constitutive elements, taken from inorganic nature, have some unique structures which cannot be ignored, and it itself possesses—or should possess—an artistic form, in which its purpose is visibly expressed. Even everyday tools are not merely things. Everything resists the fate of being considered or treated as a mere thing, as an object which has no subjectivity. This is the reason why ontology cannot begin with things and try to derive the structure of reality from them. That which is completely conditioned, which has no selfhood and subjectivity, cannot explain self and subject. Whoever attempts to do this must introduce surreptitiously into the nature of objectivity the very subjectivity which he wants to derive from it.

According to Parmenides, the basic ontological structure is not being but the unity of being and the word, the *logos* in which it is grasped. Subjectivity is not an epiphenomenon, a derived appearance. It is an original phenomenon, although only and always in polar relation with objectivity. The way in which recent naturalism has disavowed its former reductionist methods, for example, reducing everything to physical objects and their movements, suggests an increasing insight into the impossibility of deriving subjectivity from objectivity. In the practical realm the widespread resistance against the objectifying tendencies in industrial society, first in its capitalistic and then in its totalitarian forms, suggests that there is a realization that making man into a part of even the most useful machine means dehumanization, destruction of man's essential subjectivity. Past and present existentialism, in all its varieties, is united in protesting against the theoretical and practical forms of surrendering the subject to the object, the self to the thing. An ontology which begins with the self-world structure of being and the subject-object structure of reason is protected against the danger of surrendering the subject to the object.

It is also protected against the opposite danger. It is just as impossible to derive the object from the subject as it is to derive the subject from the object. Idealism in all its forms has discovered that there is no way from the "absolute ego" to the non-ego, from the absolute consciousness to the nonconscious, from the absolute self to the world, from the pure subject to the objective structure of reality. In each case that which is supposed to be derived is surreptitiously slipped into that from which it is to be derived. This trick of deductive idealism is the precise counterpart of the trick of reductive naturalism.

The motive behind the different forms of the philosophy of identity was insight into the situation. But the insight did not go far enough. The relation of subject and object is not that of an identity from which neither subjectivity nor objectivity can be derived. The relation is one of polarity. The basic ontological structure cannot be derived. It must be accepted. The question, "What precedes the duality of self and world, of subject and object?" is a question in which reason looks into its own abyss—an abyss in which distinction and derivation disappear. Only revelation can answer this question.

B. THE ONTOLOGICAL ELEMENTS

3. INDIVIDUALIZATION AND PARTICIPATION

According to Plato, the idea of difference is "spread over all things." Aristotle could call individual beings the *telos,* the inner aim, of the process of actualization. According to Leibniz, no absolutely equal things can exist, since precisely their differentiation from each other makes their independent existence possible. In the biblical creation stories God produces individual beings and not universals, Adam and Eve rather than the ideas of manhood and womanhood. Even Neo-Platonism, in spite of its ontological "realism," accepted the doctrine that there are ideas (eternal archetypes) not only of the species but also of individuals. Individualization is not a characteristic of a special sphere of beings; it is an ontological element and therefore a *quality* of everything. It is implied in and constitutive of every self, which means that at least in an analogous way it is implied in and constitutive of every being. The very term "individual" points to the interdependence of self-relatedness and individualization. A self-centered being cannot be divided. It can be destroyed, or it can be deprived of certain parts out of which new self-centered beings emerge (e.g., regeneration of structure in some lower animals). In the latter case either the old self has ceased to exist and is replaced by new selves or the old self remains, diminished in extension and power for the sake of the new selves. But in no case is the center itself divided. This is as impossible as the partition of a mathematical point. Selfhood and individualization are different conceptually, but actually they are inseparable.

Man not only is completely self-centered; he also is completely individualized. And he is the one because he is the other. The species is dominant in all nonhuman beings, even in the most highly developed animals; essentially the individual is an examplar, representing in an individual way the universal characteristics of the species. Although the individualization of a plant or an animal is expressed even in the smallest part of its centered whole, it is significant only in unity with individual persons or unique historical events. The individuality of a nonhuman being gains significance if it is drawn into the processes of human life. But only then. Man is different. Even in collectivistic societies the individual as the bearer and, in the last analysis, the aim of the collective is significant rather than the species. Even the most despotic state claims to exist for the benefit of its individual subjects. Law, by its very nature, is based on the valuation of the individual as unique, unexchangeable, inviolable, and therefore to be protected and made responsible at the same time. The individual is a person in the sight of the law. The original meaning of the word "person" (*persona, prosopon*) points to the actor's mask which makes him a definite character.

Historically this has not always been acknowledged by systems of law. In many cultures the law has not recognized everyone as a person. Anatomical equality has not been considered a sufficient basis for the valuation of every man as a person. Personal standing has been denied to slaves, children, women. They have not attained full individualization in many cultures because they have been unable to participate fully; and, conversely, they have been unable to participate fully because they have not been fully individualized. No process of emancipation was begun until the Stoic philosophers fought successfully for the doctrine that every human being participates in the universal *logos*. The uniqueness of every person was not established until the Christian church acknowledged the universality of salvation and the potentiality of every human being to participate in it. This development illustrates the strict interdependence of individuality and participation on the level of complete individualization, which is, at the same time, the level of complete participation.

The individual self participates in his environment or, in the case of complete individualization, in his world. An individual leaf participates in the natural structures and forces which act upon it and which are acted upon by it. This is the reason why philosophers like Cusanus and Leibniz have asserted that the whole universe is present in every individual, although limited by its individual limitations. There are microcosmic qualities in every being, but man alone is *microcosmos*. In him the world is present not only indirectly and unconsciously but directly and in a conscious encounter. Man participates in the universe through the rational structure of mind and reality. Considered environmentally, he participates in a very small section of reality; he is surpassed in some respects by migrating animals. Considered cosmically, he participates in the universe because the universal structures, forms, and laws are open to him. And with them everything which can be grasped and shaped through them is open to him. Actually man's participation always is limited. Potentially there are no limits he could not transcend. The universals make man universal; language proves that he is *microcosmos*. Through the universals man participates in the remotest stars and the remotest past. This is the ontological basis for the assertion that knowledge is union and that it is rooted in the *erōs* which reunites elements which essentially belong to each other.

When individualization reaches the perfect form which we call a "person," participation reaches the perfect form which we call "communion." Man participates in all levels of life, but he participates fully only in that level of life which he is himself—he has communion only with persons. Communion is participation in another completely centered and completely individual self. In this sense communion is not something an individual might or might not have. Participation is essential for the individual, not accidental. No individual exists without participation, and no personal being exists without communal being. The person as the fully developed individual self is impossible without other fully developed selves. If he did not meet the resistance of other selves, every self would try to make himself absolute. But the resistance of the other selves is unconditional. One individual can conquer the entire world of objects, but he cannot conquer another person without destroying him as a person. The individual discovers himself through this resistance. If he does not want to destroy the other person, he must enter into communion with him. In the resistance of the other person the person is born. Therefore, there is no person without an encounter with other persons. Persons can grow only in the communion of personal encounter. Individualization and participation are interdependent on all levels of being.

The concept of participation has many functions. A symbol participates in the reality it symbolizes; the knower participates in the known; the lover participates in the beloved; the existent participates in the essences which make it what it is, under the condition of existence; the individual participates in the destiny of separation and guilt; the Christian participates in the New Being as it is manifest in Jesus the Christ. In polarity with individualization, participation underlies the category of relation as a basic ontological element. Without individualization nothing would exist to be related. Without participation the category of relation would have no basis in reality. Every relation includes a kind of participation. This is true even of indifference or hostility. Nothing can make one hostile in which one does not somehow participate, perhaps in the form of being excluded from it. And nothing can produce the attitude of indifference whose existence has not made some difference to one. The element of participation guarantees the unity of a disrupted world and makes a universal system of relations possible.

The polarity of individualization and participation solves the problem of nominalism and realism which has shaken and almost disrupted Western civilization. According to nominalism, only the individual has ontological reality; universals are verbal signs which point to similarities between individual things. Knowledge, therefore, is not participation. It is an external act of grasping and controlling things. Controlling knowledge is the epistemological expression of a nominalistic ontology; empiricism and positivism are its logical consequences. But pure nominalism is untenable. Even the empiricist must acknowledge that everything approachable by knowledge must have the structure of "being knowable." And this structure includes by definition a mutual participation of the knower and the known. Radical nominalism is unable to make the process of knowledge understandable.

"Realism" must be subjected to the same scrutiny. The word indicates that the universals, the essential structures of things, are the really real in them.[2] "Mystical realism" emphasizes participation over against individualization, the participation of the individual in the universal and the participation of the knower in the known. In this respect realism is correct and able to make knowledge understandable. But it is wrong if it establishes a second reality behind empirical reality and makes of the structure of participation a level of being in which individuality and personality disappear.

4. DYNAMICS AND FORM

Being is inseparable from the logic of being, the structure which makes it what it is and which gives reason the power of grasping and shaping it. "Being something" means having a form. According to the polarity of individualization and participation, there are special and general forms, but in actual being these never are separated. Through their union every being becomes a definite being. Whatever loses its form loses its being. Form should not be contrasted with content. The form which makes a thing what it is, is its content, its *essentia,* its definite power of being. The form of a tree is what makes it a tree, what gives it the general character of treehood as well as the special and unique form of an individual tree.

The separation of form and content becomes a problem in man's cultural activity. Here given materials, things, or events which have their natural form are transformed by man's rational functions. A landscape has a natural form which is, at the same time, its content. The artist uses the natural form of a landscape as material for an artistic creation whose content is not the material but rather what has been made of the material. One can distinguish (as Aristotle did) between form and material. But even in the cultural sphere a distinction between form and content cannot be made. The problem of formalism (see above, pp. 89 ff.) is a problem of attitude. The question is not whether a certain form is adequate to a certain material. The question is whether a cultural creation is the expression of a spiritual substance or whether it is a mere form without such substance. Every type of material can be shaped by every form as long as the form is genuine, that is, as long as it is an

---

2. The word "realism" means today almost what "nominalism" meant in the Middle Ages, while the "realism" of the Middle Ages expresses almost exactly what we call "idealism" today. It might be suggested that, whenever one speaks of classical realism, one should call it "mystical realism."

immediate expression of the basic experience out of which the artist lives—in unity with his period as well as in conflict with it. If he fails to use such forms and instead uses forms which have ceased to be expressive, the artist is a formalist irrespective of whether the forms are traditional or revolutionary. A revolutionary style can become as formalistic as a conservative style. The criterion is the expressive power of a form and not a special style.

These considerations point to the other element in the polarity of form and dynamics. Every form forms something. The question is: What is this "something"? We have called it "dynamics," a very complex concept with a rich history and many connotations and implications. The problematic character of this concept, and of all concepts related to it, is due to the fact that everything which can be conceptualized must have being and that there is no being without form. Dynamics, therefore, cannot be thought as something that is; nor can it be thought as something that is not. It is the *me on,* the potentiality of being, which is nonbeing in contrast to things that have a form, and the power of being in contrast to pure nonbeing. This highly dialectical concept is not an invention of the philosophers. It underlies most mythologies and is indicated in the chaos, the *tohu-va-bohu,* the night, the emptiness, which precedes creation. It appears in metaphysical speculations as *Urgrund* (Böhme), will (Schopenhauer), will to power (Nietzsche), the unconscious (Hartmann, Freud), *élan vital* (Bergson), strife (Scheler, Jung). None of these concepts is to be taken conceptually. Each of them points symbolically to that which cannot be named. If it could be named properly, it would be a formed being beside other beings instead of an ontological element in polar contrast with the element of pure form. Therefore, it is unfair to criticize these concepts on the basis of their literal meaning. Schopenhauer's "will" is not the psychological function called "will." And the "unconscious" of Hartmann and Freud is not a "room" which can be described as though it were a cellar filled with things which once belonged to the upper rooms in which the sun of consciousness shines. The unconscious is mere potentiality, and it should not be painted in the image of the actual. The other descriptions of "that which does not yet have being" must be interpreted in the same way, that is, analogically.

In Greek philosophy nonbeing, or matter, was an ultimate principle—the principle of resistance against form. Christian theology, however, has had to try to deprive it of its independence and to seek a place for it in the depth of the divine life. The doctrine of God as *actus purus* prevented Thomism from solving the problem, but Protestant mysticism, using motifs of Duns Scotus and Luther, tried to introduce a dynamic element into the vision of the divine life. Late Romanticism as well as the philosophies of life and of process have followed this line, though always in danger of losing the divinity of the divine in their attempts to transform the static God of the *actus purus* into the living God. It is obvious, however, that any ontology which suppresses the dynamic element in the structure of being is unable to explain the nature of a life-process and to speak meaningfully of the divine life.

The polarity of dynamics and form appears in man's immediate experience as the polar structure of vitality and intentionality. Both terms need justification and explanation. Vitality is the power which keeps a living being alive and growing. *Élan vital* is the creative drive of the living substance in everything that lives toward new forms. However, a narrower use of the term is more frequent. Ordinarily one speaks of the vitality of men, not of the vitality of animals or plants. The meaning of the word is colored by its polar contrast. Vitality, in the full sense of the word, is human because man has intentionality. The dynamic element in man is open in all directions; it is bound by no a priori limiting structure. Man is able to create a world beyond the given world; he creates the technical and the spiritual realms. The dynamics of subhuman life remain within the limits of natural necessity, notwithstanding the infinite variations it produces and notwithstanding the new forms created by the evolutionary process. Dynamics reaches out beyond nature only in man. This is his vitality, and therefore man alone has vitality in the full sense of the word.

Man's vitality lives in contrast with his intentionality and is conditioned by it. On the human level form is the rational structure of subjective reason actualized in a life-process. One could call this pole "rationality," but rationality means having reason, not actualizing reason. One could call it "spirituality," but spirituality means the unity of dynamics and form in man's moral and cultural acts. Therefore, we recommend the use of the term "intentionality," which means being related to meaningful structures, living in universals, grasping and shaping reality. In this context "intention" does not mean the will to act for a purpose; it means living in tension with (and toward) something objectively valid. Man's dynamics, his creative vitality, is not undirected, chaotic, self-contained activity. It is directed, formed; it transcends itself toward meaningful contents. There is no vitality as such and no intentionality as such. They are interdependent, like the other polar elements.

The dynamic character of being implies the tendency of everything to transcend itself and to create new forms. At the same time everything tends to conserve its own form as the basis of its self-transcendence. It tends to unite identity and difference, rest and movement, conservation and change. Therefore, it is impossible to speak of being without also speaking of becoming. Becoming is just as genuine in the structure of being as is that which remains unchanged in the process of becoming. And, vice versa, becoming would be impossible if nothing were preserved in it as the measure of change. A process philosophy which sacrifices the persisting identity of that which is in process sacrifices the process itself, its continuity, the relation of what is conditioned to its conditions, the inner aim (*telos*) which makes a process a whole. Bergson was right when he combined the *élan vital,* the universal tendency toward self-transcendence, with duration, with continuity and self-conservation in the temporal flux.

The growth of the individual is the most obvious example of self-transcendence based on self-conservation. It shows very clearly the simultaneous interdependence of the two poles. Inhibition of growth ultimately destroys the being which does not grow. Misguided growth destroys itself and that which transcends itself without self-conservation. An example of wider scope is biological evolution from lower or less complex forms of life to higher and more complex forms. It is this example, more than anything else, which has inspired the philosophy of process and of creative evolution.

Self-transcendence and self-conservation are experienced immediately by man in man himself. Just as the self on the subhuman level is imperfect and in correlation with an environment, while on the human level the self is perfect and in correlation with a world, so self-transcendence on the subhuman level is limited by a constellation of conditions, while self-transcendence on the human level is limited only by the structure which makes man what he is—a complete self which has a world. On the basis of achieving self-conservation (the preservation of his humanity), man can transcend any given situation. He can transcend himself without limits in all directions just because of this basis. His creativity breaks through the biological realm to which he belongs and establishes new realms never attainable on a nonhuman level. Man is able to create a new world of technical tools and a world of cultural forms. In both cases something new comes into being through man's grasping and shaping activity. Man uses the material given by nature to create technical forms which transcend nature, and he creates cultural forms which have validity and meaning. Living in these forms, he transforms himself, while originating them. He is not only a tool for their creation; he is at the same time their bearer and the result of their transforming effect upon him. His self-transcendence in this direction is indefinite, while the biological self-transcendence has reached its limits in him. Any step beyond that biological structure which makes intentionality and historicity possible would be a relapse, a false growth, and a destruction of man's power of indefinite cultural self-transcendence. "Super-man," in a biological sense, would be less than man, for man has freedom, and freedom cannot be trespassed biologically.

5. FREEDOM AND DESTINY

The third ontological polarity is that of freedom and destiny, in which the description of the basic ontological structure and its elements reaches both its fulfilment and its turning point. Freedom in polarity with destiny is the structural element which makes existence possible because it transcends the essential necessity of being without destroying it. In view of the immense role the problem of freedom has played in the history of theology, it is surprising to see how little ontological inquiry into the meaning and nature of freedom is carried on by modern theologians, or even how little the results of previous inquiry are used by them, for a concept of freedom is just as important for theology as a concept of reason. Revelation cannot be understood without a concept of freedom.

Man is man because he has freedom, but he has freedom only in polar interdependence with destiny. The term "destiny" is unusual in this context. Ordinarily one speaks of freedom and necessity. However, necessity is a category and not an element. Its contrast is possibility, not freedom. Whenever freedom and necessity are set over against each other, necessity is understood in terms of mechanistic determinacy and freedom is thought of in terms of indeterministic contingency. Neither of these interpretations grasps the structure of being as it is experienced immediately in the one being who has the possibility of experiencing it because he is free, that is, in man. Man experiences the structure of the individual as the bearer of freedom within the larger structures to which the individual structure belongs. Destiny points to this situation in which man finds himself, facing the world to which, at the same time, he belongs.[3]

The methodological perversion of much ontological inquiry is more obvious in the doctrine of freedom than at any other point. The traditional discussion of determinism and indeterminism necessarily is inconclusive because it moves on a level which is secondary to the level on which the polarity of freedom and destiny lies. Both conflicting parties presuppose that there is a *thing* among other things called "will," which may or may not have the quality of freedom. But by definition a *thing* as a completely determined object lacks freedom. The *freedom* of a *thing* is a contradiction in terms. Therefore, determinism always is right in this kind of discussion; but it is right because, in the last analysis, it expresses the tautology that a thing is a thing. Indeterminism protests against the deterministic thesis, pointing to the fact that the moral and the cognitive consciousness presupposes the power of responsible decision. However, when it draws the consequences and attributes freedom to an object or a function called "will," indeterminism falls into a contradiction in terms and inescapably succumbs to the deterministic tautology. Indeterministic freedom is the negation of deterministic necessity. But the negation of necessity never constitutes experienced freedom. It asserts something absolutely contingent, a decision without motivation, an unintelligible accident which is in no way able to do justice to the moral and the cognitive consciousness for the sake of which it is invented. Both determinism and indeterminism are theoretically impossible because by implication they deny their claim to express truth. Truth presupposes a decision for the true against the false. Both determinism and indeterminism make such a decision unintelligible.

Freedom is not the freedom of a function (the "will") but of man, that is, of that being who is not a thing but a complete self and a rational person. It is possible, of course, to call the "will" the personal center and to substitute it for the totality of the self. Voluntaristic psychologies would support such a procedure. But it has proved to be very misleading, as the deadlock in the traditional controversy about freedom indicates. One should speak of the freedom of *man,* indicating that every part and every function which constitutes man a personal self participates in his freedom. This includes even the cells of his body, in so far as they participate in the constitution of his personal center. That which is not centered, that which is isolated from the total process of the self,

3. For further explanation see below.

either by natural or by artificial separation (disease or laboratory situations, for instance), is determined by the mechanism of stimulus and
response or by the dynamism of the relation between the unconscious
and the conscious. However, it is impossible to derive the determinacy
of the whole, including its nonseparated parts, from the determinacy of
isolated parts. Ontologically the whole precedes the parts and gives them
their character as parts of this special whole. It is possible to understand
the determinacy of isolated parts in the light of the freedom of the
whole—namely, as a partial disintegration of the whole—but the converse is not possible.

Freedom is experienced as deliberation, decision, and responsibility.
The etymology of each of these words is revealing. Deliberation points
to an act of weighing (*librare*) arguments and motives. The person who
does the weighing is above the motives; as long as he weighs them, he is
not identical with any of the motives but is free from all of them. To say
that the stronger motive always prevails is an empty tautology, since the
test by which a motive is proved stronger is simply that it prevails. The
self-centered person does the weighing and reacts as a whole, through his
personal center, to the struggle of the motives. This reaction is called
"decision." The word "decision," like the word "incision," involves the
image of cutting. A decision cuts off possibilities, and these were real
possibilities; otherwise no cutting would have been necessary.[4] The person who does the "cutting" or the "excluding" must be beyond what he
cuts off or excludes. His personal center has possibilities, but it is not
identical with any of them. The word "responsibility" points to the
obligation of the person who has freedom to respond if he is questioned
about his decisions. He cannot ask anyone else to answer for him. He
alone must respond, for his acts are determined neither by something
outside him nor by any part of him but by the centered totality of his
being. Each of us is responsible for what has happened through the
center of his self, the seat and organ of his freedom.

In the light of this analysis of freedom the meaning of destiny becomes understandable. Our destiny is that out of which our decisions
arise; it is the indefinitely broad basis of our centered selfhood; it is the
concreteness of our being which makes all our decisions *our* decisions.
When I make a decision, it is the concrete totality of everything that

---

4. In the German word *Ent-Scheidung* the image of *scheiden* ("to separate") is implied, pointing to the fact that in every decision several possibilites are excluded—*aus-
geschieden.*

constitutes my being which decides, not an epistemological subject. This refers to body structure, psychic strivings, spiritual character. It includes the communities to which I belong, the past unremembered and remembered, the environment which has shaped me, the world which has made an impact on me. It refers to all my former decisions. Destiny is not a strange power which determines what shall happen to me. It is myself as given, formed by nature, history, and myself. My destiny is the basis of my freedom; my freedom participates in shaping my destiny.

Only he who has freedom has a destiny. Things have no destiny because they have no freedom. God has no destiny because he *is* freedom. The word "destiny" points to something which is going to happen to someone; it has an eschatological connotation. This makes it qualified to stand in polarity with freedom. It points not to the opposite of freedom but rather to its conditions and limits. *Fatum* ("that which is foreseen") or *Schicksal* ("that which is sent"), and their English correlate "fate," designate a simple contradiction to freedom rather than a polar correlation, and therefore they hardly can be used in connection with the ontological polarity under discussion. But even the deterministic use of these words usually leaves a place for freedom; one has the possibility of accepting his fate or of revolting against it. Strictly speaking, this means that only he who has this alternative has a fate. And to have this alternative means to be free.

Since freedom and destiny constitute an ontological polarity, everything that participates in being must participate in this polarity. But man, who has a complete self and a world, is the only being who is free in the sense of deliberation, decision, and responsibility. Therefore, freedom and destiny can be applied to subhuman nature only by way of analogy; this parallels the situation with respect to the basic ontological structure and the other ontological polarities.

In terms of analogy we may speak of the polarity of spontaneity and law, of which the polarity of freedom and destiny is not only the outstanding example but also the cognitive entrance. An act which originates in the acting self is spontaneous. A reaction to a stimulus is spontaneous if it comes from the centered and self-related whole of a being. This refers not only to living beings but also to inorganic *Gestalten* which react according to their individual structure. Spontaneity is interdependent with law. Law makes spontaneity possible, and law is law only because it determines spontaneous reactions. The term "law" is very revealing in this respect. It is derived from the social sphere and designates an enforceable rule by which a social group is ordered and controlled. Natural laws are based on the rational structure of man and society; therefore, they are unconditionally valid, although the positive laws of social groups may contradict them. If the concept of natural law is applied universally to nature, it designates the structural determinateness of things and events. Nature does not obey—or disobey—laws the way men do; in nature spontaneity is united with law in the way freedom is united with destiny in man. The law of nature does not remove the reactions of self-centered *Gestalten,* but it determines the limits they cannot trespass. Each being acts and reacts according to the law of its self-centered structure and according to the laws of the larger units in which it is included. It is not, however, determined in such a way that its self-relatedness, and consequently its spontaneity, is destroyed. Except in the case of the abstract equations of macrophysics, calculation deals with chance, *not* with determined mechanisms. The chances of verification may be overwhelmingly great, but they are not absolute. The analogy to freedom in all beings makes an absolute determination impossible. The laws of nature are laws for self-centered units with spontaneous reactions. The polarity of freedom and destiny is valid for everything that is.

C. BEING AND FINITUDE

6. BEING AND NONBEING

The question of being is produced by the "shock of nonbeing."[5] Only man can ask the ontological question because he alone is able to look beyond the limits of his own being and of every other being. Looked at from the standpoint of possible nonbeing, being is a mystery. Man is able to take this standpoint because he is free to transcend every given reality. He is not bound to "beingness"; he can envisage nothingness; he can ask the ontological question. In doing so, however, he also must ask a question about that which creates the mystery of being; he must consider the mystery of nonbeing. Both questions have been joined together since the beginning of human thought, first in mythological, then in cosmogonic, and finally in philosophical terms. The way in which the early Greek philosophers, above all, Parmenides, wrestled with the question of nonbeing is most impressive. Parmenides realized that in speaking of nonbeing one gives it some kind of being which contradicts its character as the negation of being. Therefore, he excluded it from rational thought. But in doing so he rendered the realm of becoming un-

5. The term "nonbeing," as used in the following sections, contains the Latin word *non,* which has lost for our feeling the power of the English word "not." The shock of nonbeing is the shock of not being in the sense of a radical negation, in the sense of "being not."

intelligible and evoked the atomistic solution which identifies nonbeing with empty space, thus giving it some kind of being. What kind of being must we attribute to nonbeing? This question never has ceased to fascinate and to exasperate the philosophical mind.

There are two possible ways of trying to avoid the question of nonbeing, the one logical and the other ontological. One can ask whether nonbeing is anything more than the content of a logical judgment—a judgment in which a possible or real assertion is denied. One can assert that nonbeing is a negative judgment devoid of ontological significance. To this we must reply that every logical structure which is more than merely a play with possible relations is rooted in an ontological structure. The very fact of logical denial presupposes a type of being which can transcend the immediately given situation by means of expectations which may be disappointed. An anticipated event does not occur. This means that the judgment concerning the situation has been mistaken, the necessary conditions for the occurrence of the expected event have been nonexistent. Thus disappointed, expectation creates the distinction between being and nonbeing. But how is such an expectation possible in the first place? What is the structure of this being which is able to transcend the given situation and to fall into error? The answer is that man, who is this being, must be separated from his being in a way which enables him to look at it as something strange and questionable. And such a separation is actual because man participates not only in being but also in nonbeing. Therefore, the very structure which makes negative judgments possible proves the ontological character of nonbeing. Unless man participates in nonbeing, no negative judgments are possible; in fact, no judgments of any kind are possible. The mystery of nonbeing cannot be solved by transforming it into a type of logical judgment. The ontological attempt to avoid the mystery of nonbeing follows the strategy of trying to deprive it of its dialectical character. If being and nothingness are placed in absolute contrast, nonbeing is excluded from being in every respect; everything is excluded except being-itself (i.e., the whole world is excluded). There can be no world unless there is a dialectical participation of nonbeing in being. It is not by chance that historically the recent rediscovery of the ontological question has been guided by pre-Socratic philosophy and that systematically there has been an overwhelming emphasis on the problem of nonbeing.[6]

The mystery of nonbeing demands a dialectical approach. The genius

6. See Heidegger's relation to Parmenides and the role of nonbeing both in his philosophy and in that of his existentialist followers.

of the Greek language has provided a possibility of distinguishing the dialectical concept of nonbeing from the nondialectical by calling the first *me on* and the second *ouk on*. *Ouk on* is the "nothing" which has no relation at all to being; *me on* is the "nothing" which has a dialectical relation to being. The Platonic school identified *me on* with that which does not yet have being but which can become being if it is united with essences or ideas. The mystery of nonbeing was not, however, removed, for in spite of its "nothingness" nonbeing was credited with having the power of resisting a complete union with the ideas. The *me-ontic* matter of Platonism represents the dualistic element which underlies all paganism and which is the ultimate ground of the tragic interpretation of life.

Christianity has rejected the concept of *me-ontic* matter on the basis of the doctrine of *creatio ex nihilo*. Matter is not a second principle in addition to God. The *nihil* out of which God creates is *ouk on*, the undialectical negation of being. Yet Christian theologians have had to face the dialectical problem of nonbeing at several points. When Augustine and many theologians and mystics who followed him called sin "nonbeing," they were perpetuating a remnant of the Platonic tradition. They did not mean by this assertion that sin has no reality or that it is a lack of perfect realization, as critics often have misrepresented their view. They meant that sin has no positive ontological standing, while at the same time they interpreted nonbeing in terms of resistance against being and perversion of being. The doctrine of man's creatureliness is another point in the doctrine of man where nonbeing has a dialectical character. Being created out of nothing means having to return to nothing. The stigma of having originated out of nothing is impressed on every creature. This is the reason why Christianity has to reject Arius' doctrine of the Logos as the highest of the creatures. As such he could not have brought eternal life. And this also is the reason why Christianity must reject the doctrine of natural immortality and must affirm instead the doctrine of eternal life given by God as the power of being-itself.

A third point at which theologians have had to face the dialectical problem of nonbeing is the doctrine of God. Here it must be stated immediately that historically it was not the theology of the *via negativa* which drove Christian thinkers to the question of God and nonbeing. The nonbeing of negative theology means "not being anything special," being beyond every concrete predicate. This nonbeing embraces everything; it means being everything; it is being-itself. The dialectical question of nonbeing was and is a problem of affirmative theology. If God is called the living God, if he is the ground of the creative processes of life, if history has significance for him, if there is no negative principle in addition to him which could account for evil and sin, how can one avoid positing a dialectical negativity in God himself? Such questions have forced theologians to relate nonbeing dialectically to being-itself and consequently to God. Böhme's *Ungrund,* Schelling's "first potency," Hegel's "antithesis," the "contingent" and the "given" in God in recent theism, Berdyaev's "meonic freedom,"—all are examples of the problem of dialectical nonbeing exerting influence on the Christian doctrine of God.

Recent existentialism has "encountered nothingness" (Kuhn) in a profound and radical way. Somehow it has replaced being-itself by non-being, giving to nonbeing a positivity and a power which contradict the immediate meaning of the word. Heidegger's "annihilating nothingness" describes man's situation of being threatened by nonbeing in an ultimately inescapable way, that is, by death. The anticipation of nothingness at death gives human existence its existential character. Sartre includes in nonbeing not only the threat of nothingness but also the threat of meaninglessness (i.e., the destruction of the structure of being). In existentialism there is no way of conquering this threat. The only way of dealing with it lies in the courage of taking it upon one's self: courage! As this survey shows, the dialectical problem of nonbeing is inescapable. It is the problem of finitude. Finitude unites being with dialectical nonbeing. Man's finitude, or creatureliness, is unintelligible without the concept of dialectical nonbeing.

7. The Finite and the Infinite

Being, limited by nonbeing, is finitude. Nonbeing appears as the "not yet" of being and as the "no more" of being. It confronts that which is with a definite end (*finis*). This is true of everything except being-itself —which is not a "thing." As the power of being, being-itself cannot have a beginning and an end. Otherwise it would have arisen out of non-being. But nonbeing is literally nothing except in relation to being. Being precedes nonbeing in ontological validity, as the word "nonbeing" itself indicates. Being is the beginning without a beginning, the end without an end. It is its own beginning and end, the initial power of everything that is. However, everything which participates in the power of being is "mixed" with nonbeing. It is being in process of coming from and going toward nonbeing. It is finite.

Both the basic ontological structure and the ontological elements imply finitude. Selfhood, individuality, dynamics, and freedom all include manifoldness, definiteness, differentiation, and limitation. To be something is not to be something else. To be here and now in the process of becoming is not to be there and then. All categories of thought and reality express this situation. To be something is to be finite.

Finitude is experienced on the human level; nonbeing is experienced as the threat to being. The end is anticipated. The process of self-transcendence carries a double meaning in each of its moments. At one and the same time it is an increase and a decrease in the power of being. In order to experience his finitude, man must look at himself from the point of view of a potential infinity. In order to be aware of moving toward death, man must look out over his finite being as a whole; he must in some way be beyond it. He must also be able to imagine infinity; and he is able to do so, although not in concrete terms, but only as an abstract possibility. The finite self faces a world; the finite individual has the power of universal participation; man's vitality is united with an essentially unlimited intentionality; as finite freedom he is involved in an embracing destiny. All the structures of finitude force finite being to transcend itself and, just for this reason, to become aware of itself as finite.

According to this analysis, infinity is related to finitude in a different way than the other polar elements are related to one another. As the negative character of the word indicates, it is defined by the dynamic and free self-transcendence of finite being. Infinity is a directing concept, not a constituting concept. It directs the mind to experience its own unlimited potentialities, but it does not establish the existence of an infinite being. On this basis it is possible to understand the classical antinomies regarding the finite and the infinite character of the world. Even a physical doctrine of the finitude of space cannot keep the mind from asking what lies behind finite space. This is a self-contradictory question; yet it is inescapable. On the other hand, it is impossible to say that the world is infinite because infinity never is given as an object. Infinity is a demand, not a thing. This is the stringency of Kant's solution of the antinomies between the finite and the infinite character of time and space. Since neither time nor space is a thing, but both are forms of things, it is possible to transcend every finite time and every finite space without exception. But this does not establish an infinite thing in an infinite time and space. The human mind can keep going endlessly by transcending finite realities in the macrocosmic or in the microcosmic direction. But the mind itself remains bound to the finitude of its individual bearer. Infinitude is finitude transcending itself without any a priori limit.

The power of infinite self-transcendence is an expression of man's belonging to that which is beyond nonbeing, namely, to being-itself. The potential presence of the infinite (as unlimited self-transcendence) is the negation of the negative element in finitude. It is the negation of nonbeing. The fact that man never is satisfied with any stage of his finite development, the fact that nothing finite can hold him, although finitude is his destiny, indicates the indissoluble relation of everything finite to being-itself. Being-itself is not infinity; it is that which lies beyond the polarity of finitude and infinite self-transcendence. Being-itself manifests itself to finite being in the infinite drive of the finite beyond itself. But being-itself cannot be identified with infinity, that is, with the negation of finitude. It precedes the finite, and it precedes the infinite negation of the finite.

Finitude in awareness is anxiety. Like finitude, anxiety is an ontological quality. It cannot be derived; it can only be seen and described. Occasions in which anxiety is aroused must be distinguished from anxiety itself. As an ontological quality, anxiety is as omnipresent as is finitude. Anxiety is independent of any special object which might produce it; it is dependent only on the threat of nonbeing—which is identical with finitude. In this sense it has been said rightly that the object of anxiety is "nothingness"—and nothingness is not an "object." Objects are feared. A danger, a pain, an enemy, may be feared, but fear can be conquered by action. Anxiety cannot, for no finite being can conquer its finitude. Anxiety is always present, although often it is latent. Therefore, it can become manifest at any and every moment, even in situations where nothing is to be feared.[7]

The recovery of the meaning of anxiety through the combined endeavors of existential philosophy, depth psychology, neurology, and the arts is one of the achievements of the twentieth century. It has become clear that fear as related to a definite object and anxiety as the awareness of finitude are two radically different concepts. Anxiety is ontological; fear, psychological.[8] Anxiety is an ontological concept because it ex-

7. Psychotherapy cannot remove ontological anxiety, because it cannot change the structure of finitude. But it can remove compulsory forms of anxiety and can reduce the frequency and intensity of fears. It can put anxiety "in its proper place."

8. The English word "anxiety" has received the connotation of *Angst* only during the past decade. Both *Angst* and anxiety are derived from the Latin word *angustiae*, which

presses finitude from "inside." Here it must be said that there is no reason for preferring concepts taken from "outside" to those taken from "inside." According to the self-world structure, both types are equally valid. The self being aware of itself and the self looking at its world (including itself) are equally significant for the description of the ontological structure. Anxiety is the self-awarness of the finite self as finite. The fact that it has a strongly emotional character does not remove its revealing power. The emotional element simply indicates that the totality of the finite being participates in finitude and faces the threat of nothingness. It would seem adequate, therefore, to give a description of finitude from both outside and inside, pointing to the special form of anxious awareness which corresponds to whatever special form of finitude is under consideration.

8. Finitude and the Categories

Categories are the forms in which the mind grasps and shapes reality. To speak of something reasonably is to speak of it by means of the categorical forms, through "ways of speaking" which are also the forms of being. The categories are to be distinguished from logical forms which determine discourse but which are only indirectly related to reality itself. The logical forms are formal in that they abstract from the content to which the discourse refers. The categories, on the other hand, are forms which determine content. They are ontological, and therefore they are present in everything. The mind is not able to experience reality except through the categorical forms. These forms are used in religious as well as in secular speech. They appear implicitly or explicitly in every thought concerning God and the world, man and nature. They are omnipresent, even in that realm from which they are excluded by definition, that is, in the realm of the "unconditional." Therefore, systematic theology must deal with them, of course not in terms of a developed system of categories but in a way which shows their significance for the question of God, the question to which the entire ontological analysis leads.

The categories reveal their ontological character through their double relation to being and to nonbeing. They express being, but at the same time they express the nonbeing to which everything that is, is subject. The categories are forms of finitude; as such they unite an affirmative

---

means "narrows." Anxiety is experienced in the narrows of threatening nothingness. Therefore, anxiety should not be replaced by the word "dread," which points to a sudden reaction to a danger but not to the ontological situation of facing nonbeing.

and a negative element. The ontological task which prepares the way for the theological question, the question of God, is an analysis of this duality. In dealing with the four main categories—time, space, causality, substance—we must in each case consider not only the positive and the negative elements "from the outside," namely, in relation to the world, but we must consider them also "from the inside," namely, in relation to the self. Each category expresses not only a union of being and nonbeing but also a union of anxiety and courage.

Time is the central category of finitude. Every philosopher has been fascinated and embarrassed by its mysterious character. Some philosophers emphasize the negative element; others, the positive element. The former point to the transitoriness of everything temporal and to the impossibility of fixing the present moment within a flux of time which never stands still. They point to the movement of time from a past that is no more toward a future that is not yet through a present which is nothing more than the moving boundary line between past and future. To be means to be present. But if the present is illusory, being is conquered by nonbeing.

Those who emphasize the positive element in time have pointed to the creative character of the temporal process, to its directness and irreversibility, to the new produced within it. But neither group has been able to maintain an exclusive emphasis. It is impossible to call the present illusory, for it is only in the power of an experienced present that past and future and the movement from the one to the other can be measured. On the other hand, it is impossible to overlook the fact that time "swallows" what it has created, that the new becomes old and vanishes, and that creative evolution is accompanied in every moment by destructive disintegration. Ontology can only state a balance between the positive and the negative character of time. A decision concerning the meaning of time cannot be derived from an analysis of time.

As experienced in immediate self-awareness, time unites the anxiety of transitoriness with the courage of a self-affirming present. The melancholy awareness of the trend of being toward nonbeing, a theme which fills the literature of all nations, is most actual in the anticipation of one's own death. What is significant here is not the fear of death, that is, the moment of dying. It is anxiety about *having* to die which reveals the ontological character of time. In the anxiety of having to die nonbeing is experienced from "the inside." This anxiety is potentially present in every moment. It permeates the whole of man's being; it shapes soul and body and determines spiritual life; it belongs to the created character of being quite apart from estrangement and sin. It is actual in "Adam" (i.e., man's essential nature) as well as in "Christ" (i.e., man's new reality). The biblical record points to the profound anxiety of having to die in him who was called the Christ. We repeat, anxiety about transitoriness, about being delivered to the negative side of temporality, is rooted in the structure of being and not in a distortion of this structure.

This anxiety concerning temporal existence is possible only because it is balanced by a courage which affirms temporality. Without this courage man would surrender to the annihilating character of time; he would resign from having a present. Yet man affirms the present moment, though analytically it seems unreal, and he defends it against the anxiety its transitoriness creates in him. He affirms the present through an ontological courage which is as genuine as his anxiety about the time process. This courage is effective in all beings, but it is radically and consciously effective only in man, who is able to anticipate his end. Therefore, man needs the greatest courage to take upon himself his anxiety. He is the most courageous of all beings because he has to conquer the deepest anxiety. It is hardest for him to affirm the present because he is able to imagine a future which is not yet his own and to remember a past which is no longer his own. He must defend his present against the vision of an infinite past and of an infinite future; he is excluded from both. Man cannot escape the question of the ultimate foundation of his ontological courage.

The present always involves man's presence in it, and presence means having something present to one's self over against one's self (in German, *gegenwaertig*). The present implies space. Time creates the present through its union with space. In this union time comes to a standstill because there is something on which to stand. Like time, space unites being with nonbeing, anxiety with courage. Like time, space is subject to contradictory valuations, for it is a category of finitude. To be means to have space. Every being strives to provide and to preserve space for itself. This means above all a physical location—the body, a piece of soil, a home, a city, a country, the world. It also means a social "space"— a vocation, a sphere of influence, a group, a historical period, a place in remembrance and anticipation, a place within a structure of values and meanings. Not to have space is not to be. Thus in all realms of life striving for space is an ontological necessity. It is a consequence of the spatial character of finite being and a quality of created goodness. It is finitude, not guilt.

But to be spatial also means to be subject to nonbeing. No finite being possesses a space which is definitely its own. No finite being can rely on space, for not only must it face losing this or that space because it is a "pilgrim on earth," but eventually it must face losing every place it has had or might have had. As the powerful symbol used by Job and the psalmist expresses it: "Its place knoweth it no more." There is no necessary relationship between any place and the being which has provided this space for itself. Finitude means having no definite place; it means having to lose every place finally and, with it, to lose being itself. This threat of nonbeing cannot be escaped by means of a flight into time without space. Without space there is neither presence nor a present. And, conversely, the loss of space includes the loss of temporal presence, the loss of the present, the loss of being.

To have no definite and no final space means ultimate insecurity. To be finite is to be insecure. This is experienced in man's anxiety about tomorrow; it is expressed in anxious attempts to provide a secure space for himself, physically and socially. Every life-process has this character. The desire for security becomes dominant in special periods and in special social and psychological situations. Men create systems of security in order to protect their space. But they can only repress their anxiety; they cannot banish it, for this anxiety anticipates the final "spacelessness" which is implied in finitude.

On the other hand, man's anxiety about having to lose his space is balanced by the courage with which he affirms the present and, with it, space. Everything affirms the space which it has within the universe. As long as it lives, it successfully resists the anxiety of not-having-a-place. It courageously faces the occasions when not-having-a-place becomes an actual threat. It accepts its ontological insecurity and reaches a security in this acceptance. Yet it cannot escape the question how such courage is possible. How can a being which cannot be without space accept both preliminary and final spacelessness?

Causality also has a direct bearing on religious symbolism and on theological interpretation. Like time and space, it is ambiguous. It expresses both being and nonbeing. It affirms the power of being by pointing to that which precedes a thing or event as its source. If something is causally explained, its reality is affirmed, and the power of its resistance against nonbeing is understood. The cause makes its effect real, in thought as well as in reality. To look for causes means to look for the power of being in a thing.

This affirmative meaning of causality, however, is the reverse side of its negative meaning. The question of the cause of a thing or event presupposes that it does not possess its own power of coming into being. Things and events have no aseity. This is characteristic only of God. Finite things are not self-caused; they have been "thrown" into being (Heidegger). The question, "Where from?" is universal. Children as well as philosophers ask it. But it cannot be answered, for every answer, every statement, about the cause of something is open to the same question in endless regression. It cannot be stopped even by a god who is supposed to be the answer to the entire series. For this god must ask himself, "Where have I come from?" (Kant). Even a highest being must ask the question of its own cause, indicating thereby its partial nonbeing. Causality expresses by implication the inability of anything to rest on itself. Everything is driven beyond itself to its cause, and the cause is driven beyond itself to its cause, and so on indefinitely. Causality powerfully expresses the abyss of nonbeing in everything.

The causal scheme must not be identified with a deterministic scheme. Causality is removed neither by the indeterminacy of subatomic processes nor by the creative character of biological and psychological processes. Nothing in these realms occurs without a preceding situation or constellation which is its cause. Nothing has the power of depending on itself without a causal nexus; nothing is "absolute." Even finite creativity cannot escape that form of nonbeing which appears in causality. If we look at a thing and ask what it is, we must look beyond it and ask what its causes are.

The anxiety in which causality is experienced is that of not being in, of, and by one's self, of not having the "aseity" which theology traditionally attributes to God. Man is a creature. His being is contingent; by itself it has no necessity, and therefore man realizes that he is the prey of nonbeing. The same contingency which has thrown man into existence may push him out of it. In this respect causality and contingent being are the same thing. The fact that man is causally determined makes his being contingent with respect to himself. The anxiety in which he is aware of this situation is anxiety about the lack of necessity of his being. He might not be! Then why is he? And why should he continue to be? There is no reasonable answer. This is exactly the anxiety implied in the awareness of causality as a category of finitude.

Courage accepts derivedness, contingency. The man who possesses this courage does not look beyond himself to that from which he comes, but he rests in himself. Courage ignores the causal dependence of everything finite. Without this courage no life would be possible, but the question how this courage is possible remains. How can a being who is dependent on the causal nexus and its contingencies accept this dependence and, at the same time, attribute to himself a necessity and self-reliance which contradict this dependence?

The fourth category which describes the union of being and nonbeing in everything finite is substance. In contrast to causality, substance points to something underlying the flux of appearances, something which is relatively static and self-contained. There is no substance without accidents. The accidents receive their ontological power from the substance to which they belong. But the substance is nothing beyond the accidents in which it expresses itself. So in both substance and accidents the positive element is balanced by the negative element.

The problem of substance is not avoided by philosophers of function or process, because questions about that which *has* functions or about that which *is* in process cannot be silenced. The replacement of static notions by dynamic ones does not remove the question of that which makes change possible by not (relatively) changing itself. Substance as a category is effective in any encounter of mind and reality; it is present whenever one speaks of some*thing*.

Therefore, everything finite is innately anxious that its substance will be lost. This anxiety refers to continuous change as well as to the final loss of substance. Every change reveals the relative nonbeing of that which changes. The changing reality lacks substantiality, the power of being, the resistance against nonbeing. It is this anxiety which drove the Greeks to ask insistently and ceaselessly the question of the unchangeable. To dismiss the question with the correct assertion that the static has neither a logical nor an ontological priority over the dynamic is not justifiable, for this anxiety about change is anxiety about the threat of nonbeing implied in change. It is manifest in all great changes of personal and social life, which produce a kind of individual or social dizziness, a feeling that the ground on which the person or group has stood is being taken away, that self-identity or group identity is being destroyed. This anxiety reaches its most radical form in the anticipation of the final loss of substance—and accidents as well. The human experience of having to die anticipates the complete loss of identity with one's self. Questions about an immortal substance of the soul express the profound anxiety connected with this anticipation.

The question of the unchangeable in our being, like the question of the unchangeable in being-itself, is an expression of the anxiety of losing substance and identity. To dismiss this question with the correct assertion that the arguments for the so-called immortality of the soul are wrong, that they are attempts to escape the seriousness of the question of substantiality by establishing an endless continuation of what is essentially finite, is unjustified. The question of unchangeable substance cannot be silenced. It expresses the anxiety implied in the always threatening loss of substance, that is, of identity with one's self and the power of maintaining one's self.

Courage accepts the threat of losing individual substance and the substance of being generally. Man attributes substantiality to something which proves ultimately to be accidental—a creative work, a love relation, a concrete situation, himself. This is not a self-elevation of the finite, but rather it is the courage of affirming the finite, of taking one's anxiety upon himself. The question is how such a courage is possible. How can a finite being, aware of the inescapable loss of his substance, accept this loss?

The four categories are four aspects of finitude in its positive and negative elements. They express the union of being and nonbeing in everything finite. They articulate the courage which accepts the anxiety of nonbeing. The question of God is the question of the possibility of this courage.

9. FINITUDE AND THE ONTOLOGICAL ELEMENTS

Finitude is actual not only in the categories but also in the ontological elements. Their polar character opens them to the threat of nonbeing. In every polarity each pole is limited as well as sustained by the other one. A complete balance between them presupposes a balanced whole. But such a whole is not given. There are special structures in which, under the impact of finitude, polarity becomes tension. Tension refers to the tendency of elements within a unity to draw away from one another, to attempt to move in opposite directions. For Heraclitus everything is in inner tension like a bent bow, for in everything there is a tendency downward (earth) balanced by a tendency upward (fire). In his view nothing whatever is produced by a process which moves in one direction only; everything is an embracing but transitory unity of two opposite processes. Things are hypostasized tensions.

Our own ontological tension comes to awareness in the anxiety of losing our ontological structure through losing one or another polar element and, consequently, the polarity to which it belongs. This anxiety is not the same as that mentioned in connection with the categories, namely, the anxiety of nonbeing simply and directly. It is the anxiety of not being what we essentially are. It is anxiety about disintegrating and falling into nonbeing through existential disruption. It is anxiety about the breaking of the ontological tensions and the consequent destruction of the ontological structure.

This can be seen in terms of each of the polar elements. Finite individualization produces a dynamic tension with finite participation; the break of their unity is a possibility. Self-relatedness produces the threat of a loneliness in which world and communion are lost. On the other hand, being in the world and participating in it produces the threat of a complete collectivization, a loss of individuality and subjectivity whereby the self loses its self-relatedness and is transformed into a mere part of an embracing whole. Man as finite is anxiously aware of this twofold threat. Anxiously he experiences the trend from possible loneliness to collectivity and from possible collectivity to loneliness. He oscillates anxiously between individualization and participation, aware of the fact that he ceases to be if one of the poles is lost, for the loss of either pole means the loss of both.

The tension between finite individualization and finite participation is the basis of many psychological and sociological problems, and for this reason it is a very important subject of research for depth psychology and depth sociology. Philosophy often has overlooked the question of essential solitude and its relation to existential loneliness and self-seclusion. It also has overlooked the question of essential belongingness and its relation to existential self-surrender to the collective. The merit of existential thinking in all centuries, but especially since Pascal, is that it has rediscovered the ontological basis of the tension between loneliness and belongingness.

Finitude also transforms the polarity of dynamics and form into a tension which produces the threat of a possible break and anxiety about this threat. Dynamics drives toward form, in which being is actual and has the power of resisting nonbeing. But at the same time dynamics is threatened because it may lose itself in rigid forms, and, if it tries to break through them, the result may be chaos, which is the loss of both dynamics and form. Human vitality tends to embody itself in cultural creations, forms, and institutions through the exercise of creative intentionality. But every embodiment endangers the vital power precisely by giving it actual being. Man is anxious about the threat of a final form in which his vitality will be lost, and he is anxious about the threat of a chaotic formlessness in which both vitality and intentionality will be lost.

There is abundant witness to this tension in literature from Greek tragedy to the present day, but it has not been given sufficient attention in philosophy except in the "philosophy of life" or in theology except by some Protestant mystics. Philosophy has emphasized the rational structure of things but has neglected the creative process through which things and events come into being. Theology has emphasized the divine "law" and has confused creative vitality with the destructive separation of vitality from intentionality. Philosophical rationalism and theological legalism have prevented a full recognition of the tension between dynamics and form.

Finally, finitude transforms the polarity of freedom and destiny into a tension which produces the threat of a possible break and its consequent anxiety. Man is threatened with the loss of freedom by the necessities implied in his destiny, and he is equally threatened with the loss of his destiny by the contingencies implied in his freedom. He is continuously in danger of trying to preserve his freedom by arbitrarily defying his destiny and of trying to save his destiny by surrendering his freedom. He is embarrassed by the demand that he make decisions implied in his freedom, because he realizes that he lacks the complete cognitive and active unity with his destiny which should be the foundation of his decisions. And he is afraid of accepting his destiny without reservations, because he realizes that his decision will be partial, that he will accept only a part of his destiny, and that he will fall under a special determination which is not identical with his real destiny. So he tries to save his freedom by arbitrariness, and then he is in danger of losing both his freedom and his destiny.

The traditional discussion between determinism and indeterminism concerning "freedom of the will" is an "objectified" form of the ontological tension between freedom and destiny. Both partners in this discussion defend an ontological element without which being could not be conceived. Therefore, they are right in what they affirm but wrong in what they negate. The determinist does not see that the very affirmation of determinism as true presupposes the freedom of decision between true and false, and the indeterminist does not see that the very potentiality of making decisions presupposes a personality structure which includes destiny. Speaking pragmatically, people always act as if they consider one another to be free and to be destined simultaneously. No one ever treats a man either as a mere locus of a series of contingent actions or as a mechanism in which calculable effects follow from calculated causes. Man always considers man—including himself—in terms of a unity of freedom and destiny. The fact that finite man is threatened with the loss of one side of the polarity—and consequently with the loss of the other, since loss of either side destroys the polarity as a whole—only confirms the essential character of the ontological structure.

To lose one's destiny is to lose the meaning of one's being. Destiny is not a meaningless fate. It is necessity united with meaning. The threat of possible meaninglessness is a social as well as an individual reality. There are periods in social life, as well as in personal life, during which this threat is especially acute. Our present situation is characterized by a profound and desperate feeling of meaninglessness. Individuals and groups have lost any faith they may have had in their destiny as well as any love of it. The question, "What for?" is cynically dismissed. Man's essential anxiety about the possible loss of his destiny has been transformed into an existential despair about destiny as such. Accordingly, freedom has been declared an absolute, separate from destiny (Sartre). But absolute freedom in a finite being becomes arbitrariness and falls under biological and psychological necessities. The loss of a meaningful destiny involves the loss of freedom also.

Finitude is the possibility of losing one's ontological structure and, with it, one's self. But this is a possibility, not a necessity. To be finite is to be threatened. But a threat is possibility, not actuality. The anxiety of finitude is not the despair of self-destruction. Christianity sees in the picture of Jesus as the Christ a human life in which all forms of anxiety are present but in which all forms of despair are absent. In the light of this picture it is possible to distinguish "essential" finitude from "existential" disruption, ontological anxiety from the anxiety of guilt which is despair.[9]

9. The material discussed in this chapter is by no means complete. Poetic, scientific, and religious psychology have made available an almost unmanageable amount of material concerning finitude and anxiety. The purpose of this analysis is to give only an ontological description of the structures underlying all these facts and to point to some outstanding confirmations of the analysis.

10. Essential and Existential Being

Finitude, in correlation with infinity, is a quality of being in the same sense as the basic structure and the polar elements. It characterizes being in its essential nature. Being is essentially related to nonbeing; the categories of finitude indicate this. And being is essentially threatened with disruption and self-destruction; the tensions of the ontological elements under the condition of finitude indicate this. But being is not essentially in a state of disruption and self-destruction. The tension between the elements does not necessarily lead to the threatened break. Since the ontological structure of being includes the polarity of freedom and destiny, nothing ontologically relevant can happen to being that is not mediated by the unity of freedom and destiny. Of course, the breaking of the ontological tensions is not a matter of accident; it is universal and is dependent on destiny. But, on the other hand, it is not a matter of structural necessity; it is mediated by freedom.

Philosophical and theological thought, therefore, cannot escape making a distinction between essential and existential being. In every philosophy there is an indication, sometimes only implicit, of an awareness of this distinction. Whenever the ideal is held against the real, truth against error, good against evil, a distortion of essential being is presupposed and is judged by essential being. It does not matter how the appearance of such a distortion is explained in terms of causality. If it is acknowledged as distortion—and even the most radical determinist accuses his opponent of an (unconscious) distortion of the truth which he himself defends—the question of the possibility of such a distortion is raised in ontological terms. How can being, including within it the whole of its actuality, contain its own distortion? This question is always present even though it is not always asked. But, if it is asked, every answer openly or secretly points to the classical distinction between the essential and the existential.

Both of these terms are very ambiguous. Essence can mean the nature of a thing without any valuation of it, it can mean the universals which characterize a thing, it can mean the ideas in which existing things participate, it can mean the norm by which a thing must be judged, it can mean the original goodness of everything created, and it can mean the patterns of all things in the divine mind. The basic ambiguity, however, lies in the oscillation of the meaning between an empirical and a valuating sense. Essence as the nature of a thing, or as the quality in which a thing participates, or as a universal, has one character. Essence as that from which being has "fallen," the true and undistorted nature of things, has another character. In the second case essence is the basis of value judgments, while in the first case essence is a logical ideal to be reached by abstraction or intuition without the interference of valuations. How can the same word cover both meanings? Why has this ambiguity persisted in philosophy since Plato? The answer to both questions lies in the ambiguous character of existence, which expresses being and at the same time contradicts it—essence as that which makes a thing *what* it is (*ousia*) has a purely logical character; essence as that which appears in an imperfect and distorted way in a thing carries the stamp of value. Essence empowers *and* judges that which exists. It gives it its power of being, and, at the same time, it stands against it as commanding law. Where essence and existence are united, there is neither law nor judgment. But existence is not united with essence; therefore, law stands against all things, and judgment is actual in self-destruction.

Existence also is used with different meanings. It can mean the possibility of finding a thing within the whole of being, it can mean the actuality of what is potential in the realm of essences, it can mean the "fallen world," and it can mean a type of thinking which is aware of its existential conditions or which rejects essence entirely. Again, an unavoidable ambiguity justifies the use of this one word in these different senses. Whatever exists, that is, "stands out" of mere potentiality, is more than it is in the state of mere potentiality and less than it could be in the power of its essential nature. In some philosophers, notably Plato, the negative judgment on existence prevails. The good is identical with the essential, and existence does not add anything. In other philosophers, notably Ockham, the positive judgment prevails. All reality exists, and the essential is nothing more than the reflex of existence in the human mind. The good is the self-expression of the highest existent—God—and it is imposed on the other existents from outside them. In a third group of philosophers, notably Aristotle, a mediating attitude prevails. The actual is the real, but the essential provides its power of being, and in the highest essence potentiality and actuality are one.

Christian theology always has used the distinction between essential and existential being and predominantly in a way which is nearer to Aristotle than to Plato or Ockham. This is not surprising. In contrast to Plato, Christianity emphasizes existence in terms of creation through God, not through a demiurge. Existence is the fulfilment of creation;

existence gives creation its positive character. In contrast to Ockham, Christianity has emphasized the split between the created goodness of things and their distorted existence. But the good is not considered an arbitrary commandment imposed by an all-powerful existent on the other existents. It is the essential structure of reality.

Christianity must take the middle road wherever it deals with the problem of being. And it *must* deal with the problem of being, for, although essence and existence are philosophical terms, the experience and the vision behind them precede philosophy. They appeared in mythology and poetry long before philosophy dealt with them rationally. Consequently, theology does not surrender its independence when it uses philosophical terms which are analogous to terms which religion has used for ages in prerational, imaginative language.

The preceding considerations are preliminary and definitory; only by implication are they more than this. A complete discussion of the relation of essence to existence is identical with the entire theological system. The distinction between essence and existence, which religiously speaking is the distinction between the created and the actual world, is the backbone of the whole body of theological thought. It must be elaborated in every part of the theological system.

D. HUMAN FINITUDE AND THE QUESTION OF GOD

11. THE POSSIBILITY OF THE QUESTION OF GOD AND THE SO-CALLED ONTOLOGICAL ARGUMENT

It is a remarkable fact that for many centuries leading theologians and philosophers were almost equally divided between those who attacked and those who defended the arguments for the existence of God. Neither group prevailed over the other in a final way. This situation admits only one explanation: the one group did not attack what the other group defended. They were not divided by a conflict over the same matter. They fought over different matters which they expressed in the same terms. Those who attacked the arguments for the existence of God criticized their argumentative form; those who defended them accepted their implicit meaning.

There can be little doubt that the arguments are a failure in so far as they claim to be arguments. Both the concept of existence and the method of arguing to a conclusion are inadequate for the idea of God. However it is defined, the "existence of God" contradicts the idea of a creative ground of essence and existence. The ground of being cannot be found within the totality of beings, nor can the ground of essence and existence participate in the tensions and disruptions characteristic of the transition from essence to existence. The scholastics were right when they asserted that in God there is no difference between essence and existence. But they perverted their insight when in spite of this assertion they spoke of the existence of God and tried to argue in favor of it. Actually they did not mean "existence." They meant the reality, the validity, the truth of the idea of God, an idea which did not carry the connotation of some*thing* or some*one* who might or might not exist. Yet this is the way in which the idea of God is understood today in scholarly as well as in popular discussions about the "existence of God." It would be a great victory for Christian apologetics if the words "God" and "existence" were very definitely separated except in the paradox of God becoming manifest under the conditions of existence, that is, in the christological paradox. God does not exist. He is being-itself beyond essence and existence. Therefore, to argue that God exists is to deny him.

The method of arguing through a conclusion also contradicts the idea of God. Every argument derives conclusions from something that is given about something that is sought. In arguments for the existence of God the world is given and God is sought. Some characteristics of the world make the conclusion "God" necessary. God is derived from the world. This does not mean that God is dependent on the world. Thomas Aquinas is correct when he rejects such an interpretation and asserts that what is first in itself may be last for our knowledge. But, if we derive God from the world, he cannot be that which transcends the world infinitely. He is the "missing link," discovered by correct conclusions. He is the uniting force between the *res cogitans* and the *res extensa* (Descartes), or the end of the causal regression in answer to the question, "Where from?" (Thomas Aquinas), or the teleological intelligence directing the meaningful processes of reality—if not identical with these processes (Whitehead). In each of these cases God is "world," a missing part of that from which he is derived in terms of conclusions. This contradicts the idea of God as thoroughly as does the concept of existence. The arguments for the existence of God neither are arguments nor are they proof of the existence of God. They are expressions of the *question* of God which is implied in human finitude. This question is their truth; every answer they give is untrue. This is the sense in which theology must deal with these arguments, which are the solid body of any natural theology. It must deprive them of their argumentative character, and it must eliminate the combination of the words "existence" and "God." If this is accomplished, natural theology becomes the elaboration of the question of God; it ceases to be the answer to this question. The following interpretations are to be understood in this sense. The arguments for the existence of God analyze the human situation in such a way that the question of God appears possible and necessary.

The question of God is possible because an awareness of God is present in the question of God. This awareness precedes the question. It is not the result of the argument but its presupposition. This certainly means that the "argument" is no argument at all. The so-called ontological argument points to the ontological structure of finitude. It shows that an awareness of the infinite is included in man's awareness of finitude. Man knows that he is finite, that he is excluded from an infinity which nevertheless belongs to him. He is aware of his potential infinity while being aware of his actual finitude. If he were what he essentially is, if his potentiality were identical with his actuality, the question of the infinite would not arise. Mythologically speaking, Adam before the fall was in an essential, though untested and undecided, unity with God. But this is not man's situation, nor is it the situation of anything that exists. Man must ask about the infinite from which he is estranged, although it belongs to him; he must ask about that which gives him the courage to take his anxiety upon himself. And he can ask this double question because the awareness of his potential infinity is included in his awareness of his finitude.

The ontological argument in its various forms gives a description of the way in which potential infinity is present in actual finitude. As far as the description goes, that is, as far as it is analysis and not argument, it is valid. The presence within finitude of an element which transcends it is experienced both theoretically and practically. The theoretical side has been elaborated by Augustine, the practical side by Kant, and behind both of them stands Plato. Neither side has constructed an argument for the reality of God, but all elaborations have shown the presence of something unconditional within the self and the world. Unless such an element were present, the question of God never could have been asked, nor could an answer, even the answer of revelation, have been received.

The unconditional element appears in the theoretical (receiving) functions of reason as *verum ipsum*, the true-itself as the norm of all approximations to truth. The unconditional element appears in the practical (shaping) functions of reason as *bonum ipsum,* the good-itself as the norm of all approximations to goodness. Both are manifestations of *esse ipsum,* being-itself as the ground and abyss of everything that is.

Augustine, in his refutation of skepticism, has shown that the skeptic acknowledges and emphasizes the absolute element in truth in his denial of the possibility of a true judgment. He becomes a skeptic precisely because he strives for an absoluteness from which he is excluded. *Veritas ipsa* is acknowledged and sought for by no one more passionately than by the skeptic. Kant has shown in an analogous way that relativism with respect to ethical content presupposes an absolute respect for ethical form, the categorical imperative, and an acknowledgment of the unconditional validity of the ethical command. *Bonum ipsum* is independent of any judgment about the *bona.* Up to this point Augustine and Kant cannot be refuted, for they do not argue; they point to the unconditional element in every encounter with reality. But both Augustine and Kant go beyond this safe analysis. They derive from it a concept of God which is more than *esse ipsum, verum ipsum,* and *bonum ipsum,* more than an analytical dimension in the structure of reality. Augustine simply identifies *verum ipsum* with the God of the church, and Kant tries to derive a lawgiver and a guarantor of the co-ordination between morality and happiness from the unconditional character of the ethical command. In both cases the starting point is right, but the conclusion is wrong. The experience of an unconditional element in man's encounter with reality is used for the establishment of an unconditional being (a contradiction in terms) within reality.

The Anselmian statement that God is a necessary thought and that therefore this idea must have objective as well as subjective reality is valid in so far as thinking, by its very nature, implies an unconditional element which transcends subjectivity and objectivity, that is, a point of identity which makes the idea of truth possible. However, the statement is not valid if this unconditional element is understood as a highest being called God. The existence of such a highest being is not implied in the idea of truth.

The same must be said of the many forms of the moral argument. They are valid in so far as they are ontological analyses (not arguments) in moral disguise, that is, ontological analyses of the unconditional element in the moral imperative. The concept of the moral world order which often has been used in this connection tries to express the unconditional character of the moral command in the face of the processes of nature and history which seem to contradict it. It points to the foundation of the moral principles in the ground of being, in being-itself. But no "divine co-ordinator" can be derived in this way. The ontological basis of the moral principles and their unconditional character cannot be used for the establishment of a highest being. *Bonum ipsum* does not imply the existence of a highest being.

The limits of the ontological argument are obvious. But nothing is more important for philosophy and theology than the truth it contains, the acknowledgment of the unconditional element in the structure of reason and reality. The idea of a theonomous culture, and with it the possibility of a philosophy of religion, is dependent on this insight. A philosophy of religion which does not begin with something unconditional never reaches God. Modern secularism is rooted largely in the fact that the unconditional element in the structure of reason and reality no longer was seen and that therefore the idea of God was imposed on the mind as a "strange body." This produced first heteronomous subjection and then autonomous rejection. The destruction of the ontological *argument* is not dangerous. What is dangerous is the destruction of an approach which elaborates the possibility of the question of God. This approach is the meaning and truth of the ontological argument.

12. The Necessity of the Question of God and the So-called Cosmological Arguments

The question of God *can* be asked because there is an unconditional element in the very act of asking any question. The question of God *must* be asked because the threat of nonbeing, which man experiences as anxiety, drives him to the question of being conquering nonbeing and of courage conquering anxiety. This question is the cosmological question of God.

The so-called cosmological and teleological arguments for the existence of God are the traditional and inadequate form of this question. In all their variations these arguments move from special characteristics of the world to the existence of a highest being. They are valid in so far as they give an analysis of reality which indicates that the cosmological question of God is unavoidable. They are not valid in so far as they claim that the existence of a highest being is the logical conclusion of their analysis, which is as impossible logically, as it is impossible existentially to derive courage from anxiety.

The cosmological method of arguing for the existence of God has taken two main paths. It has moved from the finitude of being to an infinite being (the cosmological argument in the narrower sense), and it has moved from the finitude of meaning to a bearer of infinite meaning (the teleological argument in the traditional sense). In both cases the cosmological question comes out of the element of nonbeing in beings and meanings. No question of God would arise if there were no logical and noological (relating to meaning) threat of nonbeing, for then being would be safe; religiously speaking, God would be present in it.

The first form of the cosmological argument is determined by the categorical structure of finitude. From the endless chain of causes and effects it arrives at the conclusion that there is a first cause, and from the contingency of all substances it concludes that there is a necessary substance. But cause and substance are categories of finitude. The "first cause" is a hypostasized question, not a statement about a being which initiates the causal chain. Such a being would itself be a part of the causal chain and would again raise the question of cause. In the same way, a "necessary substance" is a hypostasized question, not a statement about a being which gives substantiality to all substances. Such a being would itself be a substance with accidents and would again open the question of substantiality itself. When used as material for "arguments," both categories lose their categorical character. First cause and necessary substance are symbols which express the question implied in finite being, the question of that which transcends finitude and categories, the question of being-itself embracing and conquering nonbeing, the question of God.

The cosmological question of God is the question about that which ultimately makes courage possible, a courage which accepts and overcomes the anxiety of categorical finitude. We have analyzed the labile balance between anxiety and courage in relation to time, space, causality, and substance. In each case we finally have come face to face with the question how the courage which resists the threat of nonbeing implied in these categories is possible. Finite being includes courage, but it cannot maintain courage against the ultimate threat of nonbeing. It needs a basis for ultimate courage. Finite being is a question mark. It asks the question of the "eternal now" in which the temporal and the spatial are simultaneously accepted and overcome. It asks the question of the "ground of being" in which the causal and the substantial are simultaneously confirmed and negated. The cosmological approach cannot answer these questions, but it can and it must analyze their roots in the structure of finitude.

The basis for the so-called teleological argument for the existence of God is the threat against the finite structure of being, that is, against the unity of its polar elements. The *telos,* from which this argument has received its name, is the "inner aim," the meaningful, understandable structure of reality. This structure is used as a springboard to the conclusion that finite *teloi* imply an infinite cause of teleology, that finite and threatened meanings imply an infinite and unthreatened cause of meaning. In terms of logical argument this conclusion is as invalid as the other cosmological "arguments." As the statement of a question it is not only valid but inescapable and, as history shows, most impressive. Anxiety about meaninglessness is the characteristically *human* form of ontological anxiety. It is the form of anxiety which only a being can have in whose nature freedom and destiny are united. The threat of losing this unity drives man toward the question of an infinite, unthreatened ground of meaning; it drives him to the question of God. The teleological argument formulates the question of the ground of meaning, just as the cosmological argument formulates the question of the ground of being. In contrast to the ontological argument, however, both are in the larger sense cosmological and stand over against it.

The task of a theological treatment of the traditional arguments for the existence of God is twofold: to develop the question of God which they express and to expose the impotency of the "arguments," their inability to answer the question of God. These arguments bring the ontological analysis to a conclusion by disclosing that the question of God is implied in the finite structure of being. In performing this function, they partially accept and also partially reject traditional natural theology, and they drive reason to the quest for revelation.

II

THE REALITY OF GOD

A. THE MEANING OF "GOD"

1. A Phenomenological Description

a) God and man's ultimate concern.—"God" is the answer to the question implied in man's finitude; he is the name for that which concerns man ultimately. This does not mean that first there is a being called God and then the demand that man should be ultimately concerned about him. It means that whatever concerns a man ultimately becomes god for him, and, conversely, it means that a man can be concerned ultimately only about that which is god for him. The phrase "being ultimately concerned" points to a tension in human experience. On the one hand, it is impossible to be concerned about something which cannot be encountered concretely, be it in the realm of reality or in the realm of imagination. Universals can become matters of ultimate concern only through their power of representing concrete experiences. The more concrete a thing is, the more the possible concern about it. The completely concrete being, the individual person, is the object of the most radical concern—the concern of love. On the other hand, ultimate concern must transcend every preliminary finite and concrete concern. It must transcend the whole realm of finitude in order to be the answer to the question implied in finitude. But in transcending the finite the religious concern loses the concreteness of a being-to-being relationship. It tends to become not only absolute but also abstract, provoking reactions from the concrete element. This is the inescapable inner tension in the idea of God. The conflict between the concreteness and the ultimacy of the religious concern is actual wherever God is experienced and this experience is expressed, from primitive prayer to the most elaborate theological system. It is the key to understanding the dynamics of the history of religion, and it is the basic problem of every doctrine of God, from the earliest priestly wisdom to the most refined discussions of the trinitarian dogma.

A phenomenological description of the meaning of "God" in every religion, including the Christian, offers the following definition of the meaning of the term "god." Gods are beings who transcend the realm of ordinary experience in power and meaning, with whom men have relations which surpass ordinary relations in intensity and significance. A discussion of each element of this basic description will give a full phenomenological picture of the meaning of "god," and this will be the tool with which an interpretation of the nature and the development of the phenomena which are called "religious" may be fashioned.

Gods are "beings." They are experienced, named, and defined in concrete intuitive (*anschaulich*) terms through the exhaustive use of all the ontological elements and categories of finitude. Gods are substances, caused and causing, active and passive, remembering and anticipating, arising and disappearing in time and space. Even though they are called "highest beings," they are limited in power and significance. They are limited by other gods or by the resistance of other beings and principles, for example, matter and fate. The values they represent limit and sometimes annihilate each other. The gods are open to error, compassion, anger, hostility, anxiety. They are images of human nature or subhuman powers raised to a superhuman realm. This fact, which theologians must face in all its implications, is the basis of all theories of "projection" which say that the gods are simply imaginary projections of elements of finitude, natural and human elements. What these theories disregard is that projection always is projection *on* something—a wall, a screen, another being, another realm. Obviously, it is absurd to class that on which the projection is realized with the projection itself. A screen is not projected; it receives the projection. The realm against which the divine images are projected is not itself a projection. It is the experienced ultimacy of being and meaning. It is the realm of ultimate concern.

Therefore, not only do the images of the gods bear all the characteristics of finitude—this makes them images and gives them concreteness—but they also have characteristics in which categorical finitude is radically transcended. Their identity as finite substances is negated by all kinds of substantial transmutations and expansions, in spite of the sameness of their names. Their temporal limitations are overcome; they are called "immortals" in spite of the fact that their appearance and disappearance are presupposed. Their spatial definiteness is negated when they act as multi- or omnipresent, yet they have a special dwelling place with which they are intimately connected. Their subordination to the chain of causes and effects is denied, for overwhelming or absolute power is attributed to them in spite of their dependence on other divine powers and on the influence finite beings have on them. In concrete cases they demonstrate omniscience and perfection in spite of the struggles and betrayals going on among the gods themselves. They transcend their own finitude in power of being and in the embodiment of meaning. The tendency toward ultimacy continuously fights against the tendency toward concreteness.

The history of religion is full of human attempts to participate in divine power and to use it for human purposes. This is the point at which the magic world view enters religious practice and offers technical tools for an effective use of divine power. Magic itself is a theory and practice concerning the relation of finite beings to each other; it assumes that there are direct, physically unmediated sympathies and influences between beings on the "psychic" level, that is, on the level which comprises the vital, the subconscious, and the emotional. In so far as the gods are beings, magic relations in both directions are possible—from man to the gods and from the gods to man—and they are the basis for human participation in divine power.

Nonmagical, personalistic world views lead to a person-to-person relationship to divine power, which is appropriated through prayer, that is, through an appeal to the personal center of the divine being. The god answers in a free decision. He might or he might not use his power to fulfil the content of the prayer. In any case, he remains free, and attempts to force him to act in a particular way are considered magic. Seen in this context, every prayer of supplication illustrates the tension between the concrete element and the ultimate element in the idea of God. Theologians have suggested that this type of prayer should be replaced by thanksgiving in order to avoid magic connotations (Ritschl). But actual religious life reacts violently against such a demand. Men continue to use the power of their god by asking his favors. They demand a concrete god, a god with whom man can deal.

A third way of trying to use the divine power is through a mystical participation in it which is neither magical nor personalistic. Its main characteristic is the devaluation of the divine beings and their power over against the ultimate power, the abyss of being-itself. The Hindu doctrine that the gods tremble when a saint exercises radical asceticism is another illustration of the tension between the gods as beings with a higher, though limited, power and the ultimate power which they express and conceal at the same time. The conflict between the Brahma power and the god Brahman as an object of a concrete relation with man points to the same tension within the structure of man's ultimate concern which was noted above.

The gods are superior not only in power but also in meaning. They embody the true and the good. They embody concrete values, and as gods they claim absoluteness for them. The imperialism of the gods which follows from this situation is the basis of all other imperialisms. Imperialism is never the expression of will to power as such. It always is a struggle for the absolute victory of a special value or system of values, represented by a special god or hierarchy of gods. The ultimacy of the religious concern drives toward universality in value and in meaning; the concreteness of the religious concern drives toward particular meanings and values. The tension is insoluble. The co-ordination of all concrete values removes the ultimacy of the religious concern. The subordination of concrete values to any one of them produces anti-imperialistic reactions on the part of the others. The drowning of all concrete values in an abyss of meaning and value evokes antimystical reactions on the part of the concrete element in man's ultimate concern. The conflict between these elements is present in every act of creedal confession, in every missionary task, in every claim to possess final revelation. It is the nature of the gods which creates these conflicts, and it is man's ultimate concern which is mirrored in the nature of the gods.

We have discussed the meaning of "god" in terms of man's relation to the divine, and we have taken this relationship into the phenomenological description of the nature of the gods. This underlines the fact that the gods are not objects within the context of the universe. They are expressions of the ultimate concern which transcends the cleavage between subjectivity and objectivity. It remains to be emphasized that an ultimate concern is not "subjective." Ultimacy stands against everything which can be derived from mere subjectivity, nor can the unconditional be found within the entire catalogue of finite objects which are conditioned by each other.

If the word "existential" points to a participation which transcends both subjectivity and objectivity, then man's relation to the gods is rightly called "existential." Man cannot speak of the gods in detachment. The moment he tries to do so, he has lost the god and has established just one more object within the world of objects. Man can speak of the gods only on the basis of his relation to them. This relation oscillates between the concreteness of a give-and-take attitude, in which the divine beings

easily become objects and tools for human purposes, and the absoluteness
of a total surrender on the side of man. The absolute element of man's
ultimate concern demands absolute intensity, infinite passion (Kierkegaard), in the religious relation. The concrete element drives men
toward an unlimited amount of relative action and emotion in the cult
in which the ultimate concern is embodied and actualized, and also outside it. The Catholic system of relativities represents the concrete element
most fully, while Protestant radicalism predominantly emphasizes the
absolute element. The tension in the nature of the gods, which is the
tension in the structure of man's ultimate concern (and which, in the
last analysis, is the tension in the human situation), determines the religions of mankind in all their major aspects.

b) God and the idea of the holy.—The sphere of the gods is the sphere
of holiness. A sacred realm is established wherever the divine is manifest. Whatever is brought into the divine sphere is consecrated. The
divine is the holy.

Holiness is an experienced phenomenon; it is open to phenomenological description. Therefore, it is a very important cognitive "door-
way" to understanding the nature of religion, for it is the most adequate
basis we have for understanding the divine. The holy and the divine
must be interpreted correlatively. A doctrine of God which does not
include the category of holiness is not only unholy but also untrue. Such
a doctrine transforms the gods into secular objects whose existence is
rightly denied by naturalism. On the other hand, a doctrine of the holy
which does not interpret it as the sphere of the divine transforms the
holy into something aesthetic-emotional, which is the danger of theologies like those of Schleiermacher and Rudolf Otto. Both mistakes can
be avoided in a doctrine of God which analyzes the meaning of ultimate
concern and which derives from it both the meaning of God and the
meaning of the holy.

The holy is the *quality* of that which concerns man ultimately. Only
that which is holy can give man ultimate concern, and only that which
gives man ultimate concern has the quality of holiness.

The phenomenological description of the holy in Rudolf Otto's classical book *The Idea of the Holy* demonstrates the interdependence of the
meaning of the holy and the meaning of the divine, and it demonstrates
their common dependence on the nature of ultimate concern. When Otto
calls the experience of the holy "numinous," he interprets the holy as the
presence of the divine. When he points to the mysterious character of

holiness, he indicates that the holy transcends the subject-object structure of reality. When he describes the mystery of the holy as *tremendum* and *fascinosum,* he expresses the experience of "the ultimate" in the double sense of that which is the abyss and that which is the ground of man's being. This is not directly asserted in Otto's merely phenomenological analysis, which, by the way, never should be called "psychological." However, it is implicit in his analysis, and it should be made explicit beyond Otto's own intention.

Such a concept of the holy opens large sections of the history of religion to theological understanding, by explaining the ambiguity of the concept of holiness at every religious level. Holiness cannot become actual except through holy "objects." But holy objects are not holy in and of themselves. They are holy only by negating themselves in pointing to the divine of which they are the mediums. If they establish themselves as holy, they become demonic. They still are "holy," but their holiness is antidivine. A nation which looks upon itself as holy is correct in so far as everything can become a vehicle of man's ultimate concern, but the nation is incorrect in so far as it considers itself to be inherently holy. Innumerable things, all things in a way, have the power of becoming holy in a mediate sense. They can point to something beyond themselves. But, if their holiness comes to be considered inherent, it becomes demonic. This happens continually in the actual life of most religions. The representations of man's ultimate concern—holy objects—tend to become his ultimate concern. They are transformed into idols. Holiness provokes idolatry.

Justice is the criterion which judges idolatrous holiness. The prophets attack demonic forms of holiness in the name of justice. The Greek philosophers criticize a demonically distorted cult in the name of *Dikē.* In the name of the justice which God gives, the Reformers destroy a system of sacred things and acts which has claimed holiness for itself. In the name of social justice, modern revolutionary movements challenge sacred institutions which protect social injustice. In all these cases it is demonic holiness, not holiness as such, which comes under attack.

However, it must be said with regard to each of these cases that to the degree to which the antidemonic struggle was successful historically, the meaning of holiness was transformed. The holy became the righteous, the morally good, usually with ascetic connotations. The divine command to be holy as God is holy was interpreted as a requirement of moral perfection. And since moral perfection is an ideal and not a reality, the notion of actual holiness disappeared, both inside and outside the religious sphere. The fact that there are no "saints" in the classical sense on Protestant soil supported this development in the modern world. One of the characteristics of our present situation is that the meaning of holiness has been rediscovered in liturgical practice as well as in theological theory, although in popular language holiness still is identified with moral perfection.

The concept of the holy stands in contrast with two other concepts, the unclean and the secular. In the classical sixth chapter of Isaiah the prophet must be purified by means of a burning coal before he can endure the manifestation of the holy. The holy and the unclean seem to exclude each other. However, the contrast is not unambiguous. Before it received the meaning of the immoral, the unclean designated something demonic, something which produced taboos and numinous awe. Divine and demonic holiness were not distinguished until the contrast became exclusive under the impact of the prophetic criticism. But if the holy is completely identified with the clean, and if the demonic element is completely rejected, then the holy approximates the secular. Moral law replaces the *tremendum* and *fascinosum* of holiness. The holy loses its depth, its mystery, its numinous character.

This is not true of Luther and many of his followers. The demonic elements in Luther's doctrine of God, his occasional identification of the wrath of God with Satan, the half-divine–half-demonic picture he gives of God's acting in nature and history—all this constitutes the greatness and the danger of Luther's understanding of the holy. The experience he describes certainly is numinous, tremendous, and fascinating, but it is not safeguarded against demonic distortion and against the resurgence of the unclean within the holy.

In Calvin and his followers the opposite trend prevails. Fear of the demonic permeates Calvin's doctrine of the divine holiness. An almost neurotic anxiety about the unclean develops in later Calvinism. The word "Puritan" is most indicative of this trend. The holy is the clean; cleanliness becomes holiness. This means the end of the numinous character of the holy. The *tremendum* becomes fear of the law and of judgment; the *fascinosum* becomes pride of self-control and repression. Many theological problems and many psychotherapeutic phenomena are rooted in the ambiguity of the contrast between the holy and the unclean.

The second contrast to the holy is the secular. The word "secular" is less expressive than the word "profane," which means "in front of the doors"—of the holy. But profane has received connotations of "unclean," while the term "secular" has remained neutral. Standing outside the doors of the sanctuary does not in itself imply the state of uncleanness. The profane *might* be invaded by unclean spirits but not necessarily. The German word *profan* preserves this idea of neutrality. The secular is the realm of preliminary concerns. It lacks ultimate concern; it lacks holiness. All finite relations are in themselves secular. None of them is holy. The holy and the secular seem to exclude each other. But again the contrast is ambiguous. The holy embraces itself and the secular, precisely as the divine embraces itself and the demonic. Everything secular is implicitly related to the holy. It can become the bearer of the holy. The divine can become manifest in it. Nothing is essentially and inescapably secular. Everything has the dimension of depth, and in the moment in which the third dimension is actualized, holiness appears. Everything secular is potentially sacred, open to consecration.

Furthermore, the holy needs to be expressed and can be expressed only through the secular, for it is through the finite alone that the infinite can express itself. It is through holy "objects" that holiness must become actual. The holy cannot appear except through that which in another respect is secular. In its essential nature the holy does not constitute a special realm in addition to the secular. The fact that under the conditions of existence it establishes itself as a special realm is the most striking expression of existential disruption. The very heart of what classical Christianity has called "sin" is the unreconciled duality of ultimate and preliminary concerns, of the finite and that which transcends finitude, of the secular and the holy. Sin is a state of things in which the holy and the secular are separated, struggling with each other and trying to conquer each other. It is the state in which God is not "all in all," the state in which God is "in addition to" all other things. The history of religion and culture is a continuous confirmation of this analysis of the meaning of holiness and of its relation to the unclean and to the secular.

2. Typological Considerations

a) Typology and the history of religion.—The ultimate can become actual only through the concrete, through that which is preliminary and transitory. This is the reason why the idea of God has a history, and why this history is the basic element in the history of religion, simultaneously determining it and being determined by it. In order to understand the idea of God, the theologian must look into its history, even though he derives his doctrine of God from what he considers to be the final revelation, for the final revelation presupposes some insight into the meaning of "God" on the part of those by whom it is received. The theologian must clarify and interpret this meaning in the light of the final revelation, but also, at the same time, he must interpret it on the basis of the material given by the history of religion—including Christianity in so far as it is a religion—and the history of human culture in so far as it has a religious substance.

Systematic theology cannot produce a survey of the history of religion. Neither can it sketch a general line of religious progress in human history. There is no such line. In the history of religion, as in the history of culture, each gain in one respect is accompanied by a loss in another respect. When speaking of final revelation, the theologian naturally considers its appearance real progress over preparatory revelation; but he does not (or *should* not) call the receiving revelation in which he personally stands progress over the final revelation, for final revelation is an event which is prepared by history and is received in history, but it cannot be derived from history. It stands over against progress and regress, judging the one as severely as the other. Therefore, if the theologian speaks of elements of progress in the history of religion, he must refer to those developments in which the contradiction between the ultimate element and the concrete element in the idea of God is fragmentarily overcome. Such developments occur always and everywhere, producing the different types of expression in which the meaning of God is grasped and interpreted. Since these developments are fragmentary, progress and regress are ambiguously mixed in them, and no progressivistic interpretation of the history of religion can be derived from them.

What is possible is a description of typical processes and structures. Types are ideal structures which are approximated by concrete things or events without ever being attained. Nothing historical completely represents a particular type, but everything historical is nearer to or farther away from a particular type. Every special event is opened up for our understanding by the type to which it belongs. Historical understanding oscillates between the intuition of the special and the analysis of the typical. The special cannot be described without reference to the type. The type is unreal without the special event in which it appears. Typology cannot replace historiography; historiography cannot describe anything without typology.

The development of the meaning of God has two interdependent causes: the tension within the idea of God and the general factors determining the movement of history (e.g., economic, political, and cultural factors). The development of the idea of God is not a dialectical thread spun out of the implications of ultimate concern, independent of universal history. On the other hand, neither the rise nor the development of the idea of God can be explained in terms of social and cultural factors independent of the given structure of "ultimate concern" which logically precedes each of its historical manifestations and every particular notion of God. Historical forces determine the existence of the idea of God, not its essence; they determine its variable manifestations, not its invariable nature. The social situation of a period conditions the idea of God, but it does not produce it. A feudal order of society, for example, conditions the experience and adoration and doctrine of God hierarchically. But the idea of God is present in history before and after the feudal period. It is present in all periods, transcending them in its essence, determined by them in its existence. The Christian theologian is not exempt from this rule. However strenuously he may try to transcend his period, his concept of God is dated. But the fact that he is grasped by the idea of God is not dated. This fact transcends all dates.

A concept of God is needed to delimit the discussion of the history and typology of the idea of God. If this concept is too narrow, the question arises whether there are religions which have no god; and in view of original Buddhism, for example, it is difficult not to answer this question affirmatively. If the concept of God is too wide, the question arises whether there is a God who is not the focal point of any religion; and in view of certain moral or logical concepts of God it is difficult not to answer this question affirmatively. In both cases, however, the presupposed concept of God is inadequate. If God is understood as that which concerns man ultimately, early Buddhism has a concept of God just as certainly as does Vedanta Hinduism. And if God is understood as that which concerns man ultimately, moral or logical concepts of God are seen to be valid in so far as they express an ultimate concern. Otherwise they are philosophical possibilities but not the God of religion.

Theological interpretations of the history of religion often are misguided by the unique picture which every religion presents—a picture which can easily be criticized in the light of final revelation. The criticism is much more difficult and much more serious if the typical structures within the unique form of a non-Christian historical religion are elaborated and compared with the typical structures appearing in Christianity as a historical religion. This is the only fair and methodologically adequate way of dealing systematically with the history of religion. After this has been done, the final step can be taken; both Christianity and the non-Christian religions can and must be subjected to the criterion of final revelation. It is regrettable and altogether unconvincing if Christian apologetics begins with a criticism of the historical religions without attempting to understand the typological analogies between them and Christianity and without emphasizing the element of universal preparatory revelation which they carry within them.[1]

The general outline of the typological analysis of the history of religion follows from the tension of the elements in the idea of God. The concreteness of man's ultimate concern drives him toward polytheistic structures; the reaction of the absolute element against these drives him toward monotheistic structures; and the need for a balance between the concrete and the absolute drives him toward trinitarian structures. However, there is another factor which determines the typological structures of the idea of God, namely, the difference between the holy and the secular. We have seen that everything secular can enter the realm of the holy and that the holy can be secularized. On the one hand, this means that secular things, events, and realms can become matters of ultimate concern, become divine powers; and, on the other hand, this means that divine powers can be reduced to secular objects, lose their religious character. Both types of movement can be observed throughout the entire history of religion and culture, which indicates that there is an essential unity of the holy and the secular, in spite of their existential separation. This means that the secular ultimates (the ontological concepts) and the sacred ultimates (the conceptions of God) are interdependent. Every ontological concept has a typical manifestation of man's ultimate concern in its background, although now it has been transformed into a definite concept. And every conception of God discloses special ontological assumptions in the categorical material it uses. Therefore, systematic theologians must analyze the religious substance of the basic ontological concepts and the secular implications of the different types of

1. Cf., e.g., Brunner's way of dealing with the history of religion in his book, *Revelation and Reason* (Philadelphia: Westminster Press, 1946). Of course, he can claim that he stands in the line of Deutero-Isaiah and Calvin. But the extremely polemical situation in which these two men spoke makes them questionable guides for a theological understanding of universal revelation and the history of religion. Paul and the early church are better guides here.

the idea of God. The religious typology must be pursued in its secular transformations and implications.

b) *Types of polytheism.*—Polytheism is a qualitative and not a quantitative concept. It is not the belief in a plurality of gods but rather the lack of a uniting and transcending ultimate which determines its character. Each of the polytheistic divine powers claims ultimacy in the concrete situation in which it appears. It disregards similar claims made by other divine powers in other situations. This leads to conflicting claims and threatens to disrupt the unity of self and world. The demonic element in polytheism is rooted in the claim of each of the divine powers to be ultimate, although none of them possesses the universal basis for making such a claim. An absolute polytheism is impossible. The principle of ultimacy always reacts against the principle of concretion. Polytheism "lives on" the restricting power of monotheistic elements.

This is obvious in each of the main types of polytheism—the universalistic, the mythological, and the dualistic. In the universalistic type the special divine beings, like divinities of places and realms, numinous forces in things and persons, are embodiments of a universal, all-pervading sacred power (*mana*), which is hidden behind all things and at the same time is manifest through them. A substantial unity prevents the rise of a complete polytheism. But this unity is not a real unity. It does not transcend the manifoldness into which it is split, and it cannot control its innumerable appearances. It is dispersed among these appearances and contradicts itself in them. Some forms of pan-sacramentalism, romanticism, and pantheism are the offspring of this universalistic type of polytheism. It highlights the tension between the concrete and the ultimate, but it reaches neither down to full concreteness nor up to full ultimacy.

In the mythological type of polytheism divine power is concentrated in individual deities of a relatively fixed character who represent broad realms of being and value. The mythological gods are self-related, they transcend the realm they control, and they are related to other gods of the same character in terms of kinship, hostility, love, and struggle. This type of polytheism is characterized by the great mythologies for which this type alone gives the adequate presuppositions. In the universalistic type the divine beings are not sufficiently fixed and individualized to become the subjects of stories, while in the dualistic type the myth is transformed into a dramatic interpretation of history. In all monotheistic types the myth is broken by the radical emphasis on the element of ultimacy in the idea of God. It is true that the broken myth is still a myth, and it is true that there is no way of speaking about God except in mythological terms; but the mythical as a category of religious intuition is different from the unbroken mythology of a special type of the idea of God.

The tension in the idea of God is reflected in the mythological "imaginings" concerning the nature of the gods especially in the imagination of those who embrace the mythological type. Concrete concern impells the religious imagination to personify the divine powers, for man is radically concerned only about that which can encounter him on equal terms. Therefore, the person-to-person relationship between God and man is constitutive for religious experience. Man cannot be ultimately concerned about something which is less than he is, something impersonal. This explains the fact that all divine powers—stones and stars, plants and animals, spirits and angels, and every single one of the great mythological gods—possess a personal character. It explains the fact that actually there is a struggle for a personal God in all religions, a struggle which resists all philosophical attacks.

A personal God: this indicates the concreteness of man's ultimate concern. But his ultimate concern is not only concrete but also ultimate, and this brings another element into the mythological imagery. The gods are subpersonal and suprapersonal at one and the same time. Animal-gods are not deified brutes; they are expressions of man's ultimate concern symbolized in various forms of animal vitality. This animal vitality stands for a transhuman, divine-demonic vitality. The stars as gods are not deified astral bodies; they are expressions of man's ultimate concern symbolized in the order of the stars and in their creative and destructive power. The subhuman-superhuman character of the mythological gods is a protest against the reduction of divine power to human measure. In the moment in which this protest loses its effectiveness, the gods become glorified men rather than gods. They become individual persons who possess no divine ultimacy. This development can be studied in Homeric religion as well as in modern humanistic theism. Completely humanized gods are unreal. They are idealized men. They have no numinous power. The *fascinosum* and *tremendum* are gone. Therefore, religion imagines divine personalities whose qualities disrupt and transcend their personal form in every respect. They are subpersonal or transpersonal personalities, a paradoxical combination of words which mirrors the tension between the concrete and the ultimate in man's ultimate concern and in every type of the idea of God.

Prophets and philosophers have attacked the immorality of many myths. These attacks are only partially justified. The relations of the mythological gods are transmoral; they are ontological; they refer to structures of being and to conflicts of values. The conflicts between the gods stem from the unconditional claims which each of the gods makes. They are demonic, but they are not immoral.

The mythological type of polytheism could not live without monotheistic restrictions. One of these restrictions is manifest in the fact that the god who is addressed in a concrete situation receives all the characteristics of ultimacy. In the moment of prayer the god to whom a man prays is the ultimate, the lord of heaven and earth. This is true in spite of the fact that in the next prayer another god assumes the same role. The possibility of experiencing this kind of exclusiveness expresses a feeling for the identity of the divine in spite of the multiplicity of gods and the differences between them. The other way in which the conflicts of the mythological gods are overcome is through the hierarchical organization of the divine realm, which often is undertaken by priests in the religious-political or national-political interest. This is inadequate, but it prepares the way for the monarchical type of monotheism. Finally, one must point to the fact that in a fully developed polytheism like that of Greece the gods themselves are subject to a higher principle, fate, which they mediate but against which they are powerless. In this way the arbitrariness of their individual nature is limited, and, at the same time, the path to the abstract type of monotheism is prepared.

The third type of polytheism is the dualistic, which is based on the ambiguity in the concept of the holy and on the conflict between divine and demonic holiness. In the universalistic type the danger involved in approaching the holy discloses awareness of an element of destructiveness in the nature of the divine. The *tremendum,* as well as the *fascinosum,* however, can indicate creativity as well as destructiveness. The divine "fire" produces life as well as ashes. When the religious consciousness distinguishes between good and evil spirits, it introduces a dualism into the sphere of the holy through which it attempts to overcome the ambiguity of the numinous beings. But, as bearers of divine power, the evil spirits are not merely evil, and, as individuals with a divine claim, the good spirits are not merely good. The universalistic type of polytheism takes notice of the ambiguity in the sphere of the holy, but it does not conquer it.

This is true also of the mythological type. The ruling gods dispossess the other divine beings. The demonic forces of the past are kept down. But the victorious gods themselves are threatened by old or new divine powers. They are not unconditional, and therefore they are partially demonic. The ambiguity in the sphere of the holy is not overcome by the great mythologies.

The most radical attempt to separate the divine from the demonic is religious dualism. Although its classic expression is the religion of Zoroaster and, in a derived and rationalized form, Manichaeism, dualistic structures appear in many other religions, including Christianity. Religious dualism concentrates divine holiness in one realm and demonic holiness in another realm. Both gods are creative, and different sections of reality belong to one or the other realm. Some things are evil in their essential nature, because they are created by the evil god or because they are dependent on an ultimate principle of evil. The ambiguity in the realm of holiness has become a radical split.

However, this type of polytheism is even less able than the others to exist without monotheistic elements. The very fact that the one god is called "good" gives him a divine character superior to that of the evil god, for god as the expression of man's ultimate concern is supreme not only in power but also in value. The evil god is god only according to half the nature of divinity, and even this half is limited. Dualism envisages the ultimate victory of the divine holiness over the demonic holiness. This presupposes that divine holiness is essentially superior or, as later Parsiism has taught, that there is an ultimate principle above the struggling realms, namely, the good embracing itself and its opposite. In this form dualistic monotheism has foreshadowed the God of history, the God of exclusive and trinitarian monotheism.

c) Types of monotheism.—Polytheism could not exist unless it included monotheistic elements. But in all types of polytheism the concrete element in the idea of God prevails over the element of ultimacy. In monotheism the opposite is the case. The divine powers of polytheism are subjected to a highest divine power. However, just as there is no absolute polytheism, so there is no absolute monotheism. The concrete element in the idea of God cannot be destroyed.

Monarchic monotheism lies on the boundary line between polytheism and monotheism. The god-monarch rules over the hierarchy of inferior gods and godlike beings. He represents the power and value of the hierarchy. His end would be the end of all those ruled by him. The conflicts between the gods are reduced by his power; he determines the order of values. Therefore, he can easily be identified with the ultimate in being and value, which is what the Stoics, for example, did when they identified Zeus with the ontological ultimate. On the other hand, he is not secure against attacks from other divine powers. Like every monarch, he is threatened by revolution or by outside attack. Monarchic monotheism is too deeply involved in polytheism to be liberated from it. Nevertheless, there are elements of monarchic monotheism not only in many non-Christian religions but also in Christianity itself. The "Lord of Hosts" of whom the Old Testament and Christian liturgy often speak is a monarch who rules over heavenly beings, angels, and spirits. Several times during Christian history some members of these hosts have become dangerous for the sovereignty of the highest God.[2]

The second type of monotheism is the mystical. Mystical monotheism transcends all realms of being and value, and their divine representatives, in favor of the divine ground and abyss from which they come and in which they disappear. All conflicts between the gods, between the divine and the demonic, between gods and things, are overcome in the ultimate which transcends all of them. The element of ultimacy swallows the element of concreteness. The ontological structure, with its polarities which are applied to the gods in all forms of polytheism, has no validity for the transcendent One, the principle of mystical monotheism. The imperialism of the mythological gods collapses; no demonic claims can be made by anything finite. The power of being in its completeness and the entire sum of meanings and values are seen without differentiation and conflict in the ground of being and meaning, in the source of all values.

Yet even this most radical negation of the concrete element in the idea of God is not able to suppress the quest for concreteness. Mystical monotheism does not exclude divine powers in which the ultimate embodies itself temporally. And, once admitted, the gods can regain their lost significance, especially for people who are unable to grasp the ultimate in its purity and abstraction from everything concrete. The history of mystical monotheism in India and in Europe has shown that it is "wide open" for polytheism and that it is easily overpowered by it among the masses of the people.

2. Cf. the warning against the cult of angels in the New Testament.

Monotheism is able to resist polytheism radically only in the form of exclusive monotheism, which is created by the elevation of a concrete god to ultimacy and universality without the loss of his concreteness and without the assertion of a demonic claim. Such a possibility contradicts every expectation which can be derived from the history of religion. It is the result of an astounding constellation of objective and subjective factors in Israel, especially in the prophetic line of its religion. Theologically speaking, exclusive monotheism belongs to final revelation, for it is a direct preparation for it.

The God of Israel is the concrete God who has led his people out of Egypt, "the God of Abraham, Isaac, and Jacob." At the same time, he claims to be the God who judges the gods of the nations, before whom the nations of the world are "as a drop in a bucket." This God who is concrete and absolute at the same time is a "jealous God"; he cannot tolerate any divine claim beside his own. Of course, such a claim could be what we have called "demonic," the claim of something conditioned to be unconditioned. But this is not true in Israel. Yahweh does not claim universality in the name of a particular quality or in the name of his nation and its particular qualities. His claim is not imperialistic, for it is made in the name of that principle which implies ultimacy and universality—the principle of justice. The relation of the God of Israel to his nation is based on a covenant. The covenant demands justice, namely, the keeping of the Commandments, and it threatens the violation of justice with rejection and destruction. This means that God is independent of his nation and of his own individual nature. If his nation breaks the covenant, he still remains in power. He proves his universality by destroying his nation in the name of principles which are valid for all nations—the principles of justice. This undercuts the basis of polytheism. It breaks through the demonic implications of the idea of God, and it is the critical guardian which protects the holy against the temptation of the bearers of the holy to claim absoluteness for themselves. The Protestant principle is the restatement of the prophetic principle as an attack against a self-absolutizing and, consequently, demonically distorted church. Both prophets and reformers announced the radical implications of exclusive monotheism.

Like the God of mystical monotheism, the God of exclusive monotheism is in danger of losing the concrete element in the idea of God. His ultimacy and universality tend to swallow his character as a living God. The personal traits in his picture are removed as anthropomorphisms which contradict his ultimacy, and the historical traits of his character are forgotten as accidental factors which contradict his universality. He can be amalgamated with the God of mystical monotheism or with the transformation of this God into the philosophical absolute. But one thing cannot happen. There can be no relapse into polytheism. While mystical monotheism and its philosophical transformations are inclusive of everything finite because they are reached by elevation above it, exclusive monotheism excludes the finite against whose demonic claims it has protested. Nevertheless, exclusive monotheism needs an expression of the concrete element in man's ultimate concern. This posits the trinitarian problem.

Trinitarian monotheism is not a matter of the number three. It is a qualitative and not a quantitative characterization of God. It is an attempt to speak of the living God, the God in whom the ultimate and the concrete are united. The number three has no specific significance in itself, although it comes nearest to an adequate description of life-processes. Even in the history of the Christian doctrine of the trinity there have been vascillations between trinitarian and binitarian emphasis (the discussion about the position of the Holy Ghost) and between trinity and quaternity (the question about the relation of the Father to the common divine substance of the three *personae*). The trinitarian problem has nothing to do with the trick question how one can be three and three be one. The answer to this question is given in every life-process. The trinitarian problem is the problem of the unity between ultimacy and concreteness in the living God. Trinitarian monotheism is concrete monotheism, the affirmation of the living God.

The trinitarian problem is a perennial feature of the history of religion. Each type of monotheism is aware of it and gives implicit or explicit answers. In monarchical monotheism the highest god makes himself concrete in manifold incarnations, in the sending of lower divinities, and in the procreation of half-gods. All this is not paradoxical, for the highest gods of monarchic monotheism are not ultimate. In some cases monarchical monotheism reaches quasi-trinitarian formulas; a father-divinity, a mother-divinity, and a child-divinity are united in the same myth and in the same cult. A more profound preparation for genuine trinitarian thinking is the participation of a god in human destiny, in suffering and death, in spite of the ultimacy of the power he wields and with which he conquers guilt and death. This opens the way to the gods of the late-ancient mystery cults, in which a god whose ultimacy is acknowledged becomes radically concrete for the initiated. These cults influenced the early church not only through their ritual forms but also through their adumbration of the trinitarian problem, which reached the church through the medium of exclusive monotheism.

Mystical monotheism gives classical expression to the trend toward trinitarian monotheism in the differentiation of the god Brahma from the Brahman principle. The latter represents the element of ultimacy in the most radical way; the former is a concrete god, united with Shiva and Vishnu in a divine triad. Here again the number three is not important. It is the relation of the Brahman-Atman, the absolute, to the concrete gods of Hindu piety which is central. The question of the ontological standing of Brahma and the others in relation to Brahman, the principle of being-itself, is a genuine trinitarian question, analogous to the Origenistic question of the ontological standing of the Logos and the Spirit in relation to the abyss of the divine nature. Nevertheless, there is a decisive difference between them—the presence of exclusive monotheism in Christianity.

In exclusive monotheism an abstract transcendence of the divine develops. It is not the transcendence of the infinite abyss in which everything concrete disappears, as in mystical monotheism; rather it is the transcendence of the absolute command which empties all concrete manifestations of the divine. But since the concrete element demands its rights, mediating powers of a threefold character appear and posit the trinitarian problem. The first group of these mediators is made up of hypostasized divine qualities, like Wisdom, Word, Glory. The second group are the angels, the divine messengers who represent special divine functions. The third is the divine-human figure through whom God works the fulfilment of history, the Messiah. In all these the God who had become absolutely transcendent and unapproachable now becomes concrete and present in time and space. The significance of these mediators grows as the distance between God and man increases, and, to the degree to which they become more significant, the trinitarian problem becomes more acute, more urgent. When early Christianity calls Jesus of Nazareth the Messiah and identifies him with the divine Logos, the trinitarian problem becomes the central problem of religious existence. The basic motive and the different forms of trinitarian monotheism become effective in the trinitarian dogma of the Christian church. But the Christian solution is founded on the paradox that the Messiah, the mediator between God and man, is identical with a personal human life, the name of which is Jesus of Nazareth. With this assertion the trinitarian problem becomes a part of the christological problem.

d) Philosophical transformations.—In our basic statement about the relation of theology to philosophy[3] we have made the following distinction between the religious attitude and the philosophical attitude: religion deals existentially with the meaning of being; philosophy deals theoretically with the structure of being. But religion can express itself only through the ontological elements and categories with which philosophy deals, while philosophy can discover the structure of being only to the degree to which being-itself has become manifest in an existential experience. Basically this refers to the idea of God. Certain fundamental assertions about the nature of being are implicit in the different types of man's symbolization of his ultimate concern, assertions which may or may not be made explicit by philosophical analysis. If philosophy makes them explicit, they bear a definite analogy to the special types of the idea of God in which they have been contained. Therefore, they can be considered theoretical transformations of existential visions of what concerns man ultimately. If this is true, theology can deal with these assertions in a double way. It can discuss their philosophical truth on merely philosophical grounds, and it can struggle with them as expressions of ultimate concern on religious grounds. In the first instance, philosophical arguments alone are valid; in the second instance, existential witness alone is adequate. The following analysis develops this distinction, which is of fundamental apologetic importance.

As the section on the formal criteria of theology has shown,[4] the experience of ultimacy implies an ultimate of being and meaning which concerns man unconditionally because it determines his very being and meaning. For the philosophical approach this ultimate is being-itself, *esse ipsum*, that beyond which thought cannot go, the power of being in which everything participates. Being-itself is a necessary concept for every philosophy, even for those which reject it; for they reject it with arguments taken from a definite understanding of what it means to have being. On the basis of its dissolution of the universals, nominalism objects to the concept of a universal power of being or to the concept of being-itself. But nominalism cannot escape the implicit assertion that the nature of being and knowing is best recognized by a nominalistic epistemology. If being is radically individualized, if it lacks embracing

3. Cf. Introduction, pp. 18–28.
4. Cf. Introduction, pp. 11–14.

structures and essences, this is a character of being, valid for everything that is. The question then is not whether one can speak of being-itself but what its nature is and how it can be approached cognitively.

The same argument is valid against the attempts of some logical positivists to take the question of being away from philosophy and to surrender it to emotion and to poetic expression. Logical positivism presupposes that its prohibitions against philosophy and its rejection of all but a few preceding philosophers are not based on arbitrary preferences—that they have a *fundamentum in re.* The hidden assumption is that being-itself cannot be approached cognitively except in those of its manifestations which are open to scientific analysis and verification. Everything else may be open to the noncognitive functions of the mind. But these functions cannot provide knowledge. Therefore, being has a character which makes logical positivism the best, or the only, method of cognitive approach. If the logical positivists cared to look at their hidden ontological assumptions as inquisitively as they look at the "public" ontologies of the classical philosophers, they would no longer be able to reject the question of being-itself.

The tension in the idea of God is transformed into the fundamental philosophical question how being-itself, if taken in its absolute sense, can account for the relativities of reality. The power of being must transcend every being that participates in it. This is the motive which pushes philosophical thought to the absolute, to the negation of any content, to the transnumerical One, to pure identity. On the other hand, the power of being is the power of everything that is, in so far as it *is*. This is the motive which drives philosophical thought to pluralistic principles, to relational or process descriptions of being, to the idea of difference. The double movement of philosophical thought from the relative to the absolute and from the absolute to the relative and the many attempts to find a balance between the two movements determine much philosophical thought throughout its history. They represent a theoretical transformation of the tension within the idea of God and within man's ultimate concern. And this tension, in the last analysis, is the expression of man's basic situation: man is finite, yet at the same time he transcends his finitude.

In its philosophical transformation the universalistic type of polytheism appears as monistic naturalism. *Deus sive natura* is an expression of the universalistic feeling for the all-pervading presence of the divine. But it is an expression in which the numinous character of the universalistic idea of God has been replaced by the secular character of the monistic idea of nature. Nevertheless, the very fact that the words "God" and "nature" can be used interchangeably reveals the religious background of monistic naturalism.

In its philosophical transformation the mythological type of polytheism appears as pluralistic naturalism. The pluralism of ultimate principles for which this philosophy struggles—be it in the form of life-philosophy, or as pragmatism, or as process philosophy—rejects the monistic tendency both of universalistic polytheism and of monistic naturalism. It is naturalism, parallel to the fact that the gods of the mythological type do not radically transcend nature. But it is a naturalism which is open for the contingent and for the new, just as the gods of the corresponding type act irrationally and produce new divine figures in endless succession. But as we have seen that no absolute polytheism is possible, so no absolute pluralism is possible. The unity of being-itself and the unity of the divine press the philosophical consciousness as powerfully as they press the religious consciousness toward a monistic and monotheistic ultimate. The world which is supposed to be pluralistic is one at least in this respect—that it can be recognized as a world, an ordered unity, although it has pluralistic characteristics.

In its philosophical transformation the dualistic type of polytheism appears as metaphysical dualism. The Greek doctrine of a matter (the *me on,* or nonbeing) which resists form establishes two ontological ultimates, even though the second is described as that which has no ultimate ontological standing. That which resists the structure of being cannot be destitute of ontological power. This transformation of religious dualism in Greek philosophy corresponds with the tragic interpretation of existence in Greek art and poetry. Modern philosophy is consciously or unconsciously dependent on the Christian doctrine of creation, in which religious dualism is radically rejected. But the dualistic type of polytheism has been transformed into philosophy even in the Christian period. The duality is not that between form and matter but that between nature and freedom (Kantianism) or that between the irrational will and the rational idea (Böhme, Schelling, Schopenhauer), or that between the "given" and the personal (philosophical theism), or that between the mechanical and the creative (Nietzsche, Bergson, Berdyaev). The motive behind these dualisms is the problem of evil, a clear indication that behind these metaphysical forms of dualism lies the split in the holy and in religious dualism.

In its philosophical transformation monarchical monotheism appears as gradualistic metaphysics. The religious hierarchy is transformed into a hierarchy of powers of being ("The Great Chain of Being"). Ever since Plato wrote his *Symposium* and Aristotle his *Metaphysics* this type of thinking has influenced the Western world in many ways. The absolute is the highest in a scale of relative degrees of being (Plotinus, Dionysius, the Scholastics). The nearer a thing or a sphere of reality is to the absolute, the more being is embodied in it. God is the highest being. The terms "degrees of being," "more being," "less being," are meaningful only if being is not the predicate of an existential judgment but rather if being means "the power of being." Leibniz's monadology is an outstanding example of hierarchical thinking in modern philosophy. The degree of conscious perception determines the ontological status of a monad, from the lowest form of being to God as the central monad. The romantic philosophy of nature applies the hierarchical principle to the different levels of the natural and the spiritual world. It is a triumph of hierarchical thinking that evolutionary philosophers since Hegel's time have employed the formerly static degrees of being as standards of progress in their schemes of dynamic development.

In its philosophical transformation mystical monotheism appears as idealistic monism. The relatedness of universalistic polytheism and mystical monotheism is repeated in the relatedness of naturalistic monism and idealistic monism. The difference is that in idealistic monism the unity of being is seen in its ground, in the basic identity in which all manifoldness disappears, while in naturalistic monism the process itself, including all its variety, is considered the ultimate unity. One could say that naturalistic monism never really reaches the absolute because the absolute cannot be found in nature, while idealistic monism never really reaches manifoldness because manifoldness cannot be derived from anything outside nature. In terms of the philosophy of religion, both forms of monism are called "pantheistic." Pantheist has become a "heresy label" of the worst kind. It should be defined before it is applied aggressively. Pantheism does not mean, never has meant, and never should mean that everything that is, is God. If God is identified with nature (*deus sive natura*), it is not the totality of natural objects which is called God but rather the creative power and unity of nature, the absolute substance which is present in everything. And if God is identified with the absolute of idealistic monism, it is the essential structure of being, the essence of all essences, which is called God. Pantheism is the doctrine that God is the substance or essence of all things, not the meaningless assertion that God is the totality of things. The pantheistic element in the classical doctrine that God is *ipsum esse,* being-itself, is as necessary for a Christian doctrine of God as the mystical element of the divine presence. The danger connected with these elements of mysticism and pantheism is overcome by exclusive monotheism and its philosophical analogues.

In its philosophical transformation exclusive monotheism appears as metaphysical realism. Realism has become a badge of honor in philosophy and theology in proportion to the degree to which idealism has become a badge of dishonor. But few realists are aware of the fact that the pathos of realism is ultimately rooted in the prophetic pathos which tore the divine from its "mixture" with the real, thus liberating the real to be considered in itself. The reason why realistic philosophy is unaware of its religious background is that, with its transformation into philosophy, exclusive monotheism ceases to be theism, just because its God is separated from the reality with which philosophical realism deals. This does not mean that God is denied; he simply is pushed to the edge of reality as a boundary concept, as in deism. He is removed from the real with which man must deal—which is the most effective form of actual denial. Realism does not deny the realm of essences from which idealism sets out, but it considers them mere tools for dealing realistically with reality in thought and action. It does not attribute to them any power of being, and consequently it denies them the power of judging the real. Realism inevitably becomes positivism and pragmatism if it does not proceed to dialectical realism, the philosophical analogue of trinitarian monotheism.

In its philosophical transformation trinitarian monotheism appears, as we have just said, as dialectical realism. In some respects all thinking is dialectical. It moves through "yes" and "no" and "yes" again. It is always a dialogue, whether this proceeds between different subjects or in one subject. But the dialectical method goes beyond this. It presupposes that reality itself moves through "yes" and "no," through positive, negative, and positive again. The dialectical method attempts to mirror the movement of reality. It is the logical expression of a philosophy of life, for life moves through self-affirmation, going out of itself and returning to itself. No one can understand Hegel's dialectical method who does not recognize its roots in the analysis of "life" in Hegel's early writings, from the *Early Theological Writings* to the *Phenomenology of Mind.* Dialectical realism tries to unite the structural oneness of everything within the absolute with the undecided and unfinished manifoldness of the real. It tries to show that the concrete is present in the depth of the ultimate.

These brief indications are designed to demonstrate the fact that the tension in man's ultimate concern and the different types of the idea of God in which it is expressed are the permanent background (visible or hidden) of the way in which philosophical absolutes are conceived. "Transformation" does not mean conscious acts whereby religious symbols are changed into philosophical concepts. It means that the openness of being-itself, which is given in the basic religious experience, is the foundation for the philosophical grasp of the structure of being. This origin of the ultimate philosophical notions explains the fact that they have had and still have tremendous influence on the development of the religious ideas of God, both supporting them and conflicting with them, and affecting religious experience as well as theological conceptualization. They form an element in the history of religion because their own foundation is religious. Theology must deal with philosophical absolutes in both respects. It must ascertain their theoretical validity, which is a philosophical question, and it must seek their existential significance, which is a religious question.

B. THE ACTUALITY OF GOD

3. God as Being

a) God as being and finite being.—The being of God is being-itself. The being of God cannot be understood as the existence of a being alongside others or above others. If God is *a* being, he is subject to the categories of finitude, especially to space and substance. Even if he is called the "highest being" in the sense of the "most perfect" and the "most powerful" being, this situation is not changed. When applied to God, superlatives become diminutives. They place him on the level of other beings while elevating him above all of them. Many theologians who have used the term "highest being" have known better. Actually they have described the highest as the absolute, as that which is on a level qualitatively different from the level of any being—even the highest being. Whenever infinite or unconditional power and meaning are attributed to the highest being, it has ceased to be *a* being and has become being-itself. Many confusions in the doctrine of God and many apologetic weaknesses could be avoided if God were understood first of all as being-itself or as the ground of being. The power of being is another way of expressing the same thing in a circumscribing phrase. Ever since the time of Plato it has been known—although it often has been disregarded, especially by the nominalists and their modern followers—that the concept of being as being, or being-itself, points to the power inherent in everything, the power of resisting nonbeing. Therefore, instead of saying that God is first of all being-itself, it is possible to say that he is the power of being in everything and above everything, the infinite power of being. A theology which does not dare to identify God and the power of being as the first step toward a doctrine of God relapses into monarchic monotheism, for if God is not being-itself, he is subordinate to it, just as Zeus is subordinate to fate in Greek religion. The structure of being-itself is his fate, as it is the fate of all other beings. But God is his own fate; he is "by himself"; he possesses "aseity." This can be said of him only if he is the power of being, if he is being-itself.

As being-itself God is beyond the contrast of essential and existential being. We have spoken of the transition of being into existence, which involves the possibility that being will contradict and lose itself. This transition is excluded from being-itself (except in terms of the christological paradox), for being-itself does not participate in nonbeing. In this it stands in contrast to every being. As classical theology has emphasized, God is beyond essence and existence. Logically, being-itself is "before," "prior to," the split which characterizes finite being.

For this reason it is as wrong to speak of God as the universal essence as it is to speak of him as existing. If God is understood as universal essence, as the form of all forms, he is identified with the unity and totality of finite potentialities; but he has ceased to be the power of the ground in all of them, and therefore he has ceased to transcend them. He has poured all his creative power into a system of forms, and he is bound to these forms. This is what pantheism means.

On the other hand, grave difficulties attend the attempt to speak of God as existing. In order to maintain the truth that God is beyond essence and existence while simultaneously arguing for the existence of God, Thomas Aquinas is forced to distinguish between two kinds of divine existence: that which is identical with essence and that which is not. But an existence of God which is not united with its essence is a contradiction in terms. It makes God a being whose existence does not fulfil his essential potentialities; being and not-yet-being are "mixed" in him, as they are in everything finite. God ceases to be God, the ground of being and meaning. What really has happened is that Thomas has had to unite two different traditions: the Augustinian, in which the divine existence is included in his essence, and the Aristotelian, which derives the existence of God from the existence of the world and which then asserts, in a second step, that his existence is identical with his essence. Thus the question of the existence of God can be neither asked nor answered. If asked, it is a question about that which by its very nature is above existence, and therefore the answer—whether negative or affirmative—implicitly denies the nature of God. It is as atheistic to affirm the existence of God as it is to deny it. God is being-itself, not *a* being. On this basis a first step can be taken toward the solution of the problem which usually is discussed as the immanence and the transcendence of God. As the power of being, God transcends every being and also the totality of beings—the world. Being-itself is beyond finitude and infinity; otherwise it would be conditioned by something other than itself, and the real power of being would lie beyond both it and that which conditioned it. Being-itself infinitely transcends every finite being. There is no proportion or gradation between the finite and the infinite. There is an absolute break, an infinite "jump." On the other hand, everything finite participates in being-itself and in its infinity. Otherwise it would not have the power of being. It would be swallowed by nonbeing, or it never would have emerged out of nonbeing. This double relation of all beings to being-itself gives being-itself a double characteristic. In calling it creative, we point to the fact that everything participates in the infinite power of being. In calling it abysmal, we point to the fact that everything participates in the power of being in a finite way, that all beings are infinitely transcended by their creative ground.

Man is bound to the categories of finitude. He uses the two categories of relation—causality and substance—to express the relation of being-itself to finite beings. The "ground" can be interpreted in both ways, as the cause of finite beings and as their substance. The former has been elaborated by Leibniz in the line of the Thomistic tradition, and the latter has been elaborated by Spinoza in the line of the mystical tradition. Both ways are impossible. Spinoza establishes a naturalistic pantheism, in contrast to the idealistic type which identifies God with the universal essence of being, which denies finite freedom and in so doing denies the freedom of God. By necessity God is merged into the finite beings, and their being is his being. Here again it must be emphasized that pantheism does not say that God is everything. It says that God is the substance of everything and that there is no substantial independence and freedom in anything finite.

Therefore, Christianity, which asserts finite freedom in man and spontaneity in the nonhuman realm, has rejected the category of substance in favor of the category of causality in attempting to express the relation of the power of being to the beings who participate in it. Causality seems to make the world dependent on God, and, at the same time, to separate God from the world in the way a cause is separated from its effect. But the category of causality cannot "fill the bill," for cause and effect are not separate; they include each other and form a series which is endless in both directions. What is cause at one point in this series is effect at another point and conversely. God as cause is drawn into this series, which drives even him beyond himself. In order to disengage the divine cause from the series of causes and effects, it is called the first cause, the absolute beginning. What this means is that the category of causality is being denied while it is being used. In other words, causality is being used not as a category but as a symbol. And if this is done and is understood, the difference between substance and causality disappears, for if God is the cause of the entire series of causes and effects, he is the substance underlying the whole process of becoming. But this "underlying" does not have the character of a substance which underlies its accidents and which is completely expressed by them. It is an underlying in which substance and accidents preserve their freedom. In other words, it is substance not as a category but as a symbol. And, if taken symbolically, there is no difference between *prima causa* and *ultima substantia*. Both mean, what can be called in a more directly symbolic term, "the creative and abysmal ground of being." In this term both naturalistic pantheism, based on the category of substance, and rationalistic theism, based on the category of causality, are overcome.

Since God is the ground of being, he is the ground of the structure of being. He is not subject to this structure; the structure is grounded in him. He *is* this structure, and it is impossible to speak about him except in terms of this structure. God must be approached cognitively through the structural elements of being-itself. These elements make him a living God, a God who can be man's concrete concern. They enable us to use symbols which we are certain point to the ground of reality.

b) God as being and the knowledge of God.—The statement that God is being-itself is a nonsymbolic statement. It does not point beyond itself. It means what it says directly and properly; if we speak of the actuality of God, we first assert that he is not God if he is not being-itself. Other assertions about God can be made theologically only on this basis. Of course, religious assertions do not require such a foundation for what they say about God; the foundation is implicit in every religious thought concerning God. Theologians must make explicit what is implicit in religious thought and expression; and, in order to do this, they must begin with the most abstract and completely unsymbolic statement which is possible, namely, that God is being-itself or the absolute.

However, after this has been said, nothing else can be said about God as God which is not symbolic. As we already have seen, God as being-itself is the ground of the ontological structure of being without being subject to this structure himself. He *is* the structure; that is, he has the power of determining the structure of everything that has being. Therefore, if anything beyond this bare assertion is said about God, it no longer is a direct and proper statement, no longer a concept. It is indirect, and it points to something beyond itself. In a word, it is symbolic.

The general character of the symbol has been described. Special emphasis must be laid on the insight that symbol and sign are different; that, while the sign bears no necessary relation to that to which it points, the symbol participates in the reality of that for which it stands. The sign can be changed arbitrarily according to the demands of expediency, but the symbol grows and dies according to the correlation between that which is symbolized and the persons who receive it as a symbol. Therefore, the religious symbol, the symbol which points to the divine, can be a true symbol only if it participates in the power of the divine to which it points.

There can be no doubt that any concrete assertion about God must be symbolic, for a concrete assertion is one which uses a segment of finite experience in order to say something about him. It transcends the content of this segment, although it also includes it. The segment of finite reality which becomes the vehicle of a concrete assertion about God is affirmed and negated at the same time. It becomes a symbol, for a symbolic expression is one whose proper meaning is negated by that to which it points. And yet it also is affirmed by it, and this affirmation gives the symbolic expression an adequate basis for pointing beyond itself.

The crucial question must now be faced. Can a segment of finite reality become the basis for an assertion about that which is infinite? The answer is that it can, because that which is infinite is being-itself and because everything participates in being-itself. The *analogia entis* is not the property of a questionable natural theology which attempts to gain knowledge of God by drawing conclusions about the infinite from the finite. The *analogia entis* gives us our only justification of speaking at all about God. It is based on the fact that God must be understood as being-itself.

The truth of a religious symbol has nothing to do with the truth of the empirical assertions involved in it, be they physical, psychological, or historical. A religious symbol possesses some truth if it adequately expresses the correlation of revelation in which some person stands. A religious symbol *is* true if it adequately expresses the correlation of some person with final revelation. A religious symbol can die only if the correlation of which it is an adequate expression dies. This occurs whenever the revelatory situation changes and former symbols become obsolete. The history of religion, right up to our own time, is full of dead symbols which have been killed not by a scientific criticism of assumed superstitions but by a religious criticism of religion. The judgment that a religious symbol *is* true is identical with the judgment that the revelation of which it is the adequate expression is true. This double meaning of the truth of a symbol must be kept in mind. A symbol *has* truth: it is adequate to the revelation it expresses. A symbol *is* true: it is the expression of a true revelation.

Theology as such has neither the duty nor the power to confirm or to negate religious symbols. Its task is to interpret them according to theological principles and methods. In the process of interpretation, however, two things may happen: theology may discover contradictions between symbols within the theological circle and theology may speak not only as theology but also as religion. In the first case, theology can point out the religious dangers and the theological errors which follow from the use of certain symbols; in the second case, theology can become prophecy, and in this role it may contribute to a change in the revelatory situation.

Religious symbols are double-edged. They are directed toward the infinite which they symbolize *and* toward the finite through which they symbolize it. They force the infinite down to finitude and the finite up to infinity. They open the divine for the human and the human for the divine. For instance, if God is symbolized as "Father," he is brought down to the human relationship of father and child. But at the same time this human relationship is consecrated into a pattern of the divine-human relationship. If "Father" is employed as a symbol for God, fatherhood is seen in its theonomous, sacramental depth. One cannot arbitrarily "make" a religious symbol out of a segment of secular reality. Not even the collective unconscious, the great symbol-creating source, can do this. If a segment of reality is used as a symbol for God, the realm of reality from which it is taken is, so to speak, elevated into the realm of the holy. It no longer is secular. It is theonomous. If God is called the "king," something is said not only about God but also about the holy character of kinghood. If God's work is called "making whole" or "healing," this not only says something about God but also emphasizes the theonomous character of all healing. If God's self-manifestation is called "the word," this not only symbolizes God's relation to man but also emphasizes the holiness of all words as an expression of the spirit. The list could be continued. Therefore, it is not surprising that in a secular culture both the symbols for God and the theonomous character of the material from which the symbols are taken disappear.

A final word of warning must be added in view of the fact that for many people the very term "symbolic" carries the connotation of nonreal. This is partially the result of confusion between sign and symbol and partially due to the identification of reality with empirical reality, with the entire realm of objective things and events. Both reasons have been undercut explicitly and implicitly in the foregoing chapters. But one reason remains, namely, the fact that some theological movements, such as Protestant Hegelianism and Catholic modernism, have interpreted religious language symbolically in order to dissolve its realistic meaning and to weaken its seriousness, its power, and its spiritual impact. This was not the purpose of the classical essays on the "divine names," in which the symbolic character of all affirmations about God was strongly emphasized and explained in religious terms, nor was it a consequence of these essays. Their intention and their result was to give to God and to all his relations to man more reality and power than a nonsymbolic and therefore easily superstitious interpretation could give them. In this sense symbolic interpretation is proper and necessary; it enhances rather than diminishes the reality and power of religious language, and in so doing it performs an important function.

4. God as Living

a) *God as being and God as living.*—Life is the process in which potential being becomes actual being. It is the actualization of the structural elements of being in their unity and in their tension. These elements move divergently and convergently in every life-process; they separate and reunite simultaneously. Life ceases in the moment of separation without union or of union without separation. Both complete identity and complete separation negate life. If we call God the "living God," we deny that he is a pure identity of being as being; and we also deny that there is a definite separation of being from being in him. We assert that he is the eternal process in which separation is posited and is overcome by reunion. In this sense, God lives. Few things about God are more emphasized in the Bible, especially in the Old Testament, than the truth that God is a living God. Most of the so-called anthropomorphisms of the biblical picture of God are expressions of his character as living. His actions, his passions, his remembrances and anticipations, his suffering and joy, his personal relations and his plans—all these make him a living God and distinguish him from the pure absolute, from being-itself.

Life is the actuality of being, or, more exactly, it is the process in which potential being becomes actual being. But in God as God there is no distinction between potentiality and actuality. Therefore, we cannot speak of God as living in the proper or nonsymbolic sense of the word "life." We must speak of God as living in symbolic terms. Yet every true symbol participates in the reality which it symbolizes. God lives in so far as he is the ground of life.[5] Anthropomorphic symbols are adequate for speaking of God religiously. Only in this way can he be the living God for man. But even in the most primitive intuition of the divine a feeling should be, and usually is, present that there is a mystery about divine names which makes them improper, self-transcending, symbolic. Religious instruction should deepen this feeling without depriving the divine names of their reality and power. One of the most surprising qualities of the prophetic utterances in the Old Testament is that, on the one hand, they always appear concrete and anthropomorphic and that, on the other hand, they preserve the mystery of the divine ground. They never deal with being as being or with the absolute as the absolute; nevertheless, they never make God a being alongside others, into something conditioned by something else which also is conditioned. Nothing is more inadequate and disgusting than the attempt to translate the concrete symbols of the Bible into less concrete and less powerful symbols. Theology should not weaken the concrete symbols, but it must analyze them and interpret them in abstract ontological terms. Nothing is more

5. "He that formed the eye, shall he not see?" (Ps. 94:9).

inadequate and confusing than the attempt to restrict theological work to half-abstract, half-concrete terms which do justice neither to existential intuition nor to cognitive analysis.

The ontological structure of being supplies the material for the symbols which point to the divine life. However, this does not mean that a doctrine of God can be derived from an ontological system. The character of the divine life is made manifest in revelation. Theology can only explain and systematize the existential knowledge of revelation in theoretical terms, interpreting the symbolic significance of the ontological elements and categories.

While the symbolic power of the categories appears in the relation of God to the creature, the elements give symbolic expression to the nature of the divine life itself. The polar character of the ontological elements is rooted in the divine life, but the divine life is not subject to this polarity. Within the divine life, every ontological element includes its polar element completely, without tension and without the threat of dissolution, for God is being-itself. However, there is a difference between the first and the second elements in each polarity with regard to their power of symbolizing the divine life. The elements of individualization, dynamics, and freedom represent the self or subject side of the basic ontological structure within the polarity to which they belong. The elements of participation, form, and destiny represent the world or object side of the basic ontological structure within the polarity to which they belong. Both sides are rooted in the divine life. But the first side determines the existential relationship between God and man, which is the source of all symbolization. Man is a self who has a world. As a self he is an individual person who participates universally, he is a dynamic self-transcending agent within a special and a general form, and he is freedom which has a special destiny and which participates in a general destiny. Therefore, man symbolizes that which is his ultimate concern in terms taken from his own being. From the subjective side of the polarities he takes—or more exactly, receives—the material with which he symbolizes the divine life. He sees the divine life as personal, dynamic, and free. He cannot see it in any other way, for God is man's ultimate concern, and therefore he stands in analogy to that which man himself is. But the religious mind—theologically speaking, man in the correlation of revelation—always realizes implicitly, if not explicitly, that the other side of the polarities also is completely present in the side he uses as symbolic material. God is called a person, but he is a person not in finite separation but in an absolute and unconditional participation in everything. God is called dynamic, but he is dynamic not in tension with form but in an absolute and unconditional unity with form, so that his self-transcendence never is in tension with his self-preservation, so that he always remains God. God is called "free," but he is free not in arbitrariness but in an absolute and unconditional identity with his destiny, so that he himself is his destiny, so that the essential structures of being are not strange to his freedom but are the actuality of his freedom. In this way, although the symbols used for the divine life are taken from the concrete situation of man's relationship to God, they imply God's ultimacy, the ultimacy in which the polarities of being disappear in the ground of being, in being-itself.

The basic ontological structure of self and world is transcended in the divine life without providing symbolic material. God cannot be called a self, because the concept "self" implies separation from and contrast to everything which is not self. God cannot be called the world even by implication. Both self and world are rooted in the divine life, but they cannot become symbols for it. But the elements which constitute the basic ontological structure can become symbols because they do not speak of kinds of being (self and world) but of qualities of being which are valid in their proper sense when applied to all beings and which are valid in their symbolic sense when applied to being-itself.

b) *The divine life and the ontological elements.*—The symbols provided by the ontological elements present a great number of problems for the doctrine of God. In every special case it is necessary to distinguish between the proper sense of the concepts and their symbolic sense. And it is equally necessary to balance one side of the ontological polarity against the other without reducing the symbolic power of either of them. The history of theological thought is a continuous proof of the difficulty, the creativeness, and the danger of this situation. This is obvious if we consider the symbolic power of the polarity of individualization and participation. The symbol "personal God" is absolutely fundamental because an existential relation is a person-to-person relation. Man cannot be ultimately concerned about anything that is less than personal, but since personality (*persona, prosopon*) includes individuality, the question arises in what sense God can be called an individual. Is it meaningful to call him the "absolute individual"? The answer must be that it is meaningful only in the sense that he can be called the "absolute participant." The one term cannot be applied without the other. This can only mean that both individualization and participation are rooted in the ground of the divine life and that God is equally "near" to each of them while transcending them both.

The solution of the difficulties in the phrase "personal God" follows from this. "Personal God" does not mean that God is *a* person. It means that God is the ground of everything personal and that he carries within himself the ontological power of personality. He is not a person, but he is not less than personal. It should not be forgotten that classical theology employed the term *persona* for the trinitarian hypostases but not for God himself. God became "a person" only in the nineteenth century, in connection with the Kantian separation of nature ruled by physical law from personality ruled by moral law. Ordinary theism has made God a heavenly, completely perfect person who resides above the world and mankind. The protest of atheism against such a highest person is correct. There is no evidence for his existence, nor is he a matter of ultimate concern. God is not God without universal participation. "Personal God" is a confusing symbol.

God is the principle of participation as well as the principle of individualization. The divine life participates in every life as its ground and aim. God participates in everything that is; he has community with it; he shares in its destiny. Certainly such statements are highly symbolic. They can have the unfortunate logical implication that there is something alongside God in which he participates from the outside. But the divine participation creates that in which it participates. Plato uses the word *parousia* for the presence of the essences in temporal existence. This word later becomes the name for the preliminary and final presence of the transcendent Christ in the church and in the world. *Par-ousia* means "being by," "being with"—but on the basis of being absent, of being separated. In the same way God's participation is not a spatial or temporal presence. It is meant not categorically but symbolically. It is the parousia, the "being with" of that which is neither here nor there. If applied to God, participation and community are not less symbolic than individualization and personality. While active religious communication between God and man depends on the symbol of the personal God, the symbol of universal participation expresses the passive experience of the divine parousia in terms of the divine omnipresence.

The polarity of dynamics and form supplies the material basis for a group of symbols which are central for any present-day doctrine of God. Potentiality, vitality, and self-transcendence are indicated in the term "dynamics," while the term "form" embraces actuality, intentionality, and self-preservation.

Potentiality and actuality appear in classical theology in the famous formula that God is *actus purus,* the pure form in which everything potential is actual, and which is the eternal self-intuition of the divine fulness (*pleroma*). In this formula the dynamic side in the dynamics-form polarity is swallowed by the form side. Pure actuality, that is, actuality free from any element of potentiality, is a fixed result; it is not alive. Life includes the separation of potentiality and actuality. The nature of life is actualization, not actuality. The God who is *actus purus* is not the living God. It is interesting that even those theologians who have used the concept of *actus purus* normally speak of God in the dynamic symbols of the Old Testament and of Christian experience. This situation has induced some thinkers—partly under the influence of Luther's dynamic conception of God and partly under the impact of the problem of evil—to emphasize the dynamics in God and to depreciate the stabilization of dynamics in pure actuality. They try to distinguish between two elements in God, and they assert that, in so far as God is a living God, these two elements must remain in tension. Whether the first element is called the *Ungrund* or the "nature in God" (Böhme), or the first potency (Schelling), or the will (Schopenhauer), or the "given" in God (Brightman), or *me-onic* freedom (Berdyaev), or the contingent (Hartshorne)—in all these cases it is an expression of what we have called "dynamics," and it is an attempt to prevent the dynamics in God from being transformed into pure actuality.

Theological criticism of these attempts is easy if the concepts are taken in their proper sense, for then they make God finite, dependent on a fate or an accident which is not himself. The finite God, if taken literally, is a finite god, a polytheistic god. But this is not the way in which these concepts should be interpreted. They point symbolically to a quality of the divine life which is analogous to what appears as dynamics in the ontological structure. The divine creativity, God's participation in history, his outgoing character, are based on this dynamic element. It includes a "not yet" which is, however, always balanced by an "already" within the divine life. It is not an absolute "not yet," which would make it a divine-demonic power, nor is the "already" an absolute already. It also can be expressed as the negative element in the ground of being which is overcome as negative in the process of being-itself. As such it is the basis of the negative element in the creature, in which it is not overcome but is effective as a threat and a potential disruption.

These assertions include a rejection of a nonsymbolic, ontological doctrine of God as becoming. If we say that being is actual as life, the element of self-transcendence is obviously and emphatically included. But it is included as a symbolic element in balance with form. Being is not in balance with becoming. Being comprises becoming and rest, becoming as an implication of dynamics and rest as an implication of form. If we say that God is being-itself, this includes both rest and becoming, both the static and the dynamic elements. However, to speak of a "becoming" God disrupts the balance between dynamics and form and subjects God to a process which has the character of a fate or which is completely open to the future and has the character of an absolute accident. In both cases the divinity of God is undercut. The basic error of these doctrines is their metaphysical-constructive character. They apply the ontological elements to God in a nonsymbolic manner and are driven to religiously offensive and theologically untenable consequences.

If the element of form in the dynamics-form polarity is applied symbolically to the divine life, it expresses the actualization of its potentialities. The divine life inescapably unites possibility with fulfilment. Neither side threatens the other, nor is there a threat of disruption. In terms of self-preservation one could say that God cannot cease to be God. His going-out from himself does not diminish or destroy his divinity. It is united with the eternal "resting in himself."

The divine form must be conceived in analogy with what we have called "intentionality" on the human level. It is balanced with vitality, the dynamic side on the human level. The polarity in this formulation appears in classical theology as the polarity of will and intellect in God. It is consistent that Thomas Aquinas had to subordinate the will in God to the intellect when he accepted the Aristotelian *actus purus* as the basic character of God. And it must be remembered that the line of theological thought which tries to preserve the element of dynamics in God actually begins with Duns Scotus, who elevated the will in God ·over the intellect. Of course, both will and intellect in their application to God express infinitely more than the mental acts of willing and understanding as these appear in human experience. They are symbols for dynamics in all its ramifications and for form as the meaningful structure of being-itself. Therefore, it is not a question of metaphysical psychology, whether Aquinas or Duns Scotus is right. It is a question of the way in which psychological concepts should be employed as symbols for the divine life. And with respect to this question it is obvious that for more than a century a decision has been made in favor of the dynamic element. The philosophy of life, existential philosophy, and process philosophy agree on this point. Protestantism has contributed strong motives for this decision, but theology must balance the new with the old (predominantly Catholic) emphasis on the form character of the divine life.

If we consider the polarity of freedom and destiny in its symbolic value, we find that there hardly is a word said about God in the Bible which does not point directly or indirectly to his freedom. In freedom he creates, in freedom he deals with the world and man, in freedom he saves and fulfils. His freedom is freedom from anything prior to him or alongside him. Chaos cannot prevent him from speaking the word which makes light out of darkness; the evil deeds of men cannot prevent him from carrying through his plans; the good deeds of men cannot force him to reward them; the structure of being cannot prevent him from revealing himself; etc. Classical theology has spoken in more abstract terms of the aseity of God, of his being *a se,* self-derived. There is no ground prior to him which could condition his freedom; neither chaos nor nonbeing has power to limit or resist him. But aseity also means that there is nothing given in God which is not at the same time affirmed by his freedom. If taken nonsymbolically, this naturally leads to an unanswerable question, whether the structure of freedom, because it constitutes his freedom, is not itself something given in relation to which God has no freedom. The answer can only be that freedom, like the other ontological concepts, must be understood symbolically and in terms of the existential correlation of man and God. If taken in this way, freedom means that that which is man's ultimate concern is in no way dependent on man or on any finite being or on any finite concern. Only that which is unconditional can be the expression of unconditional concern. A conditioned God is no God.

Can the term "destiny" be applied symbolically to the divine life? The gods of polytheism have a destiny—or, more correctly, a fate—because they are not ultimate. But can one say that he who is unconditional and absolute has a destiny in the same manner in which he has freedom? Is it possible to attribute destiny to being-itself? It is possible, provided the connotation of a destiny-determining power above God is avoided and provided one adds that God is his own destiny and that in God freedom and destiny are one. It may be argued that this truth is more adequately expressed if destiny is replaced by necessity, not mechanical necessity, but structural necessity, of course, or if God is spoken of as being his own law. Such phrases are important as interpretations, but they lack two elements of meaning which are present in the word "destiny." They lack the mystery of that which precedes any structure and law, being-itself; and they lack the relation to history which is included in the term "destiny." If we say that God is his own destiny, we point both to the infinite mystery of being and to the participation of God in becoming and in history.

c) God as spirit and the trinitarian principles.—Spirit is the unity of the ontological elements and the *telos* of life. Actualized as life, being-itself is fulfilled as spirit. The word *telos* expresses the relation of life and spirit more precisely than the words "aim" or "goal." It expresses the inner directedness of life toward spirit, the urge of life to become spirit, to fulfil itself as spirit. *Telos* stands for an inner, essential, necessary aim, for that in which a being fulfils its own nature. God as living is God fulfilled in himself and therefore spirit. God *is* spirit. This is the most embracing, direct, and unrestricted symbol for the divine life. It does not need to be balanced with another symbol, because it includes all the ontological elements.

Some anticipatory remarks about spirit must be made at this point, although the doctrine of the spirit is the subject of a separate part of systematic theology. The word "spirit" (with a lower-case *s*) has almost disappeared from the English language as a significant philosophical term, in contrast to German, French, and Italian, in which the words *Geist, esprit,* and *spirito* have preserved their philosophical standing. Probably this is a result of the radical separation of the cognitive function of the mind from emotion and will, as typified in English empiricism. In any case, the word "spirit" appears predominantly in a religious context, and here it is spelled with a capital *S*. But it is impossible to understand the meaning of Spirit unless the meaning of spirit is understood, for Spirit is the symbolic application of spirit to the divine life.

The meaning of spirit is built up through the meaning of the ontological elements and their union. In terms of both sides of the three polarities one can say that spirit is the unity of power and meaning. On the side of power it includes centered personality, self-transcending vitality, and freedom of self-determination. On the side of meaning it includes universal participation, forms and structures of reality, and limiting and directing destiny. Life fulfilled as spirit embraces passion as much as truth, libido as much as surrender, will to power as much as justice. If one of these sides is absorbed by its correlate, either abstract law or choatic movement remains. Spirit does not stand in contrast to body. Life as spirit transcends the duality of body and mind. It also transcends the triplicity of body, soul, and mind, in which soul is actual life-power and mind and body are its functions. Life as spirit is the life of the soul, which includes mind and body, but not as realities alongside the soul. Spirit is not a "part," nor is it a special function. It is the all-embracing function in which all elements of the structure of being participate. Life as spirit can be found by man only in man, for only in him is the structure of being completely realized.

The statement that God is Spirit means that life as spirit is the inclusive symbol for the divine life. It contains all the ontological elements. God is not nearer to one "part" of being or to a special function of being than he is to another. As Spirit he is as near to the creative darkness of the unconscious as he is to the critical light of cognitive reason. Spirit is the power through which meaning lives, and it is the meaning which gives direction to power. God as Spirit is the ultimate unity of both power and meaning. In contrast to Nietzsche, who identified the two assertions that God is Spirit and that God is dead, we must say that God is the living God because he is Spirit.

Any discussion of the *Christian* doctrine of the Trinity must begin with the christological assertion that Jesus is the Christ. The Christian doctrine of the Trinity is a corroboration of the christological dogma. The situation is different if we do not ask the question of the Christian doctrines but rather the question of the *presuppositions* of these doctrines in an idea of God. Then we must speak about the trinitarian principles, and we must begin with the Spirit rather than with the Logos. God is Spirit, and any trinitarian statement must be derived from this basic assertion.

God's life is life as spirit, and the trinitarian principles are moments within the process of the divine life. Human intuition of the divine always has distinguished between the abyss of the divine (the element of power) and the fulness of its content (the element of meaning), between the divine depth and the divine *logos*. The first principle is the basis of Godhead, that which makes God God. It is the root of his majesty, the unapproachable intensity of his being, the inexhaustible ground of being in which everything has its origin. It is the power of being infinitely resisting nonbeing, giving the power of being to every-thing that is. During the past centuries theological and philosophical rationalism have deprived the idea of God of this first principle, and by doing so they have robbed God of his divinity. He has become a hypostasized moral ideal or another name for the structural unity of reality. The power of the Godhead has disappeared.

The classical term *logos* is most adequate for the second principle, that of meaning and structure. It unites meaningful structure with crea-tivity. Long before the Christian Era—in a way already in Heraclitus—*logos* received connotations of ultimacy as well as the meaning of being as being. According to Parmenides, being and the *logos* of being cannot be separated. The *logos* opens the divine ground, its infinity and its darkness, and it makes its fulness distinguishable, definite, finite. The *logos* has been called the mirror of the divine depth, the principle of God's self-objectification. In the *logos* God speaks his "word," both in himself and beyond himself. Without the second principle the first prin-ciple would be chaos, burning fire, but it would not be the creative ground. Without the second principle God is demonic, is characterized by absolute seclusion, is the "naked absolute" (Luther).

As the actualization of the other two principles, the Spirit is the third principle. Both power and meaning are contained in it and united in it. It makes them creative. The third principle is in a way the whole (God *is* Spirit), and in a way it is a special principle (God *has* the Spirit as he has the *logos*). It is the Spirit in whom God "goes out from" himself, the Spirit proceeds from the divine ground. He gives actuality to that which is potential in the divine ground and "outspoken" in the divine *logos*. Through the Spirit the divine fulness is posited in the divine life as something definite, and at the same time it is reunited in the divine ground. The finite is posited as finite within the process of the divine life, but it is reunited with the infinite within the same process. It is dis-tinguished from the infinite, but it is not separated from it. The divine life is infinite mystery, but it is not infinite emptiness. It is the ground of all abundance, and it is abundant itself.

The consideration of the trinitarian principles is not the Christian doc-trine of the Trinity. It is a preparation for it, nothing more. The dogma of the Trinity can be discussed only after the christological dogma has been elaborated. But the trinitarian principles appear whenever one speaks meaningfully of the living God.

The divine life is infinite, but in such a way that the finite is posited in it in a manner which transcends potentiality and actuality. Therefore, it is not precise to identify God with the infinite. This can be done on some levels of analysis. If man and his world are described as finite, God is infinite in contrast to them. But the analysis must go beyond this level in both directions. Man is aware of his finitude because he has the power of transcending it and of looking at it. Without this awareness he could not call himself mortal. On the other hand, that which is infinite would not be infinite if it were limited by the finite. God is infinite because he has the finite (and with it that element of nonbeing which belongs to finitude) within himself united with his infinity. One of the functions of the symbol "divine life" is to point to this situation.

5. God as Creating

Introduction: creation and finitude.—The divine life is creative, actualizing itself in inexhaustible abundance. The divine life and the divine creativity are not different. God is creative because he is God. Therefore, it is meaningless to ask whether creation is a necessary or a contingent act of God. Nothing is necessary for God in the sense that he is dependent on a necessity above him. His aseity implies that everything which he is he is through himself. He eternally "creates himself," a paradoxical phrase which states God's freedom. Nor is creation contingent. It does not "happen" to God, for it is identical with his life. Creation is not only God's freedom but also his destiny. But it is not a fate; it is neither a necessity nor an accident which determines him.

The doctrine of creation is not the story of an event which took place "once upon a time." It is the basic description of the relation between God and the world. It is the correlate to the analysis of man's finitude. It answers the question implied in man's finitude and in finitude generally. In giving this answer, it discovers that the meaning of finitude is creatureliness. The doctrine of creation is the answer to the question implied in the creature as creature. This question is asked continually and is always answered in man's essential nature. The question and the answer are beyond potentiality and actuality, as all things are in the process of the divine life. But actually the question is asked and is *not* answered in man's existential situation. The character of existence is that man asks the question of his finitude without receiving an answer. It follows that even if there were such a thing as natural theology, it could not reach the truth of God's creativity and man's creatureliness. The doctrine of creation does not describe an event. It points to the situation of creatureliness and to its correlate, the divine creativity.

Since the divine life is essentially creative, all three modes of time must be used in symbolizing it. God *has* created the world, he *is* creative in the present moment, and he *will* creatively fulfil his *telos*. Therefore, we must speak of originating creation, sustaining creation, and directing creation. This means that not only the preservation of the world but also providence is subsumed under the doctrine of the divine creativity.

a) God's originating creativity.—(1) Creation and Nonbeing: The classical Christian doctrine of creation uses the phrase *creatio ex nihilo*. The first task of theology is an interpretation of these words. Their obvious meaning is a critical negation. God finds nothing "given" to him which influences him in his creativity or which resists his creative *telos*. The doctrine of *creatio ex nihilo* is Christianity's protection against any type of ultimate dualism. That which concerns man ultimately can only be that on which he ultimately depends. Two ultimates destroy the ultimacy of concern. This negative meaning of *creatio ex nihilo* is clear and decisive for every Christian experience and assertion. It is the mark of distinction between paganism, even in its most refined form, and Christianity, even in its most primitive form.

The question arises, however, whether the term *ex nihilo* points to more than the rejection of dualism. The word *ex* seems to refer to the origin of the creature. "Nothing" is what (or where) it comes from. Now "nothing" can mean two things. It can mean the absolute negation of being (*ouk on*), or it can mean the relative negation of being (*me on*). If *ex nihilo* meant the latter, it would be a restatement of the Greek doctrine of matter and form against which it is directed. If *ex nihilo* meant the absolute negation of being, it could not be the origin of the creature. Nevertheless, the term *ex nihilo* says something fundamentally important about the creature, namely, that it must take over what might be called "the heritage of nonbeing." Creatureliness implies nonbeing, but creatureliness is more than nonbeing. It carries in itself the power of being, and this power of being is its participation in being-itself, in the creative ground of being. Being a creature includes both the heritage of nonbeing (anxiety) and the heritage of being (courage). It does not include a strange heritage originating in a half-divine power which is in conflict with the power of being-itself.

The doctrine of creation out of nothing expresses two fundamental truths. The first is that the tragic character of existence is not rooted in the creative ground of being; consequently, it does not belong to the essential nature of things. In itself finitude is not tragic, that is, it is not doomed to self-destruction by its very greatness. Therefore, the tragic is not conquered by avoiding the finite as much as possible, that is, by ontological asceticism. The tragic is conquered by the presence of being-itself within the finite.[6] The second truth expressed in this doctrine is that there is an element of nonbeing in creatureliness; this gives insight into the natural necessity of death and into the potentiality but not necessity of the tragic.

Two central theological doctrines are based on the doctrine of creation, namely, incarnation and eschatology. God can appear within finitude only if the finite as such is not in conflict with him. And history can be fulfilled in the *eschaton* only if salvation does not presuppose elevation above finitude. The formula *creatio ex nihilo* is not the title of a story. It is the classical formula which expresses the relation between God and the world.

(2) Creation, Essence, and Existence: In the Nicene Creed, God is called the creator of "everything visible and invisible." Like the formula just discussed, this phrase also has, first of all, a protective function. It is directed against the Platonic doctrine that the creator-god is dependent on the eternal essences or ideas, the powers of being which make a thing what it is. These eternal powers of being could receive a kind of divine honor in opposition to, or at least in distinction from, the adoration due God alone. They could be identified with the angels of Middle Eastern tradition (who often are dispossessed gods) and made the objects of a cult. This occurred even within Christianity, as the New Testament shows. Neo-Platonism, and with it much Christian theology, taught that the essences are ideas in the divine mind. They are the patterns according to which God creates. They are themselves dependent on God's internal creativity; they are not independent of him, standing in some heavenly niche as models for his creative activity. The essential powers of being belong to the divine life in which they are rooted, created by him who is everything he is "through himself."

There is no difference in the divine life between potentiality and actuality. This solves one of the most difficult problems connected with the ontology of essences, namely, how essences are related to universals, on the one hand, and to individuals, on the other hand. The more individualized the conception of the essences, the more they constitute a

6. Christian asceticism is functional rather than ontological; it serves self-discipline and self-surrender; it does not seek an escape from finitude.

duplicate of reality. This is radically carried through in the view which the later Platonists taught that there is an idea of every individual thing in the divine mind. Here the ideas lose the function they had in the original conception, which was to describe the eternally true within the flux of reality. It is understandable that nominalism abolished this duplication of the world and attributed being only to individual things, but nominalism cannot deny the power of the universals which reappear in every individual exemplar and which determine its nature and its growth. And even in the individual, notably in the individual man, there is an inner *telos* which transcends the various moments of the process of his life.

The creative process of the divine life precedes the differentiation between essences and existents. In the creative vision of God the individual is present as a whole in his essential being and inner *telos* and, at the same time, in the infinity of the special moments of his life-process. Of course, this is said symbolically, since we are unable to have a perception or even an imagination of that which belongs to the divine life. The mystery of being beyond essence and existence is hidden in the mystery of the creativity of the divine life.

But man's being is not only hidden in the creative ground of the divine life; it also is manifest to itself and to other life within the whole of reality. Man does exist, and his existence is different from his essence. Man and the rest of reality are not only "inside" the process of the divine life but also "outside" it. Man is grounded in it, but he is not kept within the ground. Man has left the ground in order to "stand upon" himself, to actualize what he essentially is, in order to be *finite freedom*. This is the point at which the doctrine of creation and the doctrine of the fall join. It is the most difficult and the most dialectical point in the doctrine of creation. And, as every existential analysis of the human situation shows, it is the most mysterious point in human experience. Fully developed creatureliness is fallen creatureliness. The creature has actualized its freedom in so far as it is outside the creative ground of the divine life. This is the difference between being inside and being outside the divine life. "Inside" and "outside" are spatial symbols, but what they say is not spatial. They refer to something qualitative rather than quantitative. To be outside the divine life means to stand in actualized freedom, in an existence which is no longer united with essence. Seen from one side, this is the end of creation. Seen from the other side, it is the beginning of the fall. Freedom and destiny are correlates. The point at which creation and fall coincide is as much a matter of destiny as it is a matter of freedom. The fact that it is a universal situation proves that it is not a matter of individual contingency, either in "Adam" or in anyone else. The fact that it separates existence from its unity with essence indicates that it is not a matter of structural necessity. It is the actualization of ontological freedom united with ontological destiny.

Every theologian who is courageous enough to face the twofold truth that nothing can happen to God accidentally and that the state of existence is a fallen state must accept the point of coincidence between the end of creation and the beginning of the fall. Those theologians who are not willing to interpret the biblical creation story and the story of the fall as reports about two actual events should draw the consequence and posit the mystery where it belongs—in the unity of freedom and destiny in the ground of being. The supralapsarian Calvinists, who asserted that Adam fell by divine decree, had the courage to face this situation. But they did not have the wisdom to formulate their insight in such a way that the seemingly demonic character of this decree was avoided.

To sum up the discussion: being a creature means both to be rooted in the creative ground of the divine life and to actualize one's self through freedom. Creation is fulfilled in the creaturely self-realization which simultaneously is freedom and destiny. But it is fulfilled through separation from the creative ground through a break between existence and essence. Creaturely freedom is the point at which creation and the fall coincide.

This is the background of what is called "human creativity." If creativity means "to bring the new into being," man is creative in every direction—with respect to himself and his world, with respect to being and with respect to meaning. However, if creativity means "to bring into being that which had no being," then divine and human creativity differ sharply. Man creates new syntheses out of given material. This creation really is transformation. God creates the material out of which the new syntheses can be developed. God creates man; he gives man the power of transforming himself and his world. Man can transform only what is given to him. God is primarily and essentially creative; man is secondarily and existentially creative. And, beyond this, in every act of human creativity the element of separation from the creative ground is effective. Human creation is ambiguous.[7]

(3) Creation and the Categories: The primacy of time as a category of

7. See Part IV, Sec. 1.

finitude is expressed in the fact that the question of creation and the categories usually is discussed as the question of the relation between creation and time. If creation is symbolized as a past event, it is natural to ask what happened before this event took place. Certainly the question is absurd; it has been rejected on philosophical as well as on religious grounds, with arguments as well as with "holy wrath" (Luther). But the absurdity does not lie in the question as such; it lies in its presupposition: creation is an event in the past. This presupposition subjects creation to time, and time inescapably implies "before" and "after." The traditional theological formula since Augustine has been that time was created *with* the world, of which it is the basic categorical form. Sometimes, however, theologians have suspected that this formula implies an eternal creation, that creation is coeternal with God although temporal in its content. They assert creation *in* time while rejecting a pre-creation time. Karl Barth is a contemporary example. Yet this position seems to differ from the Augustinian only in vocabulary, not in substance.

The answer to the question of creation and time must be derived from the creative character of the divine life. If the finite is posited within the process of the divine life, the forms of finitude (the categories) also are present in it. The divine life includes temporality, but it is not subject to it. The divine eternity includes time and transcends it. The time of the divine life is determined not by the negative element of creaturely time but by the present, not by the "no longer" and the "not yet" of our time. Our time, the time which is determined by nonbeing, is the time of existence. It presupposes the separation of existence from essence and the existential disruption of the moments of time which are essentially united within the divine life.

Time, then, has a double character with respect to creation. It belongs to the creative process of the divine life as well as to the point of creation which coincides with the fall. Time participates in the destiny of everything created to be rooted in the divine ground beyond essence and existence and to be separated from the divine ground through creaturely freedom and creaturely destiny. Therefore, if one speaks of time before creation, this can only mean the divine time which is not "before" in any sense of temporal existence. And if one speaks of creation *in* time, this can only mean the transformation of the time which belongs to the divine life into the time which belongs to creaturely existence. It is more adequate to speak of creation *with* time, for time is the form of finitude in the creative ground of the divine life as well as in creaturely existence.

Analogous statements can be made with regard to the other categories. All of them are present within the creative ground of the divine life in a manner which must be indicated symbolically. And all of them are present in the way we experience them in the existence of actualized freedom, in the fulfilment and the self-estrangement of creaturely being.

(4) The Creature: In maintaining that the fulfilment of creation is the actualization of finite freedom, we affirm implicitly that man is the *telos* of creation. Of no other being that is known can it be said that finite freedom is actualized within it. In other beings there are preformations of freedom, such as Gestalt and spontaneity, but the power of transcending the chain of stimulus and response by deliberation and decision is absent. No other being has a complete self and a complete world; no other being is aware of finitude on the basis of an awareness of potential infinity. If another being were found which, in spite of biological differences, had these qualities, it would be human. And if among men a being were found of a like biological nature, but without the previously mentioned qualities, it would not be called "man." But both cases are imaginary, since biological structure and ontological character cannot be separated.

Man as creature has been called the "image of God." This biblical phrase is interpreted as differently as the Christian doctrine of man. The discussion is complicated by the fact that the biblical report uses two terms for this idea, which were translated as *imago* and *similitudo*. These were distinguished in their meaning (Irenaeus). *Imago* was supposed to point to the natural equipment of man; *similitudo*, to the special divine gift, the *donum superadditum,* which gave Adam the power of adhering to God. Protestantism, denying the ontological dualism between nature and supranature, rejected the *donum superadditum* and with it the distinction between *imago* and *similitudo*. Man in his pure nature is not only the image of God; he has also the power of communion with God and therefore of righteousness toward other creatures and himself (*justitia originalis*). With the fall this power has been lost. Man is separated from God, and he has no freedom of return. For the Roman Catholic doctrine the power of communion with God is only weakened, and some freedom of turning toward God remains. The difference between Protestantism and Roman Catholicism here is dependent on a whole group of decisions, basically on the interpretation of grace. If grace is supranatural substance, the Catholic position is consistent. If it is forgiveness received in the center of one's personality, the Protestant position is necessary. The criticism of an ontological supranaturalism in the previous chapters implies the rejection of the Catholic doctrine.

But two problems remain in spite of much discussion on Protestant soil, namely, the exact meaning of "image of God" and the nature of man's created goodness. An adequate handling of the first problem demands avoidance of a confusion between image of God and relation to God. Certainly man can have communion with God only because he is made in his image, but this does not mean that the image can be defined by communion with God. Man is the image of God in that in which he differs from all other creatures, namely, his rational structure. Of course, the term "rational" is subject to many misinterpretations. Rational can be defined as technical reason in the sense of arguing and calculating. Then the Aristotelian definition of man as *animal rationale* is as wrong as the description of the image of God in man in terms of his rational nature. But reason is the structure of freedom, and it implies potential infinity. Man is the image of God because in him the ontological elements are complete and united on a creaturely basis, just as they are complete and united in God as the creative ground. Man is the image of God because his *logos* is analogous to the divine *logos,* so that the divine *logos* can appear as man without destroying the humanity of man.

The second frequently discussed and differently answered question in Protestant theology is that of man's created goodness. The early theologians attributed to Adam as the representative of man's essential nature all perfections otherwise reserved for Christ or to man in his eschatological fulfilment. Such a description made the fall entirely unintelligible. Therefore, recent theology rightly attributes to Adam a kind of dreaming innocence, a stage of infancy before contest and decision. This interpretation of the "original state" of man makes the fall understandable and its occurrence existentially unavoidable. It has much more symbolic truth than the "praise of Adam" before the fall. The goodness of man's created nature is that he is given the possibility and necessity of actualizing himself and of becoming independent by his self-actualization, in spite of the estrangement unavoidably connected with it. Therefore, it is inadequate to ask questions concerning Adam's actual state before the fall; for example, if he was mortal or immortal, whether or not he was in communion with God, whether or not he was in a state of righteousness. The verb "was" presupposes actualization in time. But this is exactly what cannot be asserted of the state which transcends potentiality and actuality. This is true even if we use a psychological symbol and speak of the state of dreaming innocence, or if we use a theological symbol and speak of the state of being hidden in the ground of the divine life. One can speak of "was" only after the moment in which the divine command threw Adam into self-actualization through freedom and destiny.

Man is the creature in which the ontological elements are complete. They are incomplete in all creatures, which (for this very reason) are called "subhuman." Subhuman does not imply less perfection than in the case of the human. On the contrary, man as the essentially threatened creature cannot compare with the natural perfection of the subhuman creatures. Subhuman points to a different ontological level, not to a different degree of perfection. The question has to be asked whether there are superhuman beings in an ontological sense. From the standpoint both of religious imagination and of philosophical construction (Neo-Platonism, Leibniz), an affirmative answer has to be given. In these approaches the universe has been pictured as populated with spirits, angels, higher monads. Whether such beings, if they exist, should be called "superhuman" depends on one's judgment about the ultimate significance of freedom and history. If, according to Paul, the angels desire to look into the mystery of salvation, they are certainly no higher than those who experience this mystery in their own salvation. The most adequate solution of this question is given by Thomas Aquinas when he declares that the angels transcend the polarity of individuality and universality. In our terminology we could say that the angels are concrete-poetic symbols of the structures or powers of being. They are not beings but participate in everything that is. Their "epiphany" is a revelatory experience determining the history of religion and culture. They underlie the figures of the great mythological gods as well as the decisive cultural symbolism before and within the Christian Era. They are subjected to the Christ. They must serve him, though they often revolt against him. They are as effective as when they first appeared. They appear again and again with different faces but with the same substance and power.[8]

A last question must be asked, namely, how does man participate in the subhuman creature and vice versa? The classical answer is that man is the microcosmos because in him all levels of reality are present. In the

8. Their rediscovery from the psychological side as archetypes of the collective unconscious and the new interpretation of the demonic in theology and literature have contributed to the understanding of these powers of being, which are not beings, but structures.

myths of the "original man," the "man from above," "The Man" (cf. especially the Persian tradition and I Corinthians, chap. 15) and in similar philosophical ideas (cf. Paracelsus, Böhme, Schelling) the mutual participation of man and nature is symbolically expressed. The myth of the curse over nature and its potential participation in salvation points in the same direction. All this is hard to understand in a culture which is determined by nominalism and individuals. But it belongs to a heritage which the Western mind is about to reconquer. The problem is most urgent when Christian theology deals with the fall and the salvation of the world. Does "world" refer to the human race alone? And, if so, can the human race be separated from other beings? Where is the boundary line in the general biological development; where is the boundary line in the development of the individual man? Is it possible to separate the nature which belongs to him through his body from universal nature? Does the unconscious realm of man's personality belong to nature or to man? Does the collective unconscious admit of the isolation of the individual from the other individuals and from the whole of the living substance? These questions show that the element of participation in the polarity of individualization and participation must be considered much more seriously with respect to the mutual participation of nature and man. Here theology should learn from modern naturalism, which at this point can serve as an introduction to a half-forgotten theological truth. What happens in the microcosm happens by mutual participation in the macrocosmos, for being itself is one.

b) God's sustaining creativity.—Man actualizes his finite freedom in unity with the whole of reality. This actualization includes structural independence, the power of standing upon one's self, and the possibility of resisting the return to the ground of being. At the same time, actualized freedom remains continuously dependent on its creative ground. Only in the power of being-itself is the creature able to resist nonbeing. Creaturely existence includes a double resistance, that is, resistance against nonbeing as well as resistance against the ground of being in which it is rooted and upon which it is dependent. Traditionally the relation of God to the creature in its actualized freedom is called the preservation of the world. The symbol of preservation implies the independent existence of that which is preserved as well as the necessity of protection against threats of destruction. The doctrine of the preservation of the world is the door through which deistic concepts easily creep into the theological system. The world is conceived as an independent structure which moves according to its own laws. God certainly created the world "in the beginning" and gave it the laws of nature. But after its beginning he either does not interfere at all (consistent deism) or only occasionally through miracles and revelation (theistic deism), or he acts in a continual interrelationship (consistent theism). In these three cases, it would not be proper to speak of sustaining creation.

Since the time of Augustine, another interpretation of the preservation of the world is given. Preservation is continuous creativity, in that God out of eternity creates things and time together. Here is the only adequate understanding of preservation. It was accepted by the Reformers; it was powerfully expressed by Luther and radically worked out by Calvin, who added a warning against the deistic danger which he anticipated. This line of thought must be followed and made into a line of defense against the contemporary half-deistic, half-theistic way of conceiving God as a being alongside the world. God is essentially creative, and therefore he is creative in every moment of temporal existence, giving the power of being to everything that has being out of the creative ground of the divine life. There is, however, a decisive difference between originating and sustaining creativity. The latter refers to the given structures of reality, to that which continues within the change, to the regular and calculable in things. Without the static element, finite being would not be able to identify itself with itself or anything with anything. Without it, neither expectation, nor action for the future, nor a place to stand upon would be possible; and therefore being would not be possible. The faith in God's sustaining creativity is the faith in the continuity of the structure of reality as the basis for being and acting.

The main current of the modern world view completely excluded the awareness of God's sustaining creativity. Nature was considered a system of measurable and calculable laws resting in themselves without beginning or end. The "well-founded earth" was a safe place within a safe universe. Although no one would deny that every special thing was threatened by nonbeing, the structure of the whole seemed beyond such a threat. Consequently, one could speak of *deus sive natura,* a phrase which indicates that the name "God" does not add anything to what is already involved in the name "nature." One may call such ideas "pantheistic"; but, if one does, one must realize that they are not much different from a deism which consigns God to the fringe of reality and relegates to the world the same independence which it has in naturalistic pantheism. The symbol of God's sustaining creativity has disappeared in both cases. Today the main trend of the modern world view has been reversed. The foundations of the self-sufficient universe have been shaken. The questions of its beginning and end have become theoretically significant, pointing to the element of nonbeing in the universe as a whole. At the same time, the feeling of living in an ultimately secure world has been destroyed through the catastrophes of the twentieth century and the corresponding existentialist philosophy and literature. The symbol of God's sustaining creativity received a new significance and power.

The question whether the relation between God and the world should be expressed in terms of immanence or transcendence is usually answered by an "as well as." Such an answer, although it is correct, does not solve any problem. Immanence and transcendence are spatial symbols. God is *in* or *above* the world or both. The question is what does this mean in nonspatial terms? Certainly, God is neither in another nor in the same space as the world. He is the creative ground of the spatial structure of the world, but he is not bound to the structure, positively or negatively. The spatial symbol points to a qualitative relation: God is immanent in the world as its permanent creative ground and is transcendent to the world through freedom. Both infinite divinity and finite human freedom make the world transcendent to God and God transcendent to the world. The religious interest in the divine transcendence is not satisfied where one rightly asserts the infinite transcendence of the infinite over the finite. This transcendence does not contradict but rather confirms the coincidence of the opposites. The infinite is present in everything finite, in the stone as well as in the genius. Transcendence demanded by religious experience is the freedom-to-freedom relationship which is actual in every personal encounter. Certainly, the holy is the "quite other." But the otherness is not really conceived as otherness if it remains in the aesthetic-cognitive realm and is not experienced as the otherness of the divine "Thou," whose freedom may conflict with my freedom. The meaning of the spatial symbols for the divine transcendence is the possible conflict and the possible reconciliation of infinite and finite freedom.

c) God's directing creativity.—(1) Creation and Purpose: "The purpose of creation" is such an ambiguous concept that it should be avoided. Creation has no purpose beyond itself. From the point of view of the creature, the purpose of creation is the creature itself and the actualization of its potentialities. From the point of view of the creator, the purpose of creation is the exercise of his creativity, which has no purpose beyond itself because the divine life is essentially creative. If "the glory of God" is designated as the purpose of creation, as it is in Calvinist theologies, it is necessary, first of all, to understand the highly symbolic character of such a statement. No Calvinist theologian will admit that God lacks something which he must secure from the creature he has created. Such an idea is rejected as pagan. In creating the world, God is the sole cause of the glory he wishes to secure through his creation. But if he is the sole cause of his glory, he does not need the world to give him glory. He possesses it eternally in himself. In Lutheran theologies God's purpose is to have a communion of love with his creatures. God creates the world because the divine love wishes an object of love in addition to itself. Here again the implication is that God needs something he could not have without creation. Reciprocal love is interdependent love. Yet, according to Lutheran theology, there is nothing which the created world can offer God. He is the only one who gives.

The concept "the purpose of creation" should be replaced by "the *telos* of creativity"—the inner aim of fulfilling in actuality what is beyond potentiality and actuality in the divine life. One function of the divine creativity is to drive every creature toward such a fulfilment. Thus directing creativity must be added to originating and sustaining creation. It is the side of the divine creativity which is related to the future. The traditional term for directing creativity is "providence."

(2) Fate and Providence: Providence is a paradoxical concept. Faith in providence is faith "in spite of"—in spite of the darkness of fate and of the meaninglessness of existence. The term *pronoia* ("providence") appears in Plato in the context of a philosophy which has overcome the darkness of transhuman and transdivine fate by means of the idea of the good as the ultimate power of being and of knowing. Faith in historical providence is the triumph of the prophetic interpretation of history—an interpretation which gives meaning to historical existence in spite of never ending experiences of meaninglessness. In the late ancient world fate conquered providence and established a reign of terror among the masses; but Christianity emphasized the victory of Christ over the forces of fate and fear just when they seemed to have overwhelmed him at the cross. Here faith in providence was definitively established.

Within the Christian Era, however, there has been a development toward the transformation of providence into a rational principle at the expense of its paradoxical character. Although man does not know the reasons for God's providential activity, it was emphasized that there *are* reasons, known by God, and that man is able to participate in this knowledge at least fragmentarily. In modern philosophy the development moved beyond this point. It attempted to set itself on the throne of God and to lay down definitive descriptions of the reasons for God's providential activity. These have been expressed in three forms: the teleological, the harmonistic, and the dialectical.

The teleological way is an attempt to demonstrate that all things are so constructed and ordered that they serve the purpose of God's action, which purpose is human happiness. A careful analysis of everything teleological in nature and in man gives rise to innumerable arguments for divine providence. However, since man's happiness is the ultimate criterion, every event in nature which reveals its opposition to human happiness has a catastrophic effect on this teleological optimism.

The second way of pointing to providence in rational terms is the harmonistic. Most of the philosophers of the Enlightenment used this method implicitly or explicitly. In their thought harmony does not mean that everything is "sweetness and light." It means that a law of harmony works "behind the backs" of people and their egoistic intentions. The laws of the market, as developed by the classical economists, are the model of this type of secularized providence. But the principle has been effective in all realms of life. Liberalism, the doctrine of individual freedom, is a rational system of providence. The law of harmony regulates the innumerable conflicting trends, purposes, and activities of all individuals without human interference. Even Protestantism uses the principle of harmony when it opens the Bible to every Christian and denies ecclesiastical authorities the right to interfere. Behind the Protestant doctrine that the Bible interprets itself (*scriptura suae ipsium interpres*) lies an early liberal belief in harmony, which itself is a rationalized form of the faith in providence. The progressivistic optimism of the nineteenth century is a direct consequence of the general acceptance of the principle of harmony.

The third form of the rational idea of providence, both more profound and more pessimistic, is historical dialectics. It is aware of the depth of negativity in being and existence. This is true both of its idealistic and of its realistic modes of expression. Hegel introduces nonbeing and conflict into the process of divine self-realization. Marx points to the dehumanization and the self-estrangement of historical existence as a refutation of the liberal belief in an automatic harmony. Fate begins to appear again as the dark background of a rationalized providence and as its perennial threat. Nevertheless, dialectics leads to synthesis, logically as well as actually. Providence still triumphs for both Hegel and Marx. For Hegel it triumphs in his own era; for Marx it will triumph in an indefinite future. For neither of them, however, does providence offer consolation to the individual. Marx sees no fulfilment of individual destiny except in the collective fulfilment, while Hegel does not look upon history as the locus for individual happiness in the past, present, or future.

The catastrophes of the twentieth century have shattered even this limited belief in rational providence. Fate overshadows the Christian world, as it overshadowed the ancient world two thousand years ago. The individual man passionately asks that he be allowed the possibility of believing in a personal fulfilment in spite of the negativity of his historical existence. And the question of historical existence again has become a struggle with the darkness of fate; it is the same struggle in which originally the Christian victory was won.

(3) The Meaning of Providence: Providence means a fore-seeing (*pro-videre*) which is a fore-ordering ("seeing to it"). This ambiguity of meaning expresses an ambiguous feeling toward providence, and it corresponds to different interpretations of the concept. If the element of foreseeing is emphasized, God becomes the omniscient spectator who knows what will happen but who does not interfere with the freedom of his creatures. If the element of foreordering is emphasized, God becomes a planner who has ordered everything that will happen "before the foundations of the world"; all natural and historical processes are nothing more than the execution of this supratemporal divine plan. In the first interpretation the creatures make their world, and God remains a spectator; in the second interpretation the creatures are cogs in a universal mechanism, and God is the only active agent. Both interpretations of providence must be rejected. Providence is a permanent activity of God. He never is a spectator; he always directs everything toward its fulfilment. Yet God's directing creativity always creates through the freedom of man and through the spontaneity and structural wholeness of all creatures. Providence works through the polar elements of being. It works through the conditions of individual, social, and universal existence, through finitude, nonbeing, and anxiety, through the interdependence of all finite things, through their resistance against the divine activity and through the destructive consequences of this resistance. All existential conditions are included in God's directing creativity. They are not increased or decreased in their power, nor are they canceled.

Providence is not interference; it is creation. It uses all factors, both those given by freedom and those given by destiny, in creatively directing everything toward its fulfilment. Providence is a *quality* of every constellation of conditions, a quality which "drives" or "lures" toward fulfilment. Providence is "the divine condition" which is present in every group of finite conditions and in the totality of finite conditions. It is not an additional factor, a miraculous physical or mental interference in terms of supranaturalism. It is the quality of inner directedness present in every situation. The man who believes in providence does not believe that a special divine activity will alter the conditions of finitude and estrangement. He believes, and asserts with the courage of faith, that no situation whatsoever can frustrate the fulfilment of his ultimate destiny, that nothing can separate him from the love of God which is in Christ Jesus (Romans, chap. 8).

What is valid for the individual is valid for history as a whole. Faith in historical providence means the certainty that history in each of its moments, in eras of progress and eras of catastrophe, contributes to the ultimate fulfilment of creaturely existence, although this fulfilment does not lies in an eventual time-and-space future.

God's directing creativity is the answer to the question of the meaning of prayer, especially prayers of supplication and prayers of intercession. Neither type of prayer can mean that God is expected to acquiesce in interfering with existential conditions. Both mean that God is asked to direct the given situation toward fulfilment. The prayers are an element in this situation, a most powerful factor if they are true prayers. As an element in the situation a prayer is a condition of God's directing creativity, but the form of this creativity may be the complete rejection of the manifest content of the prayer. Nevertheless, the prayer may have been heard according to its hidden content, which is the surrender of a fragment of existence to God. This hidden content is always decisive. It is the element in the situation which is used by God's directing creativity. Every serious prayer contains power, not because of the intensity of desire expressed in it, but because of the faith the person has in God's directing activity—a faith which transforms the existential situation.

(4) Individual and Historical Providence: Providence refers to the individual as well as to history. Special providence (*providentia specialis*) gives the individual the certainty that under any circumstances, under any set of conditions, the divine "factor" is active and that therefore the road to his ultimate fulfilment is open. In the late ancient world special

providence was the practical meaning of providence. In a period in which for the individual history was nothing more than fortune and fate (*tychē* and *haimarmene*), a power above him which he could not change and to which he could contribute nothing, faith in special providence was a liberating faith cultivated in most of the philosophical schools. The only thing a man could do was to accept his situation and by this acceptance transcend it in Stoic courage, in skeptical resignation, or in mystical elevation. In Christianity providence is an element in the person-to-person relationship between God and man; it carries the warmth of belief in loving protection and personal guidance. It gives the individual the feeling of transcendent security in the midst of the necessities of nature and history. It is confidence in "the divine condition" within every set of finite conditions. This is its greatness, but it also is its danger. Confidence in divine guidance can become a conviction that God must change the conditions of a situation in order to make his own condition effective. And if this does not occur, confidence and faith break down. But it is the paradox of the belief in providence that, just when the conditions of a situation are destroying the believer, the divine condition gives him a certainty which transcends the destruction.

Christianity has done more than change the meaning of special providence. Following Judaism, it has added to special providence faith in historical providence. This was impossible for the ancient world, but it was real for Jewish prophetism and is necessary for Christianity, for God establishes his kingdom through history. Experience of the great empires with their fateful power does not shake the Jewish and Christian confidence in God's historical providence. The empires are stages in the world historical process, whose fulfilment is the reign of God through Israel or through the Christ. Of course, this faith is no less paradoxical than the individual person's faith in God's directing creativity within his life. And whenever the paradoxical character of historical providence is forgotten, whenever historical providence is tied to special events or special expectations, whether in religious or in secular terms, disappointment follows as inescapably as it does in the life of the individual. The misunderstanding of historical providence which looks for the fulfilment of history in history itself is utopian. But that which fulfils history transcends it, just as that which fulfils the life of the individual transcends him. Faith in providence is paradoxical. It is an "in spite of." If this is not understood, faith in providence breaks down, taking with it faith in God and in the meaning of life and of history. Much cynicism is the result of an erroneous and therefore disappointed confidence in individual or historical providence.

(5) Theodicy: The paradoxical character of faith in providence is the answer to the question of theodicy. Faith in God's directing creativity always is challenged by man's experience of a world in which the conditions of the human situation seem to exclude many human beings from even an anticipatory and fragmentary fulfilment. Early death, destructive social conditions, feeble-mindedness and insanity, the undiminished horrors of historical existence—all these seem to verify belief in fate rather than faith in providence. How can an almighty God be justified (*theos-dikē*) in view of realities in which no meaning whatsoever can be discovered?

Theodicy is not a question of physical evil, pain, death, etc., nor is it a question of moral evil, sin, self-destruction, etc. Physical evil is the natural implication of creaturely finitude. Moral evil is the tragic implication of creaturely freedom. Creation is the creation of finite freedom; it is the creation of life with its greatness and its danger. God lives, and his life is creative. If God is creative in himself, he cannot create what is opposite to himself; he cannot create the dead, the object which is merely object. He must create that which unites subjectivity and objectivity—life, that which includes freedom and with it the dangers of freedom. The creation of finite freedom is the risk which the divine creativity accepts. This is the first step in arriving at an answer to the question of theodicy.

However, this does not answer the question why it seems that some beings are excluded from any kind of fulfilment, even from free resistance against their fulfilment. Let us first inquire by whom and under what conditions this central question of theodicy can be asked. All theological statements are existential; they imply the man who makes the statement or who asks the question. The creaturely existence of which theology speaks is "my" creaturely existence, and only on this basis is the consideration of creatureliness in general meaningful. This existential correlation is abandoned if the question of theodicy is raised with respect to persons other than the questioner. The situation here is the same as that encountered when the question of predestination is applied to persons other than the questioner. This question also breaks out of the existential correlation, which makes any theological assertion on the subject questionable. A man can say with the paradoxical confidence of faith, "Nothing can separate *me* from the Love of God" (Romans, chap. 8), but he cannot say with any degree of confidence that other persons are or are not separated from the Love of God or from ultimate fulfilment. No man can make a general or an individual judgment on this question when it falls outside the correlation of faith.

If we wish to answer the question of the fulfilment of other persons, and with it the questions of theodicy and predestination, we must seek the point at which the destiny of others becomes our own destiny. And this point is not hard to find. It is the participation of their being in our being. The principle of participation implies that every question concerning individual fulfilment must at the same time be a question concerning universal fulfilment. Neither can be separated from the other. The destiny of the individual cannot be separated from the destiny of the whole in which it participates. One might speak of a representative fulfilment and nonfulfilment, but beyond this one must refer to the creative unity of individualization and participation in the depth of the divine life. The question of theodicy finds its final answer in the mystery of the creative ground. This answer, however, involves a decision which is very definite. The division of mankind into fulfilled and unfulfilled individuals, or into objects of predestination either to salvation or to condemnation, is existentially and, therefore, theologically impossible. Such a division contradicts the ultimate unity of individualization and participation in the creative ground of the divine life.

The principle of participation drives us one step further. God himself is said to participate in the negativities of creaturely existence. This idea is supported by mystical as well as by christological thought. Nevertheless, the idea must be stated with reservations. Genuine patripassianism (the doctrine that God the Father has suffered in Christ) rightly was rejected by the early church. God as being-itself transcends nonbeing absolutely. On the other hand, God as creative life includes the finite and, with it, nonbeing, although nonbeing is eternally conquered and the finite is eternally reunited within the infinity of the divine life. Therefore, it is meaningful to speak of a participation of the divine life in the negativities of creaturely life. This is the ultimate answer to the question of theodicy. The certainty of God's directing creativity is based on the certainty of God as the ground of being and meaning. The confidence of every creature, its courage to be, is rooted in faith in God as its creative ground.

6. GOD AS RELATED

a) The divine holiness and the creature.—"Relation" is a basic ontological category. It is valid of the correlation of the ontological elements as well as of the interrelations of everything finite. The distinctly theological question is: "Can God be related and, if so, in what sense?" God as being-itself is the ground of every relation; in his life all relations are present beyond the distinctions between potentiality and actuality. But they are not the relations of God with something else. They are the inner relations of the divine life. The internal relations are, of course, not conditioned by the actualization of finite freedom. But the question is whether there are external relations between God and the creature. The doctrine of creation affirms that God is the creative ground of everything in every moment. In this sense there is no creaturely independence from which an external relation between God and the creature could be derived. If God is said to be in relation, this statement is as symbolic as the statement that God is a living God. And every special relation participates in this symbolic character. Every relation in which God becomes an object to a subject, in knowledge or in action, must be affirmed and denied at the same time. It must be affirmed because man is a centered self to whom every relation involves an object. It must be denied because God can never become an object for man's knowledge or action. Therefore, mystical theology, inside and outside Christian theology, speaks of God's recognizing and loving himself through man. This means that if God becomes an object, nevertheless he remains a subject.

The unapproachable character of God, or the impossibility of having a relation with him in the proper sense of the word, is expressed in the word "holiness." God is essentially holy, and every relation with him involves the consciousness that it is paradoxical to be related to that which is holy. God cannot become an object of knowledge or a partner in action. If we speak, as we must, of the ego-thou relation between God and man, the thou embraces the ego and consequently the entire relation. If it were otherwise, if the ego-thou relation with God was proper rather than symbolic, the ego could withdraw from the relation. But there is no place to which man can withdraw from the divine thou, because it includes the ego and is nearer to the ego than the ego to itself. Ultimately, it is an insult to the divine holiness to talk about God as we do of objects whose existence or nonexistence can be discussed. It is an insult to the divine holiness to treat God as a partner with whom one collaborates or as a superior power whom one influences by rites and prayers. The holiness of God makes it impossible to draw him into the context of the ego-world and the subject-object correlation. He himself is the ground and meaning of this correlation, not an element within it. The holiness of God requires that in relation to him we leave behind the totality of finite relations and enter into a relation which, in the categorical sense of the word, is not a relation at all. We can bring all our relations into the sphere of the holy; we can consecrate the finite, including its internal and external relations, through the experience of the holy; but to do so we must first transcend all these relations. Theology, which by its nature is always in the danger of drawing God into the cognitive relation of the subject-object structure of being, should strongly point to the holiness of God and his unapproachable character in judgment of itself.

Symbols for the "all-transcending" holiness of God are "majesty" and "glory." They appear most conspicuously in the exclusive monotheism of the Old Testament and of Calvinism. For Calvin and his followers the glory of God is the purpose of creation and fall, of damnation and salvation. The majesty of God excludes creaturely freedom and overshadows the divine love. This was and is a corrective against the sentimental picture of a God who serves as the fulfilment of human desires. But it was and is, at the same time, an object for justifiable criticism. An affirmation of the glory of God at the expense of the elimination of the divine love is not glorious. And a majesty which characterizes him as a suppressive tyrant is not majestic. The majesty and glory of God should not be separated from the other qualities of the divine life. God's holiness is not a quality in and of itself; it is that quality which qualifies all other qualities as divine. His power is holy power; his love is holy love. Men are never merely means for the divine glory; they are also ends. Since men are rooted in the divine life and are supposed to return to it, they participate in its glory. In the praise of the divine majesty, praise of creaturely destiny is included. This is why the praise of God plays such a decisive role in all liturgies, hymns, and prayers. Certainly, man does not praise himself when he praises God's majesty; but he praises the glory in which he participates through his praise.

b) The divine power and the creature.—(1) The Meaning of Omnipotence: God is the power of being, resisting and conquering nonbeing. In relation to the creature, the divine power is expressed in the symbol of omnipotence. The "almighty God" is the first subject of the Christian credo. It separates exclusive monotheism from all religion in which God is less than being-itself or the power of being. Only the almighty God can be man's ultimate concern. A very mighty God may claim to be of ultimate concern; but he is not, and his claim comes to naught, because he cannot resist nonbeing and therefore he cannot supply the ultimate courage which conquers anxiety. The confession of the creed concerning "God the Father almighty" expresses the Christian consciousness that the anxiety of nonbeing is eternally overcome in the divine life. The symbol of omnipotence gives the first and basic answer to the question implied in finitude. Therefore, most liturgical and free prayers begin with the invocation "Almighty God."

This is the religious meaning of omnipotence, but how can it be expressed theologically? In popular parlance the concept "omnipotence" implies a highest being who is able to do whatever he wants. This notion must be rejected, religiously as well as theologically. It makes God into a being alongside others, a being who asks himself which of innumerable possibilities he shall actualize. It subjects God to the split between potentiality and actuality—a split which is actually the heritage of finitude. It leads to absurd questions about God's power in terms of logically contradictory possibilities. Opposing such a caricature of God's omnipotence, Luther, Calvin, and others interpreted omnipotence to mean the divine power through which God is creative in and through everything in every moment. The almighty God is the omniactive God. There is, however, a difficulty in such an interpretation. It tends to identify the divine power with actual happenings in time and space, and thereby it suppresses the transcendent element in God's omnipotence. It is more adequate to define divine omnipotence as the power of being which resists nonbeing in all its expressions and which is manifest in the creative process in all its forms.

Faith in the almighty God is the answer to the quest for a courage which is sufficient to conquer the anxiety of finitude. Ultimate courage is based upon participation in the ultimate power of being. When the invocation "Almighty God" is seriously pronounced, a victory over the threat of nonbeing is experienced, and an ultimate, courageous affirmation of existence is expressed. Neither finitude nor anxiety disappears, but they are taken into infinity and courage. Only in this correlation should the symbol of omnipotence be interpreted. It is magic and an absurdity if it is understood as the quality of a highest being who is able to do what he wants.

With respect to time, omnipotence is eternity; with respect to space, it is omnipresence; and with respect to the subject-object structure of being, it is omniscience. These symbols must now be interpreted. Causality and substance in relation to being-itself were discussed in the symbol of God as the "creative ground" of being, in which the term "creative" contained and transcended causality, while the term "ground" contained and transcended substance. Their interpretation preceded the interpretation of the three other symbols because the divine creativity logically precedes the relation of God to the created.

(2) The Meaning of Eternity: "Eternity" is a genuine religious word. It takes the place of something like omni- or all-temporality, which would be the analogy to omnipotence, omnipresence, etc. This may be a consequence of the outstanding character of time as a category of finitude. Only that is divine which gives the courage to endure the anxiety of temporal existence. Where the invocation "Eternal God" means participation in that which conquers the nonbeing of temporality, there eternity is experienced.

The concept of eternity must be protected against two misinterpretations. Eternity is neither timelessness nor the endlessness of time. The meaning of *olim* in Hebrew and of *aiones* in Greek does not indicate timelessness; rather it means the power of embracing all periods of time. Since time is created in the ground of the divine life, God is essentially related to it. In so far as everything divine transcends the split between potentiality and actuality, the same must be said of time as an element of the divine life. Special moments of time are not separated from each other; presence is not swallowed by past and future; yet the eternal keeps the temporal within itself. Eternity is the transcendent unity of the dissected moments of existential time. It is not adequate to identify simultaneity with eternity. Simultaneity would erase the different modes of time; but time without modes is timelessness. It is not different from the timeless validity of a mathematical proposition. If we call God a living God, we affirm that he includes temporality and with this a relation to the modes of time. Even Plato could not exclude temporality from eternity; he called time the moving image of eternity. It would have been foolish to imply that time is the image of timelessness. For Plato eternity included time, even though it was the time of circular movement. Hegel was criticized on logical grounds by Trendelenburg and on religious grounds by Kierkegaard for introducing movement into the realm of logical forms. But for Hegel the logical forms whose movement he described were powers of being, beyond actuality within the life of the "absolute spirit" (usually but unfortunately translated as "absolute mind"), but actualized in nature and history. Hegel pointed to a temporality within the Absolute, of which time as we know it is at once an image and a distortion. Nevertheless, Kierkegaard's criticism was justified in so far as Hegel did not realize that the human situation, which includes distorted temporality, invalidates his attempt to give a final and complete interpretation of history. But his idea of a dialectical movement within the Absolute is in agreement with the genuine meaning of eternity. Eternity is not timelessness.

And eternity is not the endlessness of time. Endless time, correctly called "bad infinity" by Hegel, is the endless reiteration of temporality. To elevate the dissected moments of time to infinite significance by demanding their endless reduplication is idolatry in the most refined sense. For every finite being, eternity in this sense would be identical with condemnation, whatever the content of never ending time (cf. the myth of the eternal Jew). For God it would mean his subjection to a superior power, namely, to the structure of dissected temporality. It would deprive him of his eternity and make him an everliving entity of subdivine character. Eternity is not the endlessness of time.

On the basis of these considerations and the assertion that eternity includes temporality, the question must still be asked: "What is the relation of eternity to the modes of time?" An answer demands use of the only analogy to eternity found in human experience, that is, the unity of remembered past and anticipated future in an experienced present. Such an analogy implies a symbolic approach to the meaning of eternity. In accord with the predominance of the present in temporal experience, eternity must first be symbolized as an eternal present (*nunc eternum*). But this *nunc eternum* is not simultaneity or the negation of an independent meaning of past and future. The eternal present is moving from past to future but without ceasing to be present. The future is genuine only if it is open, if the new can happen and if it can be anticipated. This is the motive which led Bergson to insist upon the absolute openness of the future to the point of making God dependent on the unforeseen that might happen. But in teaching the absolute openness of the future, Bergson devaluated the present by denying the possibility of its anticipation. A God who is not able to anticipate every possible future is dependent on an absolute accident and cannot be the foundation of an ultimate courage. This God would himself be subject to the anxiety of the unknown. He would not be being-itself. Therefore, a relative although not an absolute openness to the future is the characteristic of eternity. The new is beyond potentiality and actuality in the divine life and becomes actual as new in time and history. Without the element of openness, history would be without creativity. It would cease to be history. On the other hand, without that which limits openness, history would be without direction. It would cease to be history.

Further, God's eternity is not dependent on the completed past. For God the past is not complete, because through it he creates the future; and, in creating the future, he re-creates the past. If the past were only the sum total of what happened, such an assertion would be meaningless. But the past includes its own potentialities. The potentialities which will become actual in the future determine not only the future but also the past. The past becomes something different through everything new which happens. Its aspects change—a fact upon which the significance of the historical interpretation of the past is based. The potentialities included in the past, however, are not manifest before they determine the future. They may determine it through a new interpretation given by historical remembrance. Or they may determine it by developments which make effective some hidden potentialities. From the point of view of eternity, both past and future are open. The creativity which leads into the future also transforms the past. If eternity is conceived in terms of creativity, the eternal includes past and future without absorbing their special character as modes of time.

Faith in the eternal God is the basis for a courage which conquers the negativities of the temporal process. Neither the anxiety of the past nor that of the future remains. The anxiety of the past is conquered by the freedom of God toward the past and its potentialities. The anxiety of the future is conquered by the dependence of the new on the unity of the divine life. The dissected moments of time are united in eternity. Here, and not in a doctrine of the human soul, is rooted the certainty of man's participation in eternal life. The hope of eternal life is based not on a substantial quality of man's soul but on his participation in the eternity of the divine life.

(3) The Meaning of Omnipresence: God's relation to space, as his relation to time, must be interpreted in qualitative terms. God is neither endlessly extended in space nor limited to a definite space; nor is he

spaceless. A theology inclined toward pantheist formulation prefers the first alternative, while a theology with deistic tendencies chooses the second alternative. Omnipresence can be interpreted as an extension of the divine substance through all spaces. This, however, subjects God to dissected spatiality and puts him, so to speak, alongside himself sacrificing the personal center of the divine life. It must be rejected as much as the attempt to subject him to dissected temporality in terms of endless reiteration. Further, omnipresence can be interpreted to mean that God is present "personally" in a circumscribed place (in heaven above) but also simultaneously present with his power every place (in the earth beneath). But this is equally inadequate. The spatial symbols of above and below should not be taken literally in any respect. When Luther said that the "right hand of God" is not on a *locus circumscriptus* but everywhere, since God's power and creativity act at every place, he destroyed the traditional interpretation of God's omnipresence and expressed the doctrine of Nicolaus Cusandus that God is in everything, in that which is central as well as in that which is peripheral. In a vision of the universe which has no basis for a tripartite view of cosmic space in terms of earth, heaven, and underworld, theology must emphasize the symbolic character of spatial symbols, in spite of their rather literal use in Bible and cult. Almost every Christian doctrine has been shaped by these symbols and needs reformulation in the light of a spatially monistic universe. "God is in heaven"; this means that his life is qualitatively different from creaturely existence. But it does not mean that he "lives in" or "descends from" a special place.

Omnipresence, finally, is not spacelessness. We must reject punctuality in the divine life as much as simultaneity and timelessness. God creates extension in the ground of his life, in which everything spatial is rooted. But God is not subject to it; he transcends it and participates in it. God's omnipresence is his creative participation in the spatial existence of his creatures.

It has been suggested that because of his spirituality God has a relation to time but not to space. It is affirmed that extension characterizes bodily existence, which cannot be asserted of God, even symbolically. But such an argument is based on an improper ontology. Certainly one cannot say that God is body. But if it is said that he is Spirit, the ontological elements of vitality and personality are included and, with them, the participation of bodily existence in the divine life. Both vitality and personality have a bodily basis. Therefore, it is legitimate for Christian art to include the bodily resurrected Christ in the trinity; therefore, Christianity prefers the symbol of resurrection to other symbols of eternal life; therefore, some Christian mystics and philosophers have emphasized that "corporality is the end of the ways of God" (Ötinger). This is a necessary consequence of the Christian doctrine of creation, with the rejection of the Greek doctrine of *materia* as an antispiritual principle. Only on this basis can the eternal presence of God be affirmed, for presence combines time with space.[9]

God's omnipresence overcomes the anxiety of not having a space for one's self. It provides the courage to accept the insecurities and anxieties of spatial existence. In the certainty of the omnipresent God we are always at home and not at home, rooted and uprooted, resting and wandering, being placed and displaced, known by one place and not known by any place.

And in the certainty of the omnipresent God we are always in the sanctuary. We are in a holy place when we are in the most secular place, and the most holy place remains secular in comparison with our place in the ground of the divine life. Whenever omnipresence is experienced, it breaks down the difference between the sacred and the profane. The sacramental presence of God is a consequence of his omnipresence. It is an actual manifestation of his omnipresence, dependent of course on the history of revelation and the concrete symbols which have been created by it. His sacramental presence is not the appearance of somebody who is ordinarily absent and occasionally comes. If one always experienced the divine presence, there would be no difference between sacred and secular places. The difference does not exist in the divine life.

(4) The Meaning of Omniscience: The symbol of omniscience expresses the spiritual character of the divine omnipotence and omnipresence. It is related to the subject-object structure of reality and points to the divine participation in and transcendence over this structure.

The first theological task is the removal of absurdities in interpretation. Omniscience is not the faculty of a highest being who is supposed to know all objects, past, present, and future, and, beyond this, everything that might have happened if what has happened had not happened. The absurdity of such an image is due to the impossibility of subsuming God under the subject-object scheme, although this structure is grounded in the divine life. If one speaks, therefore, of divine knowledge and of the

9. The Latin word *presentia* as well as the German word *Gegenwart* contain a spatial image: "A thing which stands before one."

unconditional character of the divine knowledge, one speaks symbolically, indicating that God is not present in an all-permeating manner but that he is present spiritually. Nothing is outside the centered unity of his life; nothing is strange, dark, hidden, isolated, unapproachable. Nothing falls outside the *logos* structure of being. The dynamic element cannot break the unity of the form; the abysmal quality cannot swallow the rational quality of the divine life.

This certainty has implications for man's personal and cultural existence. In personal life it means that there is no absolute darkness in one's being. There is nothing absolutely hidden within it. The hidden, the dark, the unconscious, is present in God's spiritual life. There is no escape from it. And, on the other hand, the anxiety of the dark and the hidden is overcome in the faith of the divine omniscience. It excludes ultimate duality. It does not exclude pluralism of powers and forms; but it does exclude a split of being which makes things strange and unrelated to each other. Therefore, the divine omniscience is the logical (though not always conscious) foundation of the belief in the openness of reality to human knowledge. We *know* because we participate in the divine knowledge. Truth is not absolutely removed from the outreach of our finite minds, since the divine life in which we are rooted embodies all truth. In the light of the symbol of divine omniscience we experience the fragmentary character of all finite knowledge, but not as a threat against our participation in truth; and we experience the broken character of every finite meaning, but not as a cause for ultimate meaninglessness. The doubt about truth and meaning which is the heritage of finitude is incorporated in faith through the symbol of the divine omniscience.

c) *The divine love and the creature.*—(1) The Meaning of the Divine Love: Love is an ontological concept. Its emotional element is a consequence of its ontological nature. It is false to define love by its emotional side. This leads necessarily to sentimental misinterpretations of the meaning of love and calls into question its symbolic application to the divine life. But God is love. And, since God is being-itself, one must say that being-itself is love. This, however, is understandable only because the actuality of being is life. The process of the divine life has the character of love. According to the ontological polarity of individualization and participation, every life-process unites a trend toward separation with a trend toward reunion. The unbroken unity of these two trends is the ontological nature of love. Its awareness as fulfilment of life is the emotional nature of love. Reunion presupposes separation. Love is absent where there is no individualization, and love can be fully realized only where there is full individualization, in man. But the individual also longs to return to the unity to which he belongs, in which he participates by his ontological nature. This longing for reunion is an element in every love, and its realization, however fragmentary, is experienced as bliss.

If we say that God *is* love, we apply the experience of separation and reunion to the divine life. As in the case of life and spirit, one speaks symbolically of God as love. He *is* love; this means that the divine life has the character of love but beyond the distinction between potentiality and actuality. This means therefore that it is mystery for finite understanding. The New Testament uses the term *agapē* for divine love. But it uses the same term also for man's love to man and man's love to God. There must be something in common in the three love relations. In order to discover it, one must compare the *agapē* type of love with the other types. One can say in abbreviated form: Love as *libido* is the movement of the needy toward that which fulfils the need. Love as *philia* is the movement of the equal toward union with the equal. Love as *erōs* is the movement of that which is lower in power and meaning to that which is higher. It is obvious that in all three the element of desire is present. This does not contradict the created goodness of being, since separation and the longing for reunion belong to the essential nature of creaturely life. But there is a form of love which transcends these, namely, the desire for the fulfilment of the longing of the other being, the longing for *his* ultimate fulfilment. All love, except *agapē,* is dependent on contingent characteristics which change and are partial. It is dependent on repulsion and attraction, on passion and sympathy. *Agapē* is independent of these states. It affirms the other unconditionally, that is, apart from higher or lower, pleasant or unpleasant qualities. *Agapē* unites the lover and the beloved because of the image of fulfilment which God has of both. Therefore, *agapē* is universal; no one with whom a concrete relation is technically possible ("the neighbor") is excluded; nor is anyone preferred. *Agapē* accepts the other in spite of resistance. It suffers and forgives. It seeks the personal fulfilment of the other. *Caritas* is the Latin translation of *agapē;* from it comes the English word "charity," which has deteriorated to the level of "charitable enterprises." But, even in this dubious meaning, it points to the *agapē* type of love which seeks the other because of the ultimate unity of being with being within the divine ground.

From what has been said about God's providential creativity, it is obvious that this type of love is the basis for the assertion that God is love. God works toward the fulfilment of every creature and toward the bringing-together into the unity of his life all who are separated and disrupted. Since *agapē* is usually (though not always and not necessarily) connected with the other types of love, it is natural that Christian symbolism has used these types in order to make the divine love concrete. In so far as devotional language speaks of the longing of God for his creature and in so far as mystical language speaks of the need that God has for man, the *libido* element is introduced into the notion of the divine love, but in poetic-religious symbolism, for God is not in need of anything. When biblical and devotional language suggest that the disciples are the "friends of God" (or Christ), the *philia* element is introduced into the notion of the divine love, although in a metaphorical symbolic way, for there is no equality between God and man. If God is described in religious and theological language as driving toward the *eschaton,* i.e., the ultimate fulfilment in which he is "all in all," it can be compared with the *erōs* type of love, the striving for the *summum bonum;* but it can only be compared, not equated, with *erōs,* for God in his eternity transcends the fulfilment and nonfulfilment of reality. The three types of love contribute to the symbolization of the divine love, but the basic and only adequate symbol is *agapē.*

Agapē between men and the *agapē* of God toward man correspond with each other, since the one is the ground of the other. But the *agapē* of man toward God falls outside this strict correlation. Affirming God's ultimate meaning and longing for his ultimate fulfilment is not love in the same way as *agapē.* Here one does not love God "in spite of," or in forgiveness, as in *agapē* toward man. Therefore, the word can be used here only in the general sense of love, with an emphasis on voluntary union with the divine will. The Latin word *dilectio,* which points to the element of choice in the act of love, is more descriptive of this situation. Basically, however, one's love to God is of the nature of *erōs.* It involves elevation from the lower to the higher, from lower goods to the *summum bonum.* An affirmation concerning the irreconcilable conflict between *erōs* and *agapē* will not keep theologians from asserting that man reaches his highest good in God and that he longs for his fulfilment in God. If *erōs* and *agapē* cannot be united, *agapē* toward God is impossible.

It has been said that man's love of God is the love with which God loves himself. This is an expression of the truth that God is a subject even where he seems to be an object. It points directly to a divine self-love and indirectly, by analogy, to a divinely demanded human self-love. Where the relation of the trinitarian *personae* is described in terms of love (*amans, amatus, amor*—Augustine), it is a statement about God loving himself. The trinitarian distinctions (separation and reunion) make it possible to speak of divine self-love. Without separation from one's self, self-love is impossible. This is even more obvious, if the distinction within God includes the infinity of finite forms, which are separated and reunited in the eternal process of the divine life. The divine life is the divine self-love. Through the separation *within* himself God loves himself. And through separation *from* himself (in creaturely freedom) God fulfils his love of himself—primarily because he loves that which is estranged from himself.

This makes it possible also to apply the term *agapē* to the love wherein man loves himself, that is, himself as the eternal image in the divine life. Man can have the other forms of love toward himself, such as simple self-affirmation, *libido*, friendship, and *erōs*. None of these forms is evil as such. But they become evil where they are not under the criterion of self-love in the sense of *agapē*. Where this criterion is lacking, proper self-love becomes false self-love, namely, a selfishness which is always connected with self-contempt and self-hate. The distinction between these two contradictory forms of self-love is extremely important. The one is an image of the divine self-love; the other contradicts the divine self-love. The divine self-love includes all creatures; and proper human self-love includes everything with which man is existentially united.

(2) The Divine Love and the Divine Justice: Justice is that side of love which affirms the independent right of object and subject within the love relation. Love does not destroy the freedom of the beloved and does not violate the structures of the beloved's individual and social existence. Neither does love surrender the freedom of him who loves, and it does not violate the structures of his individual and social existence. Love as the reunion of those who are separate does not distort or destroy in its union. There is a love, however, which is chaotic self-surrender or chaotic self-imposition; it is not a real love but a "symbiotic" love (Erich Fromm). Much romantic love has this character. Nietzsche was right when he emphasized that a love relation is creative only if an independent self enters the relation from both sides. Divine love includes the jus-

tice which acknowledges and preserves the freedom and the unique character of the beloved. It does justice to man while it drives him toward fulfilment. It neither forces him nor leaves him; it attracts him and lures him toward reunion.

But in this process justice not only affirms and lures; it also resists and condemns. This fact has led to the theory of the conflict between love and justice in God. Jewish-Christian conversations often have suffered under this assumption. Political attacks upon the Christian idea of love are unaware of the relation between love and justice in God and man. And so is much Christian pacifism in its attacks on political struggles for justice.

It has been asked how divine love is related to divine power, especially to the power which carries through the demands of justice. And a conflict between the divine love and the divine wrath against those who violate justice has been noted. All these questions are answered in principle by the interpretation of love in ontological terms and of the divine love in symbolic terms. But special answers are demanded in systematic theology, and, although it cannot go into the actual problems of social ethics, it must show that every ethical answer is based on an implicit or explicit assertion about **God**.

It must be emphasized that it is not the divine power as such which is thought to be in conflict with the divine love. The divine power is the power of being-itself, and being-itself is actual in the divine life whose nature is love. A conflict can be imagined only in relation to the creature who violates the structure of justice and so violates love itself. When this happens—and it is the character of creaturely existence that it happens universally—judgment and condemnation follow. But they do not follow by a special act of divine wrath or retribution; they follow by the reaction of God's loving power against that which violates love. Condemnation is not the negation of love but the negation of the negation of love. It is an act of love without which nonbeing would triumph over being. It is the way in which that which resists love, namely, the reunion of the separated in the divine life, is left to separation, with an implied and inescapable self-destruction. The ontological character of love solves the problem of the relation of love and retributive justice. Judgment is an act of love which surrenders that which resists love to self-destruction.

This again provides theology with the possibility of using the symbol "the wrath of God." For a long time it was felt that such a symbol meant ascribing human affects to God in the sense of the pagan stories of the "anger of the gods." But what is impossible in a literal understanding is possible and often necessary in a metaphorical symbol. The wrath of God is neither a divine affect alongside his love nor a motive for action alongside providence; it is the emotional symbol for the work of love which rejects and leaves to self-destruction what resists it. The experience of the wrath of God is the awareness of the self-destructive nature of evil, namely, of those acts and attitudes in which the finite creature keeps itself separated from the ground of being and resists God's reuniting love. Such an experience is real, and the metaphorical symbol "the wrath of God" is unavoidable.

Judgment, which includes condemnation and the wrath of God, has eschatological connotations, and the question arises of a possible limit to divine love. The threat of ultimate judgment and the symbols of eternal condemnation or eternal death point to such a limit. It is necessary, however, to distinguish between eternal and everlasting. Eternity as a quality of the divine life cannot be attributed to a being which as condemned is separated from the divine life. Where the divine love ends, being ends; condemnation can only mean that the creature is left to the nonbeing it has chosen. The symbol "eternal death" is even more expressive, where interpreted as self-exclusion from eternal life and consequently from being. If, however, one speaks of everlasting or endless condemnation, one affirms a temporal duration which is not temporal. Such a concept is contradictory by nature. An individual with concrete self-consciousness is temporal by nature. Self-consciousness as the possibility of experiencing either happiness or suffering includes temporality. In the unity of the divine life, temporality is united with eternity. If temporality is completely separated from eternity, it is mere nonbeing and is unable to give the form for experience, even the experience of suffering and despair.

It is true that finite freedom cannot be forced into unity with God because it is a unity of love. A finite being can be separated from God; it can indefinitely resist reunion; it can be thrown into self-destruction and utter despair; but even this is the work of the divine love, as the inscription which Dante saw written over the entrance of hell so well shows (Canto III). Hell has being only in so far as it stands in the unity of the divine love. It is not the limit of the divine love. The only preliminary limit is the resistance of the finite creature.

The final expression of the unity of love and justice in God is the symbol of justification. It points to the unconditional validity of the structures of justice but at the same time to the divine act in which love conquers the immanent consequences of the violation of justice. The ontological unity of love and justice is manifest in final revelation as the justification of the sinner. The divine love in relation to the unjust creature is grace.

(3) The Divine Love as Grace and Predestination: The term "grace" (*gratia, charis*) qualifies all relations between God and man in such a way that they are freely inaugurated by God and in no way dependent on anything the creature does or desires. One may distinguish two basic forms of grace—the grace which characterizes God's threefold creativity and the grace which characterizes God's saving activity. The first form of grace is simple and direct; it provides participation in being to everything that is, and it gives unique participation to every individual being. The second form of grace is paradoxical; it gives fulfilment to that which is separated from the source of fulfilment, and it accepts that which is unacceptable. It is possible to distinguish a third form of grace, one which mediates between the two preceding ones and unites elements of both, namely, God's providential grace. On the one hand, it belongs to creative grace and, on the other hand, to saving grace, since the purpose of God's directing or providential creativity is fulfilment of the creature in spite of resistance. The classical term for this kind of grace is *gratia praeveniens* ("prevenient grace"). It prepares for the acceptance of saving grace through the processes of nature and history.

Not everyone is prepared to accept saving grace. This raises the problem of the relation of divine love to man's ultimate destiny; this is the question of predestination. It cannot be fully discussed here, since it presupposes the doctrine of justification by faith, a concept for which it is an affirmative protection against both human incertitude and human arrogance. Nevertheless, it has direct implications for the doctrine of the divine love and must therefore be partially discussed. First of all, it cannot be understood as double predestination, since that violates both the divine love and the divine power. Ontologically, eternal condemnation is a contradiction in terms. It establishes an eternal split within being-itself. The demonic, whose characteristic is exactly this split, has then reached coeternity with God; then nonbeing has entered the very heart of being and of love. Double predestination is not a genuine religious symbol; it is a logical consequence drawn from the religious idea of predestination. But it is a wrong consequence, as are all logical theological consequences which are not rooted in existential participation. There is no existential participation in the eternal condemnation of others. There is the existential experience of the threat of one's own self-exclusion from eternal life. This is the basis of the symbol of condemnation. Predestination, as the religious correlate to "justification by faith alone," must, like providence, be seen in the light of the ontological polarity between freedom and destiny. Predestination is providence with respect to one's ultimate destiny. It has nothing to do with determination in terms of a deterministic metaphysics, the inadequate and obsolete character of which has already been shown. Nor is the notion of predestination related to indeterminism. Rather, it shows that the relation of God and the creature must be interpreted in symbolic terms. Thinking is demanded on two levels. On the creaturely level, ontological elements and categories are applicable in a proper and literal sense. On the level of God's relation to the creature, the categories are affirmed and negated at the same time. The word "predestination," taken literally, includes causality and determination. When it is understood in this sense, God is conceived as a physical or psychological cause of a deterministic character. Therefore, the word must be taken in the symbolic sense of pointing to the existential experience that, in relation to God, God's act always precedes and, further, that, in order to be certain of one's fulfilment, one can and must look at God's activity alone. Taken in this way, predestination is the highest affirmation of the divine love, not its negation.

The divine love is the final answer to the questions implied in human existence, including finitude, the threat of disruption, and estrangement. Actually this answer is given only in the manifestation of the divine love under the conditions of existence. It is the christological answer to which the doctrine of the divine love gives the systematic foundation, although one would not be able to speak of this foundation without having received the christological answer. But what is existentially first may be systematically last and vice versa. This is also true of the doctrine of the trinity. Its logical foundation in the structure of life has been given, but its existential foundation, the appearance of Jesus as the Christ, has not been discussed. Only after such a discussion can a fully developed doctrine of the trinity be presented.

d) God as Lord and as Father.—The symbols "life," "spirit," "power," "love," "grace," etc., as applied to God in devotional life are elements of the two main symbols of a person-to-person relationship with God, namely, God as Lord and God as Father. Other symbols which have this ego-thou character are represented by these two. Symbols like "King,"

"Judge," or the "Highest" belong to the symbolic sphere of God as Lord; symbols like "Creator," "Helper," "Savior," belong to the symbolic sphere of God as Father. There is no conflict between these two symbols or symbol spheres. If God is addressed as "My Lord," the fatherly element is included. If God is addressed as "Father in Heaven," the lord-like element is included. They cannot be separated; even the attempt to emphasize the one over against the other destroys the meaning of both. The Lord who is not the Father is demonic; the Father who is not the Lord is sentimental. Theology has erred in both directions.

God as Lord and the related symbols express the holy power of God. "Lord" is first of all a symbol for the unapproachable majesty of God, for the infinite distance between him and the creature, for his eternal glory. "Lord" is in the second place a symbol representing the Logos of being, the structure of reality, which in man's existential estrangement appears as the divine law and the expression of the divine will. In the third place, "Lord" is a symbol for God's governing of the whole of reality according to the inner *telos* of creation, the ultimate fulfilment of the creature. In these three respects, God is called the "Lord." Some theologians use the symbol "Lord" to the exclusion of all those in which the uniting love of God is expressed. But the God who is only the Lord easily becomes a despotic ruler who imposes laws on his subjects and demands heteronomous obedience and unquestioned acceptance of his sayings. Obedience to God prevails over against love of God. Man is broken by judgments and threats before he is accepted. Thus his rational autonomy as well as his will are broken. The Lord who is only Lord destroys the created nature of his subjects in order to save them. This is the authoritarian distortion of the symbol of God as Lord; but it is an almost inescapable distortion, if God is not also understood as Father.

While Lord is basically the expression of man's relation to the God who is holy power, Father is basically the expression of man's relation to the God who is holy love. The concept "Lord" expresses the distance; the concept "Father," the unity. In the first place, "Father" is a symbol for God as the creative ground of being, of man's being. God as Father is the origin upon which man is continuously dependent because he is eternally rooted in the divine ground. In the second place, "Father" is a symbol for God in so far as he preserves man by his sustaining creativity and drives him to his fulfilment by his directing creativity. In the third place, "Father" is a symbol for God in so far as he justifies man through grace and accepts him although he is unacceptable. Some theology, including much popular thinking, is inclined to emphasize the symbol "Father" in such a way that it is forgotten that it is God the Lord who is the Father. If this side is neglected, God is conceived as a friendly Father who gives what men want him to give and who forgives all who would like to be forgiven. God then stands to man in a familial relation. Sin is a private act of hurting someone who easily forgives, as in the case of human fathers who themselves need forgiveness. But God does not stand in a private relation to man, whether a familial relation or an educational relation. He represents the universal order of being and cannot act as though he were a "friendly" father, showing sentimental love toward his children. Justice and judgment cannot be suspended in his forgiveness. The sentimental interpretation of the divine love is responsible for the assertion that Paul's interpretation of the Cross of Christ and his doctrine of atonement contradict the simple prayer for forgiveness in the Lord's Prayer. This assertion is false. The consciousness of guilt cannot be overcome by the simple assurance that man is forgiven. Man can believe in forgiveness only if justice is maintained and guilt is confirmed. God must remain Lord and Judge in spite of the reuniting power of his love. The symbol "Lord" and the symbol "Father" complete each other. This is true theologically as well as psychologically. He who is only Lord cannot be man's ultimate concern. And he who is only Father cannot be man's ultimate concern. The Lord who is only Lord evokes a justified revolutionary resistance which can be broken only by threats. And, if it is broken, the repression produces a type of humility which contradicts man's dignity and freedom. On the other hand, the Father who is only Father evokes a reverence which easily turns into the desire for independence, a gratefulness which easily turns into indifference, a sentimental love which easily turns into contempt, and a naïve confidence which easily turns into disappointment. The criticism by psychology and sociology of personalistic symbols for man's relation to God must be taken seriously by theologians. It must be acknowledged that the two central symbols, Lord and Father, are stumbling blocks for many people because theologians and preachers have been unwilling to listen to the often shocking insights into psychological consequences of the traditional use of these symbols. It must be emphasized that these symbols and all other symbolic descriptions of the divine life and of our relation to it are two-sided. On one side, they are determined by the transcendent reality they express; on the other side, they are influenced by the situation of those for whom they point to this reality. Theology must look at both sides and interpret the symbols in such a way that a creative correlation can be established between them.

"Lord" and "Father" are the central symbols for the ego-thou relationship to God. But the ego-thou relation, although it is the central and most dynamic relation, is not the only one, for God is being-itself. In appellations like "Almighty God" the irresistible power of God's creativity is felt; in "Eternal God" the unchangeable ground of all life is indicated. In addition to such appellative symbols, there are symbols used in meditation in which the ego-thou relation is less explicit, although it always is implicit. Contemplating the mystery of the divine ground, considering the infinity of the divine life, intuiting the marvel of the divine creativity, adoring the inexhaustible meaning of the divine self-manifestation—all these experiences are related to God without involving an explicit ego-thou relation. Often a prayer which starts with addressing itself to God as Lord or Father moves over into a contemplation of the mystery of the divine ground. Conversely, a meditation about the divine mystery may end in a prayer to God as Lord or Father.

Here again we must stress that the possibility of using the symbols "Lord" and "Father" without rebellion or submissiveness, without ideological deception or wishful sentimentality, is provided for us by the manifestation of the Lord and Father as Son and Brother under the conditions of existence. The question with which the doctrine of God concludes is the quest for a doctrine of existence and the Christ.

INDEX

INDEX

A priori, 166–68
Absolute, the, 153, 215
Absolutism, 83, 86–87, 88–89, 97, 150–52, 167
Abstraction, 107
Abyss, the, 79, 110, 113, 119, 156, 158–59, 164, 174, 216, 226
Accidents, 197
Actuality, 246, 273–74, 280
Actus purus, 180, 246
Adam, 174, 194, 206, 256, 258–60
Aestheticism, 90, 93
Aesthetics, 13, 77
Agapē, 280–82
Alexander of Hales, 40, 155
Alexandrian school, 6, 154
All-mightiness, 273
America, 87
Amor intellectualis, 90
Analogia entis, 131, 239–40
Analogy, 179
Angels, 229, 260
Anger of the gods, 284
Angst, 191
Anselm, 207
Anthropomorphism, 227, 242
Anti-Christ, 27
Antilegomena, 5
Antinomy, 190
Anxiety, 191–201, 206, 208–10, 253, 273–74, 276, 278–79
Apocrypha, the, 51, 115
Apollo, 128
Apollonian-Dionysian culture, 27, 141
Apologetics, 31–32
Aquinas, Thomas, 6, 28, 41, 72, 85, 155, 180, 205, 236, 247, 260
Archetype, 174, 260
Argumentum ex ignorantia, 6
Arianism, 17, 188
Aristotle, 6, 19, 56, 72, 85, 157, 165, 174, 178, 203, 233, 237
Art, academic, 78
Asceticism, 213, 254
Aseity, 196, 236, 248
Athanasius, 85
Atheism, 27, 237, 245
Athens, 89

Atonement, 288
Augustine, 50, 62, 85, 188, 206–7, 257, 262, 282
Augustinian, 41, 237
Authority, 47, 49, 52, 84–85, 129, 134, 145, 148–49, 287
Autonomy, 64, 83, 84–86, 127, 147–48, 208

Bach, J. S., 90
Barth, Karl, 4–5, 7–8, 29, 36, 42, 51, 61, 122, 257
Becoming, 181
Behaviorism, 168
Being, 14, 186, 192, 194–95, 197, 202; depth of, 113, 124; new, 24, 49–50, 53, 55, 74, 93, 126–27, 136–37, 146, 148–51, 155; structure of, 20–23, 26, 168–69
Being-itself, 164, 188–89, 191, 209, 230, 234–35, 237, 242–43, 247, 261, 270–71, 273, 276, 279, 283, 285, 289
Berdyaev, Nikolai, 189, 232, 246
Bergson, Henri, 62, 100, 168, 179, 181, 232, 275
Bible, 34–35, 48, 50, 158–59, 265
Biblical disciplines, 29
Biblical records, 133
Biblicism, 21, 36–37, 52, 126
Body, 250, 277
Böhme, Jakob, 62, 141, 179, 189, 232, 246, 261
Bonaventura, 40–41, 85
Boodin, John E., 44
Brahma, 213, 229
Brahman, 132, 214, 229
Brightman, Edgar, 9, 44, 246
Brunner, Emil, 42, 57, 61, 221
Buddhism, 220

Calvin, John, 61, 63, 217, 221, 262, 272, 273
Calvinism, 47, 256, 264, 272
Canon, 51
Caritas, 280
Cartesians, 168–69
Categorical imperative, 89, 207
Categories, 82, 164–66, 192, 209, 238, 257–58, 286
Causa prima, 24
Cause (causality), 195–96, 209, 237–38

293